The Metropolitan Police and the British Film Industry, 1919–1956

The Metropolitan Police and the British Film Industry, 1919–1956

Public Relations, Collaboration and Control

Alex Rock

THE BRITISH FILM INSTITUTE
Bloomsbury Publishing Plc
50 Bedford Square, London, WC1B 3DP, UK
1385 Broadway, New York, NY 10018, USA
29 Earlsfort Terrace, Dublin 2, Ireland

BLOOMSBURY is a trademark of Bloomsbury Publishing Plc
First published in Great Britain 2023 by Bloomsbury
Paperback edition published 2024
on behalf of the
British Film Institute
21 Stephen Street, London W1T 1LN
www.bfi.org.uk

The BFI is the lead organization for film in the UK and the distributor of Lottery funds for film. Our mission is to ensure that film is central to our cultural life, in particular by supporting and nurturing the next generation of filmmakers and audiences. We serve a public role which covers the cultural, creative and economic aspects of film in the UK.

Copyright © Alex Rock, 2023

Alex Rock has asserted his right under the Copyright, Designs and Patents Act, 1988, to be identified as Author of this work.

For legal purposes the Acknowledgements on p. x constitute
an extension of this copyright page.

Cover design: Louise Dugdale

Cover image © The Blue Lamp (1950)/Studiocanal Films Ltd/Mary Evans/

All rights reserved. No part of this publication may be reproduced or transmitted in any form or by any means, electronic or mechanical, including photocopying, recording, or any information storage or retrieval system, without prior permission in writing from the publishers.

Bloomsbury Publishing Plc does not have any control over, or responsibility for, any third-party websites referred to or in this book. All internet addresses given in this book were correct at the time of going to press. The author and publisher regret any inconvenience caused if addresses have changed or sites have ceased to exist, but can accept no responsibility for any such changes.

A catalogue record for this book is available from the British Library.

A catalog record for this book is available from the Library of Congress.

ISBN: HB: 978-1-3502-9508-7
PB: 978-1-3502-9512-4
ePDF: 978-1-3502-9510-0
eBook: 978-1-3502-9509-4

Typeset by Newgen KnowledgeWorks Pvt. Ltd., Chennai, India

To find out more about our authors and books visit www.bloomsbury.com
and sign up for our newsletters.

For my parents and Hope, with love; and to Jill Mills (who started it all).

Contents

List of Tables	ix
Acknowledgements	x

1 'Now it's entertainment, now it's propaganda': The processes
 of cultural production 1
 1.1 Theorizing the control of cultural production 2
 1.2 Narratives of *Law-and-Order News* 9
 1.3 'The process of knowledge production at a mundane
  level': Methodological approaches 14
2 Transparency or control: The Metropolitan Police Press
 Bureau 1919–38 21
 2.1 'The Official Film' 29
 2.2 Keeping the secrets of Scotland Yard 35
 2.3 The '1927 principles' 39
3 A reassuring necessity: Mediating images of law and order
 in the Second World War 55
 3.1 Producing *War and Order* 60
 3.2 'Such a step might appear on the surface to be
  revolutionary': Harold Scott, Percy Fearnley and the
  New Jerusalem of post-war policing 69
 3.3 Producing police narratives: *This Modern
  Age: Scotland Yard* and *The Girl from Scotland Yard* 75
 3.4 'I agree Police "Girl" is too frightful for the title': *The
  Girl From Scotland Yard* and the Metropolitan Women
  Police 87
4 The police as producer: Percy Fearnley, the Metropolitan
 Police Press Bureau and the making of *The Blue Lamp* 115
 4.1 'Sordid, squalid, sadistic and altogether
  unpleasant': British Crime Cinema before *The Blue Lamp* 118

4.2 The scriptwriter and the commissioner's Daughter: *The Blue Lamp*'s tentative beginnings — 122
4.3 'P.C. 99 … might be dealing with sheep dipping': The Home Office suggest a crime film — 132
4.4 The Met lose control: J. Arthur Rank and the *Ad-Valorem* tax — 139
4.5 'This guinea pig film': The script and the shoot — 146
4.6 'Though very occasionally they may get killed, nothing else can ever conceivably go wrong with them': The critical reception of *The Blue Lamp* — 156

5 Real life as the Metropolitan Police insisted upon us seeing it: Division of labour and the collaborative production of *Street Corner*, 1950–3 — 169
5.1 Fearnley's influence — 172
5.2 The script — 179
5.3 Shooting *Street Corner* — 187

6 'The machine at work': Forensic filmmaking and *The Long Arm*, 1951–6 — 203
6.1 1955 — 204
6.2 'Pull it to pieces': The first stage of production — 207
6.3 The production gathers pace — 221

7 Conclusion: Further areas of research — 239
7.1 What next for the Press Bureau? — 245

Bibliography — 253
Annotated Filmography — 263
Index — 265

Tables

2.1 Record of Approaches from Film Companies to the
     Metropolitan Police Press Bureau   46
6.1 *The Long Arm* and *Street Corner* Production Timelines   215

Acknowledgements

This has been a long-gestating labour of love, written over the course of thirteen years with the support, love and enthusiasm of a number of people. I'd like to thank Professor Steve Chibnall; his work has been an inspiration for many years, and this project would not have come to fruition without his friendship, supervision and generosity. All of my colleagues and fellow PhD students at De Montfort University, Leicester, have helped progress this work, particularly Dr Johnny Walker; his advice and encouragement throughout the publication process has been invaluable. I'd like to thank the staff of the many archives I've used to source material, including the National Archives, Dudley Archives, Derbyshire Record Office, the Cinema Theatre Association Archive and the Steve Chibnall Archive. The power of the archive remains undiminished, and there are so many stories left to tell.

Finally, I'd like to thank my former colleagues at Derby QUAD – the finest independent arts centre in the UK – for their support of the project during the lockdowns of 2020, particularly Adam Buss and Adam Marsh. I'm looking forward to introducing a screening of *The Blue Lamp* in the Sir John Hurt Cinema!

An early version of Chapter 2 has been published as follows:

'"We must go about it in our own way and have complete control": The British Film Industry and The Metropolitan Police Press Bureau, 1919–1938', in Laura Mee and Johnny Walker (eds), *Cinema, Television and History: New Approaches* (Cambridge: CSP, 2014), pp. 26–47.

1

'Now it's entertainment, now it's propaganda': The processes of cultural production

The Blue Lamp (Basil Dearden, Ealing Studios, 1950) was made in 1949 and released in the following year, and has been seen as an important cultural milestone in legitimizing the role of the police in British society.[1] As announced by the film's opening title sequence, *The Blue Lamp* would not have been made without the help of the Metropolitan Police (hereafter abbreviated to 'Met'); influenced by the British Documentary Movement, the film's writers shadowed working police personnel in order to convey a sense of authenticity. The film's status as a Met collaboration which propagated that institution's idealized view of itself was picked up by contemporaneous press coverage and was not played down by the Met Commissioner, Sir Harold Scott, who, in an interview with the *Daily Mirror*, said, 'We're hoping to win recruits from this film. It shows the Yard as it really is, and is a miracle of casting.'[2] A *Daily Herald* review of *The Blue Lamp* characterized the processes of control inherent in producing a collaboration between an independent filmmaking body and a public body such as the Met as follows:

> Now it's entertainment, now it's propaganda. The quickness of the hand deceives the eye.[3]

The Blue Lamp exists on a trajectory of British crime films made collaboratively between the British entertainment film industry and the Met. The analysis of these collaborations, of which *The Blue Lamp* is the most potent, forms the central focus of this piece of research. Using the *Daily Herald* review as a point of referral, it will investigate how the processes of collaboration and control manifest in the production of a film. To what extent did the Met assume the role of producer in the films instigated by independent filmmakers for commercial purposes? How did the Met begin to experiment with these processes of collaboration and control? Why did the Met choose to work with non-state agencies to produce these films? What impact did these choices make on the films?

1.1 Theorizing the control of cultural production

I began my research with the aim of studying the production of a series of three films made by the entertainment film industry between 1949 and 1956 in collaboration with the Met. These films embraced a variety of oppositions involving the relationship between entertainment and propaganda. However, these three films were nothing new; the Met had been collaborating on film productions for thirty years prior to the release of *The Blue Lamp*. I soon became aware of the need to trace the birth of cinema's use as a means to construct a public image while also historicizing the relationship between the film industry and the Met from the moment, in 1919, that public image came formally to be considered of consequence by the Met. This relationship existed on varying levels of closeness since its instigation, beginning with a rather fractious and restrictive period between the two world wars and culminating – through circumstance rather than design – in the beginning of a hegemonic partnership during the Second World War and onwards. The construction of this history, and the analysis of the development of methods used by the Met in collaborating with the British film industry, addresses the following subsidiary research questions. Can propaganda entertain? To what extent does the institution, as a manipulator of meaning, lose *control* of its cultural productions when relying upon the independent (i.e. not state-owned or sponsored) entertainment film industry – and does the latter also lose an element of control? What messages are encoded within the text, and *from whom do they originate*? How do they get there? Does the 'quickness of the hand' (institutionally-author(iz)ed production) indeed deceive the eye (film reception)? To understand the meaning-making processes of *The Blue Lamp* and its two feature-length contemporaries, one must first acknowledge the evolution of the collaborative process between state apparatus (in this instance, the arms-length Home Office body represented by the Met) and the British film industry, which first began collaboratively producing images of law and order in the written and visual press in 1919.

Similar work has been carried out on the relationships between the police and the press, and the police and the television industry, but very little work has been conducted on the complementary and overlapping strand of collaboration between the police and the film industry. While the medium of film of course is very different to that of the written press or television, they may all nevertheless be perceived as offering similar outcomes, opportunities and threats. The positives in utilizing all three media for the police include but are not limited to: increased exposure; the strengthening of consent for the enforcement of the rule of law; and the use of popular media as recruitment platforms. Nevertheless, there are risks for the police in utilizing the media for these purposes – the encouragement and subsequent exposure of corruption causing a rupture in the consensual application of the rule of law being the most obvious. The control of the tipping point between the hegemonic strength of this relationship and its weakness was contested between the Met and British film interests. Therefore, my research also addresses the extent to which the Met sought to control the production of these collaborative film texts, taking responsibilities which normally lie with the film producer to manipulate the final film to the institution's advantage.

To understand the political and sociological implications of police-authorized images of a deviant activity such as crime, one needs to delve further into the histories of such collaborations. The production of these images is inextricably linked with the rise of the cinema and the popular press as a means of mass communication throughout the late nineteenth and early-to-mid twentieth centuries. The rise of these mass media forms not just coincided with, but also spurred on, the growth of public relations as institutions sought to control the flow of information to the mass media in an attempt to manipulate the consumption of their image and to lessen the impact of the critical press.[4] Jurgen Habermas's work has been influential in assessing the extent to which the rise of the mass media brought about the growth in public relations in Britain and the subsequent mediation processes inherent to the relationship between the private sphere of the press and the public sphere of the institution (whether that institution be the Met, as is the focus of my research, or any other organization):

> The integration of the public and private realms entailed a corresponding disorganisation of the public sphere that once was the go-between linking state and society. This mediating function passed from the public to such institutions as have arisen out of the private spheres (e.g. special interest associations) or out of the public sphere of parties; these now engage in the exercise or equilibrium of power in co-operation with the state apparatus, treating it as a matter internal to their organisations. At the same time they endeavour, via the mass media that have themselves become autonomous, to obtain the agreement, or at least the acquiescence of a mediated public. Publicity is generated from above, so to speak, in order to create an aura of good will for certain positions ... Critical publicity is supplanted by manipulative publicity![5]

Habermas's identification of the mediating function, represented in my research by the Met Press Bureau, and the extent to which this function seeks to 'supplant' critical publicity (i.e. an independent, critical eye), is of direct relevance to my research. Influenced by Habermas, my research addresses the extent to which the Met employed the mediating function of public relations to manipulate their own public image in a series of film collaborations released between 1921 and 1956.

To generalize, the early work into this field of enquiry regarding the relationship between public bodies such as the Met and the media was conducted in the 1970s by scholars making use of Marxist theory, which was the dominant paradigm within the social sciences in the post-1968 era. These studies set an interpretive framework for research into the influence of the police over the media, and it is no coincidence that running parallel to the dominance of Marxist theory within the social sciences was a major police crisis involving the discovery by the press and academics of endemic institutional corruption and heavy-handedness within the Met. This scandal culminated in the release of a book-length exposé of corruption within the Met's Vice Squad in 1977 – the same year that Steve Chibnall published his sociological exploration of the murky relationships between Fleet Street crime reporters and senior detectives within the Met.[6] The discussion below makes use of Marxist terminology to explore the approaches taken by previous studies of the relationship between the police and the media, and to make apparent the structural framework for my research.

Writers such as Robert Reiner, Steve Chibnall and Haia Shpayer-Makov have interrogated the uneasy reciprocal relationships between agents of the written press and the police at various points in time, and their output, when put together, forms a history of police/press relations from the Victorian era until the present day. These histories have focused on the institutions of Scotland Yard and Fleet Street, forming a London-centric and somewhat skewed history of the relationship between the police and the press, due to the necessities of archival document conservation and, in the case of Chibnall's *Law-and-Order News*, access to police officers and crime reporters. This centralized historical approach is not, however, without justification; Scotland Yard is home to the largest police force in Britain, and its specialized detective personnel are often farmed out to smaller provincial forces in times of need. The author Maurice Procter, himself a former constable with the Halifax constabulary, refers to Scotland Yard as 'one of the two great clearing houses of crime in England', the other being Wakefield.[7] Similarly, London was, and still is, the base for the majority of the national written press, and so the dependence of the nation upon the police and press resources of London means that, unavoidably, the histories of police/press relations in England must take London as their basis. These studies conclude that the relationships between the national, London-based media and the Met are heavily weighted in terms of benefit towards the latter, and thus the study of the Met's Press Bureau must be considered a primary objective.

The histories of the collaborative processes between the written press and the police have been covered in some detail by the aforementioned writers amongst others. However, the relationships between the film industry and the police have remained largely neglected. Margaret Dickinson and Sarah Street, in *Cinema and State: The Film Industry and the Government 1927-84*, provide an informative account of state intervention in the British film industry in the form of legislation over the period 1927-84, but avoid discussion of instances in which the state itself authorized images of its machinery to be produced by the entertainment film industry.[8] Similarly, Susan Sydney-Smith has covered in great detail the relationship between the police and the television industry, which is an ongoing process of image management as seen through a series of recent documentary productions made collaboratively between the television industry and the police.⁹ My research addresses this imbalance and, in a post-Leveson era where the propriety of the relationship between the police and the media is continually interrogated, this research addresses the prehistory of today's police-press relations, providing a long-overdue companion piece to the works of Sydney-Smith, Chibnall, Dickinson and Street.

Jacqui L'Etang has remarked that Jurgen Habermas's research has 'identified public relations as supporting the dominance of elites and reinforcing structural inequalities'.¹⁰ Raymond Williams's definition of culture provides an insight into why exactly the control of culture through the imposition of public relations policy was contested somewhat hypocritically within the context of the free-market doctrines of the British state in the twentieth century:

> Culture in all its early uses was a noun of process: the tending of something, basically crops or animals.¹¹

The study of 'culture', particularly in Marxist histories, examines the extent to which the cultural product 'tends' and cultivates a certain value system within the consumer of the product. The films I explore are cultural products, and through analyzing the processes of control involved in the collaborative process between the police and the film industry, one can identify the 'cultivation' of an ideologically loaded belief system and also trace the originator of that process. In referring to British culture, I am not solely discussing the artistic and aesthetic products of the British value system at any given point in the last century, but also the process by which these images and texts 'tend' to their audience's needs and desires. Culture, as a process, manipulates the development of those who choose, or feel compelled, to consume it. Cinema is a medium of this process and so, for a Marxist critic, it becomes readily apparent why cultural elites would wish to exert an element of control upon it. Terry Eagleton, discussing Marx's *The German Ideology*, notes that the superstructure's need to control the economic base of society leads to the ruling classes (an outdated term, of course, but one upon which these key histories have established as an interpretive framework for my research) performing one essential function: 'to legitimate the power of the social class which owns the means of economic production'.[12] This control, this performance of a function which in itself is of no value to the social or economic conditions of a nation, can be achieved through the control of culture.

Williams had earlier discussed this point in some detail in his review of Marxist criticism published in *Culture and Society 1780–1950* in 1958. Whilst pointing out the inaccuracies of R. E. Warner's polemic statement that '*capitalism has no further use for culture*' (emphasis in original), Williams does, however, acknowledge that 'his general point about culture is reasonable', and provides an excellent account of the reasoning behind the control of culture:

> The progress of culture is dependent upon the material conditions for culture; and, in particular, the social organization of any period of history limits the cultural possibilities of that period. Yet all through history there is a constant interaction between culture and social organization ... There is a continuity both between various forms of social organization and various forms of culture, but the cultural continuity is the more marked because, for one thing, it is easier to envisage possibilities than to put them into practice, and also because change and progress in society have always been resisted for as long as possible by those interested persons who, being for the moment at the top, stand to lose by any readjustment within the whole.[13]

This process of cultural production and manipulation can be perceived in the collaborative processes that lead to the production of police-author(iz)ed images of crime on the British screen in the twentieth century. The ruling classes – 'those interested persons ... being for the moment at the top' – seek to impose their own limitations upon the processes of cultural production by controlling the material conditions required to produce it; this I will provide evidence for in my analysis of the role played by the Met Police Press Bureau in the production of the film collaborations. The acknowledgement of the importance of the written and visual media in maintaining 'the social organization' (i.e. the dominant ideology of the period) resulted in closer relationships between the media and the state in the period immediately following the First World War, which of course points to the fact that 'those interested persons' were aware of the need to limit the opportunities for 'readjustment within the whole' offered by the situation following the cessation of total war. This period, and the failure of the state to successfully control the processes of cultural production in the early post-war years of social adjustment, will be discussed in depth in Chapter 1. The situation following the end of the Second World War provided a similarly tumultuous social environment, but the technological developments in travel and mass communication between the late 1910s and mid-1940s meant that, for the state, it was of increasing importance to control and manipulate the conditions of British cultural production. This, in the case of British crime cinema, was achieved through good fortune and opportunistic planning. The producers of British crime films lobbied the relevant state machinery – mainly the Home Office, Board of Trade and the Met Press Bureau – for access to the necessary 'material conditions', namely police advisors, access to vehicles and specialist equipment, and the permission to shoot films on location in, for example, police stations, courtrooms and approved schools. In exchange for some of these facilities, the state effectively 'authored' the films by making their cooperation dependent upon the alteration of narrative content to fit a hegemonic need or purpose.

1.2 Narratives of *Law-and-Order News*

Robert Reiner disputes this interpretation. He concedes that 'mass-media images of the police are of central importance in understanding the political significance and role of policing,[14] arguing that these images form an important part of the process of deterrence. These images contribute to the 'presentation of society as governed by the rule of law'[15] and, in doing so, they also assist the manufacture of consent, legitimizing the role of law and order in society:

> The media-constructed image of policing is thus vital for the attainment of that minimum of 'consent' which is essential for the preservation of police authority. The image does not float free of the actualities of policing, but it is not a mirror reflection of them either. It is a refraction of the reality, constructed from it in accordance with the organisational imperative of the media industries, the ideological frames of creative personnel and audiences, and the changing balance of political and economic forces affecting both the reality and the image of policing.[16]

Here, Reiner indicates the reasons behind the Met wanting to develop their public image through cinema. The competing sides of the police – one of a 'service' operating on a consensual level, the other as a 'force' operating as a top-down suppressive element – make apparent the need for the strengthening of consent; one would reasonably anticipate that, in times of peace, the identification of the police as a 'force' would weaken the level of consent within society. The police enact the rule of law, and the acceptance of their status as agents of the rule of law is established only through consensus. How, then, did the police attempt to manufacture the requisite level of consent through cinema?

Within this context, Reiner identifies two critical schools of thought; the 'hegemonic' school, who agree that the media *should* manufacture 'that minimum of "consent"' required for effective governance, and the 'subversives' – presumably including Raymond Williams – who believe that the manipulation of images of law-and-order stifle discourses regarding effective governance by depicting the status quo as *right*. Arguing – from a post-Marxist, post-Thatcher and largely conservative position – that both of these schools of thought simplify the issue, he states that

> very broadly the weight of images portrayed by the mass media will be supportive of the existing social order in any relatively stable society. These images reflect and reinforce the views and self-perceived interests of the majority, not just an elite.[17]

To argue that the cultural productions of a 'relatively stable' capitalist society carry the 'self-perceived interests of the majority' implies that the majority, whose interests have been self-identified, are also in control of the means of cultural production and that the elite are not. This of course is not the case with the crime films made collaboratively with the Met between 1919 and 1956, and it is also not evidenced by the culture of suppression dominant within the Press Bureau between 1919 and 1940. Whilst this issue is unacknowledged by Reiner, he does, quite reasonably, propose that the 'key to understanding the content of the media is knowledge of the organisational dynamics, ideology, and professional imperatives of the productive personnel and institutions'.[18] Therefore, locating control of production is vital in developing an understanding of narratives of law and order.

Locating control within media representations of law and order forms the central tenet of Steve Chibnall's *Law-and-Order News* and the research that has further developed Chibnall's method of approach including Leishman, Mason and Mawby.[19] Chibnall, channeling Foucault's notion of images of discipline and punishment, notes that

> the existence of crime news disseminated by the mass media means that people no longer need to gather together to witness punishments. They can remain at home for their moral instruction.[20]

This idea is valuable when considering the role of crime films in immediate post-war British society and culture. As with crime reportage, which, due to Harold Scott's post-1945 empowerment of the

Met Press Bureau, relies heavily upon the arms-length management of the Home Office, media representations of crime and images of punishment serve to reinforce the dominant ideology, particularly if these images are informed by those responsible for enforcing discipline and adherence to the rule of law.

The reinforcement of this ideology may prove reassuring in the light of the potential breakdown of law and order, as seen in the 'Age of Austerity' immediately following the end of the Second World War[21]. Mark Jarvis, quoting R. A. Butler's White Paper of 1959, *Penal Practice in a Changing Society*, notes that

> even though Britain was experiencing 'rising standards in material prosperity, education and social welfare' this had not produced a 'decrease in the high rate of crime during the war'. The disquieting feature in this growth of crime since the war was the incidence of crimes of a violent and sexual nature. Another aspect, 'perhaps even more disturbing', was the increase in convictions of young men between the ages of sixteen and twenty-one years old.[22]

The debates surrounding how best to deal with post-war criminality pervade the films of the period and also expose the threadbare ideological 'consensus' of post-war Britain. For R. A. Butler, Conservative Home Secretary under Harold Macmillan's government between 1957 and 1962, the origins of the rising crime and juvenile delinquency figures he had to tackle could be traced back to the turbulence of the Second World War and the immediate post-war period. Donald Thomas's account of this period provides further evidence for this; his study of the criminal activities of the British public during the war demonstrates how rising crime figures in the 1940s were a consequence of the call-up of large parts of the police force alongside the looting opportunities provided by sustained German bombing raids.[23]

Mawby develops the empirical research of Chibnall, noting similarities between the cultural perception of law and order in the

1970s – the period of Chibnall's study – and the 2000s. Discussing Chibnall's research and the contextual similarities between his period of study and the author's own, Mawby asserts that the period of the 1970s were a time 'when public confidence in policing had declined from its highpoint of a perceived post-war golden age'[24]. Leishman and Mason also make use of this terminology, extending it somewhat:

> The golden age of crime reporting and the golden age of policing were co-located in the consensus mood of the immediate post-war years.[25]

Kynaston, R. A. Butler and Donald Thomas dispute this conclusion, positing instead that the post-Second World War era of social readjustment was but the opposite of a golden age for policing, with a public – starved of material goods – falling victim to a thriving black market, and an under-strength police force unable to cope with the increased workload. The notion of post-war 'consensus' is also a generalization, the existence of which, as demonstrated by Kynaston above, is debatable. The 'consensus' rhetoric, much like the similar 'Dunkirk spirit' evoked whenever Britain faces a national struggle, is an ideological construction originating from the superstructure, and the ready acceptance of such falsehoods surely undercuts rigorous debate.

Mawby, however, is correct in his identification of a golden age of police/public relations. The Met Press Bureau had been reinvigorated in 1945 by the newly appointed Commissioner, Harold Scott, who had identified the need to co-opt both the written and visual media into the manufacture of consent. His strategy to boost recruitment and the public perception of the police involved encouraging the production of films about the police alongside offering increased access to Scotland Yard for crime reporters. Leishman and Mason also acknowledge the importance of the role played by Harold Scott, but seem to limit their discussion of Scott to the organizational, rather than the mundane, level of control. They credit Scott with 'promoting public confidence in the police through the maintenance of productive links with news outlets', which overstates his input.[26] While Scott should receive credit for recruiting a journalist to manage the Press Bureau, the perceived 'golden age' of 'policing consensus' was largely due to the innovation and lack of institutional restraint exhibited by that journalist.[27] Just as Scott was the first Met Commissioner appointed from a non-military background, Percy H. Fearnley was appointed Public Information Officer of the Met Press Bureau – the first journalist, and first non-policeman, given the role in the Bureau's twenty-six-year history. Fearnley's success in propagating popular, idealized images of the police force led to other front-line institutions to follow suit, most notably the Probation Service and Approved Schools, with considerably less success. The level of influence wielded by Percy Fearnley over the series of film collaborations made with the Press Bureau's assistance will be a key point of interrogation for this piece of research.

1.3 'The process of knowledge production at a mundane level': Methodological approaches

Chibnall notes that historians '[tend] to ignore the kinds of routine operations, tacit assumptions, conceptual frameworks, and occupational constraints which systematically shape the everyday production of knowledge'.[28] In order to provide an accurate history of the production of knowledge, one cannot limit oneself to a study of the processes of ownership and control, but must also incorporate a study of the processes by which cultural productions are made. Sarah Street also argues for a similar approach to the specific study of film history. Arguing for a 'cinematic histoire totale' wherein film, for the historian, must of necessity not be divorced from its cultural, political and economic contexts, she concludes that 'the institutional boundaries which have separated the study of film from the study of history are therefore collapsed: film is a part of history and history is a part of film'.[29] These thoughts have also been articulated by John Ellis and Andrew Spicer; the former stated that 'writing about film production has generally been a ghetto of cinema criticism',[30] and Spicer has further developed this statement with a specific focus upon the role of the producer of a text:

> This lack of attention to producers is largely the result of the long shadow of the *auteur* theory, which, in its conventional form, has elevated the director as the key creative influence within filmmaking, expressing a personal vision with a distinctive aesthetic 'signature'. As a consequence, the producer has been relegated to the role of organiser and financier, concerned only with a saleable product and often actively hostile to creativity, or, at best, a trimmer, fearful of the radical or the experimental, seeking an acceptable compromise.[31]

By looking at the processes of control inherent in the collaborative production of images of law and order between the police and the film industry alongside the *actual production process* – 'the process of knowledge production at a mundane level'[32] – I intend to counter this imbalance of research, ensuring that a consideration of the text itself is thoroughly grounded in a study of its cultural, political and economic processes. Indeed, in addressing the extent to which the Met lost control of a collaborative production with the entertainment film industry, I also must, of consequence, address the opposite exchange of control. Did the Met, in effectively controlling the production of a series of film collaborations, supplant the film's named producer?

To trace this control exchange, my research takes as its basis the production files housed in the Public Record Office's National Archives, London (abbreviated to PRO TNA hereafter) in order to assess the processes of control inherent in my corpus at both macro and 'mundane' levels. The PRO TNA is the government's official document repository within which are housed the surviving documents of many government departments. After a period of time, the documents are released for public inspection. However, extant material is not comprehensive and has been subject to two phases of selection:

> The first, when the records have passed out of active use, usually takes place five years after a record has been created. At this point, records which are obviously worthless are destroyed, and those which have been identified as valuable for future administrative need, or future research are kept for further review at a later date. This process, known as second review takes place when the record is 15 to 25 years old.[33]

The process of preservation, then, is a subjective rather than a comprehensive act. Methodological constraints for this form of empirical research can be readily perceived by the fact that PRO TNA's first review stage only takes place 'when the records have passed out of active use'.

I also make use of newspaper coverage of the production processes and contexts of reception where available alongside – again, where available – script drafts, treatments and the alterations made by both the Met and those in the employ of the entertainment film industry. Sarah Street has discussed methodological issues arising from the use of, and reliance on, the archive in the study of cinema:

> Documents which are relevant to a particular film, issue or personality acquire significance because of a specific set of circumstances which have determined their existence and survival. 'Dominant' discourses (for example, opinions and policies generated by politicians and civil servants) survive because of their perceived importance 'in the national interest': they are available for study in the Public Record Office and are written in language which equates with 'the voice of truth'.[34]

The processes of archiving are, then, politicized; the choices inherent in the conservation of particular source materials are themselves not without motives of control and vested interest.

Moseley and Wheatley have raised a similar issue with regards to the archiving of television, but their comment is relevant when considering wider issues of archiving:

> Archiving practices affect and produce the kinds of histories that can be written. Access to research materials is a major shaping factor in the kinds of television histories that are undertaken; there are institutional gaps in the audiovisual archive, and therefore in national histories of television ... We propose that there are also gendered gaps in the archives and histories of British television.[35]

The authors of both articles recognize that, in writing histories of visual media, the researcher is limited to a study of what has been preserved, and therefore those histories can never be complete. Street, along with Moseley and Wheatley, also acknowledges that the 'dominant' discourses are preserved before the subordinated materials, leaving gaps that are impossible to fill satisfactorily. These observations are supported by the PRO's own archival policy which, as I have discussed, is subjective and responsible for preserving 'dominant' discourses over the superficially 'mundane'. The tone of the preserved correspondence also varies wildly according to its intended audience, and therefore some documentation is of more value to the researcher than other preserved documents intended for wide dissemination. Governmental minutes and white papers maintain a front of objectivity, whereas internal memos are often passionate, vitriolic and opinionated. In undertaking the process of analysis, I have prioritized the confidential over the public, and so my analysis of newspaper reportage and governmental releases is scant.

With the approaches outlined above in mind, I will now move on to a brief historiography of the early years of the Met Press Bureau, making use of the surviving documentation surrounding its inception and its early attempts to control the processes of cultural production.

Notes

1 See Robert Reiner, *The Politics of the Police*, 3rd edn (Oxford: OUP, 2000), pp. 47–84.
2 Donald Zec, 'The Blue Lamp', *Daily Mirror*, 18 January 1950, n.p.
3 P.H., 'The Blue Lamp', *The Daily Herald*, 20 January 1950, n.p.
4 See Jeremy Tunstall, *The Media in Britain* (London: Constable, 1983) for a full account of how the rise of the mass media created a dependency on information received from official channels based within the institution under analysis.
5 Jurgen Habermas, *The Structural Transformation of the Public Sphere: An Inquiry into a Category of Bourgeois Society* (Cambridge: Polity Press, 1989), pp. 177–8.
6 Steve Chibnall, *Law-and-Order News* (London: Tavistock, 1977); Barry Cox, John Shirley and Martin Short, *The Fall of Scotland Yard* (London: Penguin, 1977).
7 Maurice Procter, *The Devil Was Handsome* (London: Hutchinson, 1962), p. 109.
8 Margaret Dickinson and Sarah Street, *Cinema and State: The Film Industry and the Government 1927–84* (London: BFI, 2005).
9 Susan Sydney-Smith, *Beyond Dixon of Dock Green: Early British Police Series* (London: I. B. Tauris, 2002).
10 L'Etang, Jacquie, *Public Relations In Britain: A History of Professional Practice in the 20th Century* (London: Lawrence Erlbaum, 2004), p. 6.
11 Raymond Williams, *Keywords* (London: Flamingo, 1988), p. 87.
12 Terry Eagleton, *Marxism and Literary Criticism* (London: Methuen, 1976), p. 5.
13 Raymond Williams, *Culture and Society 1780–1950* (London: Penguin, 1976), p. 263.
14 Robert Reiner, *The Politics of the Police*, 2nd edn (London: Harvester Wheatsheaf, 1992), p. 171.
15 Ibid.

16 Ibid., p. 172.
17 Ibid., p. 173.
18 Ibid.
19 Frank Leishman and Paul Mason, *Policing and the Media: Facts, Fictions and Factions* (Devon: Willan, 2003); Frank Leishman, 'From *Dock Green* to *Life on Mars*: Continuity and Change in TV Copland' (Gloucester: Cyder Press, 2008); Rob C. Mawby, 'Chibnall Revisited: Crime Reporters, the Police and *Law-and-Order News*', *British Journal of Criminology* (vol. 50, no. 6, 2010), pp. 1060–76.
20 Chibnall, *Law-and-Order News*, p. xi.
21 For accounts of the breakdown of law and order in the period immediately following the Second World War, see David Kynaston, *Austerity Britain 1945–51* (London: Bloomsbury, 2007), pp. 112–13; Mark Jarvis, *Conservative Governments, Morality and Social Change in Affluent Britain, 1957–64* (Manchester: MUP, 2005), p. 21; Edward Smithies, *The Black Economy in England Since 1914* (Dublin: Gill and Macmillan, 1984), pp. 84–90.
22 Jarvis, *Conservative Governments, Morality*, p. 21.
23 Donald Thomas, *An Underworld At War* (London: John Murray, 2003).
24 Rob C. Mawby, 'Chibnall Revisited: Crime Reporters, the Police and "Law-and-Order News"', p. 1062.
25 Leishman and Mason, *Policing and the Media*, p. 36.
26 Ibid.
27 Ibid.
28 Chibnall, *Law-and-Order News*, pp. 208–12.
29 Sarah Street, *British Cinema in Documents* (London: Routledge, 2000), p. 2.
30 John Ellis, 'Made in Ealing', *Screen* (vol. 16, no. 1, 1975), p. 78.
31 Andrew Spicer, *Sydney Box* (Manchester: MUP, 2006), p. 1.
32 Chibnall, *Law-and-Order News*, p. 212.
33 'The Public Records System', http://www.nationalarchives.gov.uk/info rmation-management/legislation/public-records-system.htm (accessed 2 June 2014).
34 Street, *British Cinema*, pp. 5–6.
35 Rachel Moseley and Helen Wheatley, 'Is Archiving A Feminist Issue? Historical Research and the Past, Present and Future of Television Studies', *Cinema* Journal (vol. 47, no. 3, Spring 2008), pp. 153–4.

2

Transparency or control: The Metropolitan Police Press Bureau 1919–38

Research into the role of public relations within arms-length control agencies such as the Metropolitan Police, as discussed in the previous chapter, has indicated the importance of the study of the ways in which the agency attempts to manipulate its image through the control of cultural productions. Scholars including Chibnall, Mawby and Chermak and Weiss have researched the influence of the Public Information Officer (PIO) role within police forces in various contexts and in their respective time periods, but the history of the PIO role itself is a neglected object of study.[1] Percy Fearnley, an early appointment of Harold Scott's post-1945 Metropolitan Police Commissionership, was the first head of the Metropolitan Police Press Bureau to be given the job title of PIO, which may have reflected his expertise as a professional journalist – the first civilian to be given the responsibility of managing the Press Bureau and, arguably, the first effective appointment to the Bureau in its history. However, developing an understanding of the history of the Metropolitan Police Press Bureau from its inception in 1919 until Fearnley's appointment helps to illustrate the difference in approach taken by the Bureau in the period immediately following the Second World War. Established in 1919 as a conduit for information between the Metropolitan Police (hereafter abbreviated to 'Met') and the press as a means of ostensibly improving transparency, the Bureau instead became a mechanism for control of the written and visual media. It was not until the appointment of Percy Fearnley that the opportunities for collaboration between the police and the press were fully realized, with success for both parties.

Chermak and Weiss's statistical research, conducted in 2005 in the United States, points to the importance of the role of the PIO in maintaining the public image of the police. The pervasive influence of the PIO upon the media industry permeates the responses to their survey:

> For example, media workers report that almost 75 percent of crime incident information is provided by law enforcement, 85 percent covered community policing activities, and 76 percent said that they will provide coverage of innovations when police organizations request it.[2]

For the specific social situation of the United States in 2005, the PIO acts as a controlling and collaborative presence for the media. This relationship is of mutual benefit; the PIO distributes law-and-order news to the hungry media, but in doing so, the PIO is given the opportunity to also construct a positive image of the police through coverage of 'community policing activities' – essentially reportage of a police-promotions activity – and 'coverage of innovations', which involves a propagandistic rendering of police progression and evolution. Their research, bombastic in its self-awareness, does indeed fill gaps in previous scholarship, but avoids a history of the inception of the PIO – a role so crucial to the acceptance of the police as an authoritarian body in western civilization. This chapter, then, contributes to this field by providing a brief account of the formative years of the Met Press Bureau and its early collaborative engagements with the British film industry. In doing so, the chapter makes clear the dichotomies between public/private and transparency/control upon which the Press Bureau was founded and, in light of its inability to accept the public relations (hereafter 'PR') potential of mediated images of the police, upon which it ultimately failed until its rebirth in 1945.

The Police Commissioner responsible for the formation of the Press Bureau, Nevil Macready, reflected on its efficiency and purpose in his self-aggrandizing two-volume memoir:

> Another innovation that was started during the year 1919 was the institution of a press room at Scotland Yard, where at certain hours each day pressmen could get reliable information on any subject of public interest connected with police activities in the metropolis. The leakage which occurs in all public offices was very noticeable in police circles when I first went to the Yard, and I found that it was partly due to the temptations offered to the police by people connected with the press, who paid either in cash or in kind for the information, often inaccurate, which they extracted. One well-known man in newspaper circles told me that this source of information cost him £1,000 a year. From the police point of view it was all wrong that officers should take money, or its equivalent, on any pretence whatever, as, while the information given was at times harmless enough, the principle was vicious and might at any moment lead to a public scandal.[3]

Apart from its stated intention to resolve an endemic culture of bribery within the Met, the Press Bureau – re-presenting a control agency to the written and visual media – also proposed to improve transparency between the machinery of the state and its subjects. Macready mentions, in his memoirs, that the Press Bureau 'helped in some measure to dissipate the clouds of mystery in which Scotland Yard was supposed to be enveloped,'[4] but stops short of using the word 'transparency'. Within the public forum, the Met Commissioner and the Home Office were open about these two purposes upon which the Press Bureau was founded, but private internal correspondence indicates that the Bureau was also responsible for controlling and managing public perception of the police. Instead of maintaining accountability through transparently presenting the work of Scotland Yard to the media, the Press Bureau instead managed data in order to construct an ideologically loaded depiction of the Met in the press. On 27 September 1919, Commissioner Macready wrote to Sir Edward Troup, Under-Secretary of State at the Home Office, to request permission to form the Press Bureau. To be housed in a basement room at Scotland Yard and staffed on a part-time basis by Macready's secretary, George Rivers-Bodilly (with assistance from a shorthand typist), the proposal to form the Bureau indicates the controlling ideas behind its formation. Macready wrote:

> I understand that, in the past, the policy has rather been to discourage communications with the Press, and the result has been that certain Papers spend sums of money to procure information which is often inaccurate, and which – especially in intricate cases – tends to hamper the Police in their work.[5]

The push for the introduction of the Press Bureau must be situated within the unique context of post-war Britain. After the trauma of the First World War, various British institutions – including the Bank of England – were attempting to introduce an element of transparency to their operations in the form of Press Offices, and it was felt that a similar body may assist in dissipating the culture of secrecy surrounding Scotland Yard.[6] The Police Strikes of 1918 and the ensuing campaign for the unionization of the Met provide further reasons as to why Macready chose to accommodate the media: the activities of the banned National Union of Police and Prison Officers (NUPPO) had, in calling a strike, despatched Macready's predecessor, Sir Edward Henry, and, by getting the media 'on side', he may have speculated that he could manipulate national sympathies against police unionization.

The primacy accorded to newspaper representations is evident in the title of the new Bureau, but the significance of a second mass medium could no longer be ignored. During the latter half of the First World War, the propaganda potential of the cinema for the government had also been realized. An article by Herbert Ponting, the cameraman who accompanied Captain Scott on his ill-fated South Pole expedition, was published in the *Manchester Guardian* on 11 September 1917 concerning the educational possibilities of cinema and the methods by which the British educational system may make use of it.[7] This article was passed to the War Cabinet and proved the inspiration for Sir Edward Carson, a Conservative Minister and Unionist leader, to organize a conference in January 1918 to 'consider certain questions connected with the utilization of Cinematograph films for purposes of Propaganda both at home and abroad, more particularly with the object of discussing proposals for co-ordination of the work already being done and considering suggestions for the systematic utilization of the Cinema screen for Government purposes'.[8] As a result of this conference, the government proposed the introduction of liaison officers to be appointed by 'Departments and Committees which are interested in the production or utilization [*sic*] of Cinematograph films'.[9]

> On 28 May 1917 *Topical Budget,* a minor British newsreel with an audience of little more than half a million, found itself taken over by the British government, renamed *War Office Official Topical Budget,* and over the next year and a half widening that audience to over three million at home and abroad. It became the chief channel for British film propaganda.[10]

For Luke McKernan, the takeover of the newsreel provides 'one of the first instances of the authorities accepting the popularity of the cinema and making it work for them'.[11]

The *Topical Budget* was, prior to its nationalization, controlled by William Jeapes of the Topical Film Company. Jeapes and Topical were crucial in developing the potential of cinema for domestic propaganda in the early post-war period; Topical was sold to the newspaper magnate Edward Hulton in 1919 and was almost immediately awarded the task of producing an official film of the activities of Scotland Yard. The resulting film, *Scotland Yard 1921: For the King, the Law, the People* (Edmund Distin-Maddick, Topical Film Company, 1921), forms the locus of this chapter. The 'Official Film', as it was known during production, provides the earliest example of collaboration between an independent film production company and the Met, and its primary purpose was to improve the image of the police following a period of negative press coverage involving strikes, 'Third Degree' interrogation practices and a culture of police bribery and corruption.[12] It is clear then, with regards to the nationalization of *Topical Budget*, the January 1918 conference, and the introduction of Press Offices at both the Bank of England and the Met, that a movement towards the manipulation of cultural productions by governmental control agencies was gaining momentum.

Despite this realization of the collaborative opportunities between the media and the state, the relationship between both was fractious. For example, the memo proposing the formation of the Press Bureau makes clear the level of suspicion with which the press was regarded by the Met Commissioner – a suspicion that hampered the opportunities offered by improving relations between police and press:

> I propose, therefore, to set aside one room in Scotland Yard where, at any hour of the day, Press Representatives will be interviewed by a responsible official, be given information on matters on which they seek it, and be supplied with such Police information as it may be of advantage to make public.[13]

The relationship between transparency and control is perceptible in Commissioner Macready's proposal and, as borne out by the statistical research of Chermak and Weiss, is still of relevance today. Instead of acting as a means of improving transparency and accountability by openly disclosing non-prejudicial information to the free press, the Press Bureau was instead founded upon a principle of control wherein the flow of 'such Police information as it may be of advantage to make public' – essentially, propagandist image-management data – was mediated through a partial arm of the establishment.

The Bureau itself was influenced by the prevalent tradition among the higher echelons of the Met of recruiting from the armed forces during the interwar period. Possibly as a result of this, the Bureau's impact upon the written and visual media was largely censorial – an approach that contrasted markedly with the collaborative openness fostered by post-1945, civilian Press Bureau employees. The illicit NUPPO railed against this recruitment tendency instilled in the Met by senior officers; Macready, for example, was a General in the British Expeditionary Force in France during the First World War, immediately prior to his appointment as Met Commissioner. Despite this, Macready possessed a liberal arts background; his upbringing as the son of the noted stage actor William Charles Macready and maternal grandson of an artist had instilled in him a respect for the arts, and he was a committed amateur dramatist.[14] He did, however, follow in his predecessor's footsteps by continuing to appoint former armed forces officers to influential Met positions. Brought in to assist the breaking of a strike and to dismantle the NUPPO, his decision to assign George Rivers-Bodilly the task of managing the first Press Bureau provides a pertinent and lasting example of the influence of Army culture upon the Met during the interwar years.

Rivers-Bodilly was a Captain in the British Army and had been awarded several medals in a distinguished military career.[15] He retired from the Army in January 1919 to take a post with Macready as his Private Secretary before moving on to the Press Bureau. In contrast to the personal histories of Macready and Rivers-Bodilly, Harold Scott was, in 1945, the first Met Commissioner to be appointed from outside of the military, and Percy Fearnley was a journalist before his appointment to the post of PIO. The differences between the two regimes – Macready's post-First World War Met and Scott's post-Second World War era – are marked; while Fearnley scored politically and culturally important public relations coups by encouraging collaboration between the Met and the British film industry along with constantly petitioning for increased access to information with which to brief the crime reporters of Fleet Street, Rivers-Bodilly's time at the Press Bureau was characterized by the refusal of almost all press and film company requests, as evidenced by the extant Press Bureau ledgers and files relating to this period.

Before the start of the Second World War, only one independent film was made officially depicting the work of the Met. The film – *Scotland Yard 1921: For the King, the Law, the People* – was considered a failure despite attempts at promotion by Macready's successor, William Horwood. In order to provide an element of accuracy to filmic depictions of Scotland Yard, the entertainment film industry often turned to retired Scotland Yard employees in lieu of official police assistance, offering them advisory or authorial roles in the productions. When the attention of Scotland Yard was drawn to these instances, as in 1921 with the case of ex-Chief Inspector Ernest Haigh and the serial *Secrets of Scotland Yard*, the Met responded with threats to take the ex-employee's pension away. The remainder of this chapter, then, will focus upon the interwar years of the Press Bureau in order to provide a counterpoint to the activities of the Bureau after 1945. Making use of the Press Bureau files, preserved in the National Archives, in which requests for assistance and information from the British film industry were recorded, alongside production files and correspondence regarding *Scotland Yard 1921* and *Secrets of Scotland Yard*, the chapter will examine the early attempts at collaboration between the state and the British film industry in order to demonstrate the markedly anti-media stance of the Met in the interwar period.

2.1 'The Official Film'

The first film made with the express permission and assistance of the Met did not, strangely, fall under the control of George Rivers-Bodilly. This may have been because of the fact that the seeds for the project were sown on 4 September 1919, preceding Macready's official request for the formation of the Press Bureau by just under four weeks.[16] It is also indicative of the limitations of the early Press Bureau; it would appear that Rivers-Bodilly managed the relationship between the written press and the Met, with the relatively new form of visual media embodied by the newsreel and other cinematic narratives falling under the jurisdiction of Major Edmund Distin-Maddick, a pioneer of British cinema exhibition with – again – significant military experience. Distin-Maddick approached the Topical Film Company on behalf of the Met with a view to the production of an official police film. William Jeapes, founder of Topical, agreed to the proposal put forward by Distin-Maddick:

> Conditionally that we have the exclusive right of distribution of either complete films (or short lengths for use in the Topical Budget for which royalties shall be mutually arranged) we shall be very pleased to undertake the manufacture of all films that you may produce and pay to the Commissioner 50% of all profits that may accrue from the distribution for the Commissioner to dispose of to such Police Charities as he may elect.[17]

The film, according to the Topical Film Co., was to remain 'under [the] direction'[18] of Distin-Maddick, and the Commissioner was to be provided with a copy of the film. This degree of control may, in hindsight, have led to the failure of the film; the filmmakers were effectively 'directed' by the police's public relations machinery, and so any independent insight was denied to the Topical Film Co.

The tone of the correspondence between the Met and Topical makes it quite clear that Topical were considered contractors by senior figures within the Met. The film was completed by January 1921 and Commissioner William Horwood, Macready's successor following his appointment to the Royal Ulster Constabulary, formulated the following response to Topical's William Jeapes:

> Our first view of the Official Film yesterday was most satisfactory, and I am very much obliged for the kind assistance which Major Maddick tells me that you have rendered him.[19]

Any indication of artistry is lacking in Horwood's response. The film, referred to simply as the Official Film, would appear to have been directly under the control of Distin-Maddick, with the 'kind assistance' of Topical. Edmund Distin-Maddick seems, in the records documenting the making of *Scotland Yard 1921*, to represent the interests of the Met, with William Jeapes of Topical acting in the interests of the British film industry, within which his company is a significant contributor. However, the distinction between authorial control – Edmund Distin-Maddick and the Met – and the transparent, revelatory approach of Jeapes and the Topical Film Company is superficial. Further examination reveals a complex historical series of relationships involving 'old-boys' networks and side-swapping between Topical and Distin-Maddick. Topical was founded in 1911 by William Jeapes and began producing the *Topical Budget* newsreel, a biweekly British news digest for cinematic distribution. As already mentioned, in 1917, the Topical Film Company was co-opted into the war effort by the War Office, whose Cinematograph Committee took control of the company in order to distribute official film footage of battles and other propagandist material for consumption by British cinemagoers. The Topical Budget was renamed the *War Office Official Topical Budget* and remained so until February 1919, when the Ministry of Information sold the company off as a going concern to the newspaper proprietor Edward Hulton seven months prior to the company being approached to produce what would become

Scotland Yard 1921. While, strictly speaking, Topical was at this point a privately controlled independent newsreel film company, they were, in view of their past collaborations, considered a responsible, line-towing outfit by the Met, who surely would have had the company recommended to them by the Home Office.

Similarly, Edmund Distin-Maddick, prior to his involvement with the Met, was a cinema pioneer of some note. After an illustrious career as a surgeon, he became an enthusiast of the educative possibilities heralded by the technological developments in cinema. He bought an old theatre in 1905 – the Scala in London – and converted it into a cinema. During the First World War, he was employed as the Intelligence Department's Director of Kinematography and had produced an official film of considerable repute, *The Battle of the Somme* (Geoffrey Malins and John McDowell, British Topical Committee for War Films, 1916), released in July 1916. Through his work with the Intelligence Department during the First World War, it can be safely assumed that Distin-Maddick would have developed a working relationship with the Topical Film Company, whose cameramen it was his responsibility to assign press passes to. During the war, Distin-Maddick's cinema was also noted for its exhibition of films produced by Topical:

> In November 1915, in a personal deal between William Jeapes and Frederick Wile, Berlin correspondent of the *Daily Mail*, the Topical Film Company acquired the prints of a large number of German propaganda films. Wile had secured the prints and turned to Jeapes for help in printing and distribution. Suitably edited, selected German films were the main feature of a programme of films running at the Scala cinema in London between January and June 1916, and elsewhere in the country.[20]

It is difficult here to argue for Distin-Maddick's position as a cog within the wider ideological state machinery, and similarly reductive to present Topical as an independent, sales-driven entertainment film production company. The lines between the two were blurred for a considerable period of time.

The proceeds from *Scotland Yard 1921* were directly paid to the Met Commissioner's Office whereby they were channeled into police benevolent funds.[21] From these brief summaries of the three key bodies involved in the production of the first collaborative project involving the British film industry and the police, it is apparent that the film was not commissioned with the intention of providing insight into the machinations of the Met, or with improving transparency and accountability between the police and British subjects. The two Commissioners involved in the production of the film, Nevil Macready and William Horwood, chose to retain powerful and far-reaching direct control of the project with the intention of boosting the legitimacy of the Met and the coffers of the benevolent fund. The choice of filmmakers involved in the project – Distin-Maddick and Topical – again provides an example of this; they were as firmly entrenched within the British establishment as the Commissioners themselves.

Scotland Yard 1921 succeeded in fostering the development of a more collaborative relationship between the press and the police for the short publicity period leading up to the film's release. Horwood even welcomed this, noting in a letter sent to Topical on 26 January 1921 that 'any help we can give in publicity for our mutual benefit we shall be glad to render'.[22] Despite this apparent openness towards the publicity machine, Commissioner Horwood remained deeply suspicious of the press. On 9 March 1921, in preparation for *Scotland Yard 1921*'s trade show, Horwood sent the following letter to the editors of all national papers and certain high-circulation local newspapers:

> I have caused a film to be constructed at Scotland Yard showing some of the work of the Metropolitan Police. The accompanying pamphlet will give you an idea of the object for which it has been prepared.

I shall be most grateful if you will see that the subject is treated seriously and kindly, and so help our Public and our Force to appreciate one another.[23]

The letter concludes with an invitation for the press to see the film at the trade show. The tone of the invitational letter betrays the ideological sentiment behind the film; through embracing the technologies of the cinema and manipulating their meaning-making potential, Horwood hoped to develop and promote an acceptance of the police within British society. The letter indicates his fear of a poor reception for the film, and his polite insistence regarding the kind and serious treatment of the film thinly veils a threat to the press; to lose favour with the Met in the early days of official police-press relations risked losing any limited access to the official sources of law-and-order news. Horwood, in the circular, identifies himself as the author of the film ('I') and reveals his sentiment that the press is an inconvenient buffer between the police and the public. *The Times* review published three days later demonstrates that Horwood's polite intimidation proved successful:

> [*Scotland Yard 1921*] shows the daily routine of every member of the police force from the highest to the lowest. It is a fascinating record, and will give the public the unique opportunity of appreciating the work which is carried out by the force. The earlier sections of the film deal with the work of Scotland Yard and all its specialized branches, but later on the daily life of the constable from the first moment of his entry into the force is shown in detail.[24]

The purpose of the film, as made explicit by Sir John Baird, Under-Secretary of State for the Home Department, in the opening speech given at *Scotland Yard 1921*'s trade show, was not to bolster a recruitment drive. Baird informed the press that the Met is operating at close to full strength and that, 'although recruiting is not actually closed, it is very nearly so'.²⁵ Instead, the production of the film was motivated by similar ambitions that led to the formation of the Press Bureau:

> It is a Film of propaganda to show you citizens of the Metropolis and other places where the Film may be shown exactly what the Police do for you, to create a liaison between the Public and the Force, and to increase ... that kindness of feeling and thankfulness to our 'Men in Blue'.²⁶

This need to 'create a liaison' between control agencies and British subjects necessitates the development of a relationship with the press, whether they be represented by the national or provincial newspapers or, as is the object of my study, the British film industry. However, in opening the doors to Scotland Yard, the Met Commissioner risked the 'transparency' of the free press outweighing the 'control' of the Met's agency. John Baird's choice of words is telling; he understands the need to improve the relationship between the police and the public, but fails to mention the body represented by his audience – the press – who of necessity must facilitate the building of the relationship of accountability and acquiescence between the public and the police. His ignorance of this requirement is emblematic of police policy towards the press throughout the interwar period – in producing *Scotland Yard 1921*, the Met sought to 'speak' to the British public by circumventing the press, cutting out the 'middle men'. The control maintained at the expense of transparency in the making of *Scotland Yard 1921* provides one example of this, but so too do other examples of correspondence between the Met and the British film industry.

The film was considered a failure and disowned immediately after the advent of sound in British cinema. The Chief Constable of the Cumberland and Westmorland Constabulary wrote to the then-Commissioner, Viscount Byng, in February 1931, requesting a copy of *Scotland Yard 1921* with which to illustrate a lecture he had been invited to give at a school.²⁷ H. M. Howgrave-Graham, the Secretary to the Met, wrote in reply that the film 'is out of date and as it was never regarded as a very successful or flattering production from our point of view, the Commissioner thinks that it is better forgotten.'[28] By August 1933, Howgrave-Graham had decided that the film – the only surviving copy of which belonged to the Commissioner's Office following a severe fire at Topical's premises in 1924 – should be removed from Scotland Yard. He wrote the following to the War Office:

> I have discovered in an old cupboard here an old police film which was made just after the war.
>
> It was a commercial failure and I don't suppose anybody is very likely to want it again, but I feel that it should not be destroyed and I want to ask you whether you would take it and keep it for us in your store.[29]

A reply was not filed, and the film is considered lost. The failure of the film – judged presumably in terms of both profit and positive publicity – could be attributed to the control levied by the Met through the Commissioner's Office; as demonstrated above, William Horwood was directly involved with the film, and answerable for its outcome. *Scotland Yard 1921* provides an example of the state recognizing the propaganda potential of the controlled cinematic depiction of its machinery, and also the concern surrounding the influence of the uncontrolled cinematic image. The failure of *Scotland Yard 1921* to build upon the public image of the Met, and subsequent controversies involving independent crime films depicting Scotland Yard, may have prevented the Met and the Home Office from directly collaborating with the British film industry for the remainder of the interwar years.

2.2 Keeping the secrets of Scotland Yard

A month before the trade show of *Scotland Yard 1921*, advertisements began appearing in *Kinematograph Weekly* for a serial covering a similar subject to the official film. The heavily sensationalized advertisements for this serial, produced by the Frederick White Company, presented it as an insider's tale of life in Scotland Yard, promising that 'the chief outstanding events in this great detective's life will be portrayed in this serial'.[30] The press campaign was noticed by Film Booking Offices (1919) Ltd, the distribution arm of the Topical Film Company, who, fearing significant competition to their *Scotland Yard 1921* product, drew the attention of Commissioner Horwood to the advertisements.[31] Horwood sought legal advice in an attempt to impose either an injunction upon the aforementioned 'great detective', recently retired ex-Chief Inspector Ernest Haigh, or undertake libel proceedings against the Frederick White Company.[32] Solely on the basis of the advertisements, legal counsel was unable to recommend either form of legal action, and instead, letters of varying severity were sent to ex-Chief Inspector Haigh, the publishers and editorial board of *Kinematograph Weekly*, and the Frederick White Company.

The letters express the level of anxiety felt by the Met regarding the serial, which itself was titled *Scotland Yard*. The most severe letter of the four was addressed to ex-Chief Inspector Haigh:

[The Commissioner's] attention has been drawn to an advertisement in the 'Kinematograph Weekly' for February 3rd, 1921, of a film called 'Scotland Yard' which purports to reveal official secrets of Scotland Yard and with which your name is associated.

This advertisement is calculated seriously to prejudice the Criminal Investigation Department of the Metropolitan Police Force in the estimation of the public, and to impede its work by destroying public confidence in it.

The Commissioner ... desires me in this connection to remind you of the provisions relating to the forfeiture of pension contained in Section 8 of the Police Act, 1890 as amended by Section 5 of the Police (Superannuation) Act, 1906.[33]

The unofficial *Scotland Yard* film was uncontrolled, unmediated, in sharp contrast to the sterile 'Official Film', and the Met's fear of uncontrollable images of itself in the media is tangible in this case.

Haigh's reply to the Met was apologetic. After speaking to the Frederick White Company on the Met's behalf, Haigh succeeded in preventing any further publication of the trade advertisements, and requested clarification from the Met regarding his role in the film industry:

> Before proceeding further with the series of films I should be glad to know whether there is any objection to my working as a film artist in a series of stories, all pure fiction, without disclosing my former connection with the service. The stories which I have written are all clean, of good moral tone, do not depict sordid crimes or murders and most certainly do not in any way prejudice the C. I. Department or tend in the slightest degree to destroy the public confidence that exists therein.[34]

Haigh defends his motive for working with the Frederick White Company, stating that in doing so, he is attempting to 'provide for the education and needs' of his family, which in turn implies that the pension he received was unsuited to maintaining the lifestyle to which he and his family had become accustomed. Despite this, it is clear from Haigh's correspondence that his loyalties lie with Scotland Yard, although his image and involvement in the *Scotland Yard* serial may have been exploited by the production company. In another letter, he reveals that, following his retirement, a business venture with which he was financially involved had collapsed and he had fallen on hard times, with his 'available savings ... swallowed up in paying for a few slight house repairs + alterations'.[35] It would seem that Haigh fell foul of monetary extravagance; his pension of £304. 7/6 was, by his own admission, 'a liberal one', but his inability to resist the allure of the film industry and the naivety with which he approached his film career seems to have caused him considerable embarrassment:

That I should have been so easily enmeshed in Trouble makes me ashamed. The over anxiety I have felt to relieve myself of financial embarrassment is the sole reason ... I loathe the work I have so unwittingly accepted and if the question is that my pension is to be forfeited if I continue with such work and saved to me by abandoning it I shall choose without hesitation and make the best arrangements I can with my principals.[36]

The attempted suppression of the serial continued apace following Haigh's letter. A meeting was arranged between the Frederick White Company, Haigh and Scotland Yard which, revealingly, was represented by Edmund Distin-Maddick amongst others.[37] Distin-Maddick's involvement indicates the reasoning behind the proactive suppression of the unofficial *Scotland Yard* film; as it would be released so close to the Official Film, the Commissioner seems anxious that audiences should not confuse the two. Whether Frederick White's *Scotland Yard* came to be titled so in an attempt to benefit from the publicity of the Official Film is unclear, but Horwood seems less concerned with the actual title itself as with the content of the serial whose exploitation promises an insider's view of life at Scotland Yard. However, Haigh himself, despite being the author of the serial's scenario, seemed to have very little control over the way in which it was advertised. In his defence, he wrote, 'I had no idea that my work was to be advertised as it was. I was not even consulted on the point and when the true facts came to my knowledge I took such steps as I could to put things right.'[38]

Frederick White's *Scotland Yard* serial was trade-shown in the first week of May 1921, two months after the trade show of the Official Film and three months after the initial publication of the offending *Kinematograph Weekly* advertisements. Documentation is unclear on this point, but it may be assumed that the two-month delay between the Official Film's trade-show and White's serial was caused by the negotiations between the producer and the Met. Whether or not the serial was picked up for national release is again unclear, particularly given the lukewarm reception accorded to it in the national press. The *Daily Telegraph*'s review of the serial compares it unfavourably with a Sherlock Holmes serial trade-shown in the same week but, tellingly, blames not the producers or Ernest Haigh for its 'tame and insipid' content, but the level of control held over the project by the Met:

> No doubt if [Haigh] was absolved from the trammels of professional secrecy, and given a free hand, the man from Scotland Yard could also make our flesh creep.[39]

The anonymous reviewer seems to have been in contact with a Frederick White Company insider – possibly White or Haigh himself – and has somehow been made aware of the cinematic limitations placed upon Haigh by the Met. The Met's proactive approach to the suppression of Frederick White's *Scotland Yard* contrasts with their enthusiastic embracing of Topical's production; however, the failure to prevent the release of the former, alongside the latter's inability to generate either significant income for the Benevolent Fund or the *right* kind of publicity of the police, seemed to have set in motion a hands-off approach to future projects involving the British film industry. Scotland Yard, particularly under the Commissionership of William Horwood, demonstrated an aversion towards the British film industry, setting in motion a series of policies which remained relatively untouched until the end of the Second World War and the appointment of Harold Scott to the position of Commissioner.

2.3 The '1927 principles'

In the late 1920s, public relations work in Britain began to gather pace as marketing professionals and civil servants took advantage of the new opportunities offered by developments in consumer behaviour, new technologies and cultural developments. The work of the Empire Marketing Board at this point – with innovations pushed through by Stephen Tallents and William Crawford – were key to demonstrating the potential for public relations work. Tallents joined the Empire Marketing Board in 1926; he observed that 'scarcely any British government department had ever thought about publicity and that most departments despised and were inclined to resent it'.[40] Tallents and Crawford were busy opening up new opportunities for trade drives showcasing the produce of the Empire, within a largely liberal, adventurous framework – with the approval of the Department of Overseas Trade and the Foreign Office.[41] In 1928, the Empire Marketing Board founded its own Film Unit. While the arenas of trade and commerce were busy experimenting with new modes of address – pioneered within a civil service framework – notions of bolstering consent for the rule of law through these means continued to languish. It seems that the Foreign Office was far more ready to accept change than the Home Office and the Met.

Stung by their inability to collaborate on a commercially successful film, the Met's distrust of the film industry grew under the Commissionership of William Horwood, despite the successful use of cinema within the Empire Marketing Board. Upon his retirement in November 1928, Lord Byng was appointed his replacement. With the change of regime, filmmakers again began to approach the Met for facilities, emboldened by the introduction of the Cinematograph Films Act (1927). The Act was a protectionist piece of legislation intended to reverse the decline of the British film industry, and to encourage filmmakers to produce more films in Britain and the Empire:

> The Cinematograph Films Act (1927) was the first case of the government intervening to protect the commercial film industry. [The Act] imposed a statutory obligation on renters and exhibitors

to acquire and show a minimum 'quota' of British films out of the total number they handled, British and foreign.[42]

The Act created a marketplace for British productions at a time when American imports were beginning to dominate British screens. In introducing such legislation, the state was encouraging British filmmakers to undertake a production drive; however, when producers approached state control agencies, they were met with a response that contradicted the spirit of the Films Act.

Norman Lee – co-writer of Hitchcock's *The Farmer's Wife* (Alfred Hitchcock, British International Pictures, 1928) who would later direct *Bulldog Drummond at Bay* (Norman Lee, Associated British Picture Corporation, 1937) along with a series of Edgar Wallace adaptations – was one such filmmaker. Lee, writing on behalf of H. B. Parkinson Film Productions, addressed his letter directly to the Prime Minister, Stanley Baldwin, and his complaints regarding his prior treatment were plentiful. Lee contends that Met Commissioner Horwood had not accorded 'sufficient facilities for filming London' to production companies eager to put the capital on screen.[43] He lists five experiences of such difficulties, including being 'hunted by detectives in Hyde Park' whilst attempting to film there, being refused permits to film Billingsgate Market, Westminster Abbey and Regents Park, and also being refused collaborative facilities for a film based on the work of the London fire brigade.[44] His fifth example indicates the hostility towards filmmakers from the higher echelons of the Met:

> I wrote to Scotland Yard and asked if I might make notes for a scenario connected with a river police story, such notes to be the result of a ride in a police boat. I guaranteed that the Police should appear in the very best possible light and that no interference with duty should take place while my investigations were going on. I received a blank refusal. In reply I sent a protest to Sir William Horwood who did not answer.[45]

The situation improved somewhat following Norman Lee's protestations. A series of rules, informally known as the '1927 principles', had governed the treatment of film companies by the Met since 1927. While there is no direct evidence to suggest so, these rules may well have been drawn up in response to the Cinematograph Films Act (1927), as a means by which the Met could be seen to be supporting the British film industry. These rules, reiterated by the Met Secretary H. M. Howgrave-Graham in a private memo to the Home Office, stipulate conditions under which permission for facilities and collaboration might be granted to film companies. The conditions require that prospective collaborators are affiliated with 'bona-fide firms', that only the 'ordinary work of police is portrayed', that all completed films are submitted to the Met prior to release for 'examination', that no 'stunts' are arranged as part of the filming, and also 'that photographs or films are not used as part of a story (in the sense of fiction)'.[46] Of course, compliance with these stipulations proved impossible for almost all prospective productions. These principles were drawn up with the intention of benefitting potential collaborators, but Howgrave-Graham seems to have been unaware of the impossibility of obeying such stringent stipulations. In introducing his series of rules, he declared that 'we get so much publicity of the wrong kind that I can't help feeling it might be to our advantage to have a little of the right kind'.[47] It is worth noting that the Met appeared to not differentiate between the two types of requests they received from film companies – the 1927 principles applied to both applications to film within public areas of the Metropolitan Police district and also to prospective collaborative projects involving the production of a narrative that depicts aspects of the Met on screen.

Howgrave-Graham, having played an important role in the introduction of these guidelines, defended his refusal to grant Lee production facilities for a film to be based around the work of the river police on the basis that the film would contravene the clause involving the use of images of the police in a fictional narrative.[48] However, following a meeting involving Norman Lee, H. B. Parkinson and the Permanent Under Secretary of State to the Home Office, Sir John Anderson and his Assistant, A. L. Dixon, the Home Office intimated that there was 'some little margin'[49] between the Met's position regarding the use of images of the police in a fictional narrative and the Home Office's belief that the police should 'be as helpful as possible'[50] towards British film companies. Lee was, eventually, granted permission to film a variety of street scenes, including incidental images of police patrols, in April 1929 for a film whose plot involved 'the Atlantic having been flown by two Englishmen'.[51] His project involving the work of the river police failed to come to fruition, but his earlier lobbying of the Prime Minister had led to film companies being more likely to have requests for filming in public places granted. His protestations were not enough to encourage the Met to banish the memories of the two 1921 Scotland Yard films, and to attempt a collaborative project.

The appointment of Lord Trenchard to the post of Commissioner in 1931 again led to a review of the principles introduced in 1927. Whereas, previously applications to film street scenes within the Metropolis and applications for permission to collaborate with the Met on a project involving filming the police were covered by the same rules, Trenchard began to separate these two very different types of requests for assistance. In a private minute discussing the 1927 rule that forbids applicants from taking 'films or photographs [for use as] part of a story',[52] Trenchard clarifies as follows:

> It does not matter what the rule was *supposed* to mean; what I would like it to mean is that no facilities shall be given to photograph any part of Scotland Yard if the intention is to weave such pictures into one of these horrible film plots.

It is quite another matter for film companies to take photographs in the street, and I have no objection provided obstruction is not caused. This does not involve filming the police with a view to making a 'story' about them: if they happened to come into the picture it would only be in an incidental way.[53]

As a result of this clarification, more freedom was accorded to film companies in their attempts to film the capital, but not without some controversial moments. For example, Warner Bros First National Pictures approached the Met to request permission to film 'certain exterior shots in the vicinity of Barclay's Bank, Twickenham' for their production, *The Blind Spot*.[54] The film's plot involves a bank robbery, and the exterior shots to be taken consisted of the six robbers approaching the bank – the Warners foreman responsible for hand-delivering the introductory letter to Twickenham Police Station mentioned as much to Inspector Bradford of the station, who forwarded a report of the verbal information gathered, along with Warners' introductory letter, to the Commissioner's Office.[55] Trenchard's secretary wrote in response that the Commissioner 'will raise no objection to the proposal ... provided that no obstruction is caused'.[56] However, Trenchard was concerned about the content of the film and wrote to the Home Office to recommend that they put some pressure on the British Board of Film Censors 'to stop the film being shown'[57]:

> I think that this sort of film does harm to the men of about 18 or 19, as it shows them that these sort of things are fairly easy to carry out if done with determination.[58]

However, it transpired that Barclay's had refused permission to Warner Bros to film inside the branch. Warners circumvented this refusal by filming the exterior of the bank and switching to scenes shot in their studio to represent the bank interior. Permission had been granted, in the Commissioner's name, to film the exterior of the bank for a film that neither Barclay's, the Home Office nor the Met actually wanted made. This event, occurring a mere six weeks after Trenchard expressed his openness towards film companies shooting street scenes in London, caused film companies to again be regarded with suspicion by the Commissioner's Office. Stung by the same seed of doubt as his predecessors had been, Trenchard strengthened the 1927 principles by authorizing the addition of the following clause:

> No facilities will be given to photograph scenes which are open to the objection that they suggest methods of committing crime. Although Police have no authority, provided that obstruction is not caused, to prohibit the taking of such scenes, it is probable that the withholding of Police facilities will make it impossible to continue.[59]

Once again, the possibility of the Met collaborating on an entertainment film depicting the police is prevented due to a wider suspicion of the British film industry held by the Met's higher echelons.

Unable to reconcile its twin, and contrary, approaches of transparency and control to a collaborative film project, the Met and its Press Bureau floundered until the war. The table below (Table 2.1) details all written approaches to the Press Bureau from film companies requesting assistance in the period immediately following the debacle surrounding *The Blind Spot* until the end of 1938. All requests for collaboration were refused, alongside requests for the supply of props for studio-shot films.

In 1935, Lord Trenchard retired from the post of Commissioner, and Sir Philip Game was appointed in his place. Game remained Commissioner until the cessation of hostilities in 1945, making his period in charge considerably longer than any Commissioner so far considered. With regards to the prospect of collaborating with the British film industry, Game retained the same sense of suspicion towards British film interests as his predecessor during the interwar

Table 2.1 Record of Approaches from Film Companies to the Metropolitan Police Press Bureau

Date of Approach	Studio/Applicant	Film Title	Request
14 September 1932	British and Dominions Film Corporation Ltd	*Bright Lights of London*	The supply of 'two Police notices suitable to hang on the wall in a Scotland Yard office.'*
1934	Zenifilms	Unknown	Request to film the 'activities of Police, and Scotland Yard in particular', for a twenty-minute short film.**
1935	Gaumont-British Picture Corporation	Unknown	Request for facilities to collaborate on film about the Met.**
30 October 1935	British and Dominions Film Corporation Ltd	Unknown	That the Met supply a set of notices, including 'Motor Rules and Regulations' and a 'Wanted Criminals' poster, along with holder cards for fingerprints.*
1935	National Progress Film Company	Unknown	Request for collaborative facilities to produce a film adaptation of Sir Basil Thomson's book, *The Story of Scotland Yard*. Thomson was Assistant Metropolitan Police Commissioner during the First World War.**
1936	'Mr Rose', film producer	Unknown	That the Met collaborate on a film project 'to 'tell the story of Scotland Yard'.**
1936	Universal Studios	*The March of Time* newsreel	The provision of facilities to film the work of the Met for the newsreel. Several requests were made to this effect.**
1936	Universal Studios	*The March of Time* newsreel	That the Met allow special provision for the newsreel's cameramen to film the Coronation of George VI.**
1936	National Progress Film Company	Unknown	That the Met provide facilities for a film dealing with the history of Scotland Yard.**
1936	The Criterion Films Productions	Unknown	The provision of facilities for the making of a 'crime' film.**

1937	Phoenix Films Ltd	Unknown	That the Met collaborate on a 'film on a large scale about Scotland Yard'.**
1938	British Pictorial Productions Ltd	Unknown	That the Met provide facilities for a film depicting Scotland Yard 'at work'.**
1938	British Fine Arts Pictures Ltd	*The Passing Show*	The consideration of facilities for a film depicting the work of the Met.**
6 September 1938	Welwyn Studios Ltd	Unknown	That the Met supply a poster referring to bail for display inside a studio set of Hyde Park Police Station.*

Source: Entries marked * are sourced from PRO TNA MEPO 2/5519; entries marked ** are sourced from MEPO 2/7442.

years, as seen in the table outlined above. His responses to some of the requests for collaboration from the British studios are laced with the same discourses involving the need to control, rather than mediate, independent images of the police as his predecessors. A memo, compiled in late 1938, summarized the previous six years' correspondence between various interests within the British film industry and the Met Press Bureau. This memo provides evidence of Sir Philip Game's attitude towards the British film companies so desperate to collaborate with the Met during the late interwar years. For example, the memo reports the following response to Sir Basil Thomson's request for Met collaboration on a film project adapting his memoirs:

> The Commissioner added that if and when we want an official film, we must go about it in our own way and have complete control.[60]

The memo from which this quote is taken also mentions that Game, as a result of Thomson's approach, discussed the possibility of the Met 'advantageously' producing a film with the long-serving Secretary, H. M. Howgrave-Graham, in 1935.

Howgrave-Graham set out a series of potential subjects for films that would, he felt, 'clearly be of public appeal and be of a kind which a film company could make money out of' and also propagandistically benefit the Met:

> The only subjects which occur to me as suitable for treatment in this way are (1) publicity for Information Room and wireless organisation, and (2) vulnerability of certain types of flat and jerry built houses and also of Yale locks; advantages of mortice locks.[61]

The unexciting nature of these subjects is indicative of the Met's lack of understanding of the film industry at the time. It also demonstrates their lack of ambition, in sharp contrast to the post-war PR campaign within the Met; whilst Harold Scott and Percy Fearnley maintained a firm collaborative presence with both Fleet Street and Wardour Street in order to mediate and control any images of the police in the written and visual press, the late-interwar Commissionership of Sir Philip Game maintained a culture of suspicion, reticence and secrecy with regards to the British film industry.

An analysis of the Met's attitude towards the written and visual media during the twenty years of peace separating the two world wars helps, through contrast, to illuminate the difference of approach in PR taken in the mid-to-late 1940s. The Press Bureau was established in a climate where PR opportunities were being re-evaluated by state institutions but, much to the chagrin of the film companies hoping for a new culture of openness and collaboration, the Bureau's aspirations of providing transparency and demystifying the Met were too ambitious for a body whose traditions were drawn from the military and which sought to control the public image of the police through denying access to collaborative provisions. Successive administrations viewed the British film industry with an ever-increasing degree of suspicion, reinforced by the failure of the only collaborative production of the period, *Scotland Yard 1921*, and a series of controversies surrounding the production of unauthorized depictions of the Met by British film interests intent on placing the British police on screen.

As I will demonstrate in the following chapters, the post-1945 Press Bureau regime of Percy Fearnley, augmented by the progressiveness of Commissioner Harold Scott, maximized the PR potential of depictions of the police on British screens, but the interwar failure of the Met to regard the British film industry with anything less than deep suspicion led to a series of missed opportunities to increase the legitimacy of the police in the eyes of the public. The PR failure of the Met prior to the Second World War is neatly summed up by an incident in 1937. Howgrave-Graham compiled a series of notes in preparation for a parliamentary question asked of the Home Secretary, enquiring 'if there is at present any public relations officer attached to the Metropolitan Police; and, if not, whether he will consider the appointment of such an officer'.[62] Howgrave-Graham minuted the following for the attention of the Commissioner:

> The work of a Public Relations Officer is publicity – i.e. publicity by means of liaison with the Press, Films, Advertisement, and so on.
>
> We have, as you know, our press organisation here and the assistance of the Home Office Press Officer is also available to us. We don't need advertisement in the same way as a big 'business' like the Post Office.[63]

The Commissioner and the Secretary eventually arrived at a suitable response – 'There is no person bearing the title "Public Relations Officer" attached to the Metropolitan Force, and the need for such an officer has not been felt'.[64] The war, however, forcibly began to change this perceived lack of need within the Met.

Notes

1. Rob C. Mawby, 'Chibnall Revisited: Crime Reporters, the Police and "Law-and-Order News"', *British Journal of Criminology* (vol. 6, no. 50, 2010), pp. 1060–76; Steve Chibnall, *Law-and-Order News* (London: Tavistock, 1977); Steven Chermak and Alexander Weiss, 'Maintaining Legitimacy Using External Communication Strategies: An Analysis of Police-Media Relations', *Journal of Criminal Justice* (vol. 33, no. 5, 2005), pp. 501–12.
2. Chermak and Weiss, *Maintaining Legitimacy*, p. 510.
3. General Sir Nevil Macready, *Annals of an Active Life Volume II* (London: Hutchinson, 1924), p. 416.
4. Ibid., p. 417.
5. Public Record Office, The National Archives (hereafter PRO TNA), HO 45/24442, Sir Nevil Macready, Commissioner of Police of the Metropolis, to Sir Edward Troup, Under-Secretary of State, Home Office, 27 September 1919.

6 The Bank of England – traditionally an institution which viewed the press with some scepticism – began to manage its public image in the years immediately following the First World War by control-releasing certain information to the press in order to construct a positive image of the monetary policies introduced in this period. See R. S. Sayers, *The Bank of England, 1891–1944*, vol. 1 (Cambridge: CUP, 1976), pp. 373–85.
7 Herbert Ponting, 'Education and the Film: Its Place in the Schools', *Manchester Guardian* (11 September 1917), n.p. Preserved in PRO TNA HO 45/10960/340327.
8 PRO TNA HO 45/10960/340327, Sir Edward Carson to the Home Office and Board of Trade, 11 January 1918; see also PRO TNA BT 13/83.
9 PRO TNA HO 45/10960/340327, Lieutenant Colonel John Buchan, Department of Information, to the Home Office, 28 January 1918.
10 Luke McKernan, *Topical Budget: The Great British News Film* (London: BFI, 1992), p. 19.
11 Ibid., p. 28.
12 The 'Third Degree' controversy relates to a press exposé of 'rough' police interrogation practices taking place across Britain during the 1920s. For a full account of the controversy, see John Carter Wood, '"The Third Degree": Press Reporting, Crime Fiction and Police Powers in 1920s Britain', *Twentieth Century British History* (vol. 21, no. 4, 2010), pp. 464–85.
13 PRO TNA HO 45/24442, General Sir Nevil Macready, Metropolitan Police, to Edward R. Troup, Under Secretary of State to the Home Office, 27 September 1919.
14 Nevil's father, William Charles Macready, was a leading stage actor and a close friend of Charles Dickens. His diaries provide an excellent insight into the Victorian theatrical scene. J. C. Trewin (ed.), *The Journal of William Charles Macready 1832–1851* (London: Longmans, 1967).
15 His medals were recently auctioned by Spinks' Auction House, based in London. See Lot 232, http://www.auction-net.co.uk/viewAuction.php?id=1211&offset=200&PHPSESSID=413f2c0fc4f9dce4b1636a05f7ece50c (accessed 9 January 2012).
16 A letter from William Jeapes to Major Edmund Distin-Maddick, dated 6 September 1920, makes reference to 'the proposal you [Distin-Maddick]

put to me [Jeapes] on 4 September last as to our taking films of the Metropolitan Police Force under your direction and editing'. PRO TNA MEPO 2/6207, William Jeapes, Topical Film Company, to Major Edmund Distin-Maddick, Metropolitan Police, 6 September 1920.
17 Ibid.
18 Ibid.
19 PRO TNA MEPO 2/6207, Brigadier-General Sir William Horwood, Commissioner of Police of the Metropolis, to William Jeapes, Topical Film Company, 26 January 1921.
20 McKernan, *Topical Budget*, p. 35.
21 Horwood mentions, in a press release announcing the release of *Scotland Yard 1921*, that 'I have a fund at my disposal for police organisations which I hope this film will assist to swell'. PRO TNA MEPO 2/6207, Brigadier-General Sir William Horwood, Commissioner of Police of the Metropolis, circular to the Press, 9 March 1921.
22 PRO TNA MEPO 2/6207, Brigadier-General Sir William Horwood, Commissioner of Police of the Metropolis, to William Jeapes, Topical Film Company, 26 January 1921.
23 PRO TNA MEPO 2/6207, Brigadier-General Sir William Horwood, Metropolitan Police, Press Circular, 9 March 1921.
24 Anon., 'Police Pictures: Tribute to the Work of the Force', *The Times*, 12 March 1921, p. 8.
25 PRO TNA MEPO 2/6207, Sir John Baird, Under-Secretary of State for the Home Office, 'Concerning the Importance of Being A Policeman' draft speech. Undated.
26 Ibid.
27 PRO TNA MEPO 2/6207, P. T. B. Browne, Chief Constable, Cumberland and Westmorland Constabulary, to the Viscount Byng of Remy, Commissioner of Police of the Metropolis, 10 February 1931.
28 PRO TNA MEPO 2/6207, H. M. Howgrave-Graham, Secretary of the Metropolitan Police, to P. T. B. Browne, Chief Constable, Cumberland and Westmorland Constabulary, 25 February 1931.
29 PRO TNA MEPO 2/6207, H. M. Howgrave-Graham, Secretary of the Metropolitan Police, to E. Foxen-Cooper, War Office, 29 August 1933.
30 PRO TNA MEPO 2/7442, unpaginated torn advertisements from *Kinematograph Weekly*, undated (presumably late January 1921).

31 PRO TNA MEPO 2/7442, Arthur Clavering, Film Booking Offices (1919) Ltd, to Major Edmund Distin-Maddick, Metropolitan Police, 3 February 1921.
32 PRO TNA MEPO 2/7442, handwritten note from Hugh Fraser, 8 February 1921.
33 PRO TNA MEPO 2/7442, W. H. Kendall, Secretary to the Metropolitan Police Commissioner's Office, to ex-Chief Inspector Ernest Haigh, 8 February 1921.
34 PRO TNA MEPO 2/7442, Haigh to Kendall, 9 February 1921.
35 PRO TNA MEPO 2/7442, Haigh to Kendall, 13 February 1921.
36 Ibid.
37 PRO TNA MEPO 2/7442, W. H. Kendall, account of meeting of 14 February 1921 between Ernest Haigh, H. B. Parkinson, Kendall, 'Mr. Muskett', and Major Edmund Distin-Maddick. Account dated 15 February 1921.
38 PRO TNA MEPO 2/7442, Haigh to Kendall, 13 February 1921.
39 Anon., untitled review of new serials, *Daily Telegraph*, 5 May 1921, n.p. Preserved in PRO TNA MEPO 2/7442.
40 Scott Anthony, *Public Relations and the Making of Modern Britain: Stephen Tallents and the Birth of a Progressive Media Profession* (Manchester: MUP, 2012), p. 15.
41 See ibid., pp. 37–41, for a full account of Tallents's work during this time.
42 Margaret Dickinson and Sarah Street, *Cinema and State: The Film Industry and the British Government 1927–84* (London: BFI, 1985), p. 5.
43 PRO TNA MEPO 2/2259, Norman Lee, Director for H. B. Parkinson Film Productions Ltd, to Stanley Baldwin, Prime Minister, 11 January 1929.
44 Ibid.
45 Ibid.
46 PRO TNA MEPO 2/2259, Memo from H. M. Howgrave-Graham, Secretary, Metropolitan Police, to 'S. of S.' (presumably the Under-Secretary of State for the Home Office), 23 February 1929.
47 PRO TNA MEPO 2/6978, Howgrave-Graham to Horwood, private minute, 6 December 1927.

48 PRO TNA MEPO 2/2259, Howgrave-Graham to A. L. Dixon CBE, Assistant Permanent Secretary at the Home Office, 26 February 1929.
49 PRO TNA MEPO 2/2259, Dixon to Howgrave-Graham, 5 April 1929.
50 Ibid.
51 PRO TNA MEPO 2/2259, Inspector W. Irwin, Police Report filed at Bow Street Station, 9 April 1929.
52 PRO TNA MEPO 2/7442, anonymous memo headed 'Summary of applications for facilities to make films depicting Police work, etc.', undated (possibly 1938, or early 1939).
53 PRO TNA MEPO 2/6978, Lord Trenchard, Commissioner of Police of the Metropolis, Minute 2, 19 February 1932.
54 PRO TNA MEPO 2/7392, Mr Royce, Secretary and Controller, Warner Bros. First National Productions Ltd, to Twickenham Police Station, 12 April 1932.
55 PRO TNA MEPO 2/7392, Inspector H. Bradford, Police Report filed at Twickenham Station, 13 April 1932.
56 PRO TNA MEPO 2/7392, 'S. R.' on behalf of the Commissioner's Office, Metropolitan Police, to Mr Royce, Warner Bros. First National, 16 April 1932.
57 PRO TNA MEPO 2/7392, Lord Trenchard, Commissioner of Police of the Metropolis, to R. R. Scott, Permanent Under-Secretary at the Home Office, 7 May 1932.
58 Ibid.
59 PRO TNA MEPO 2/7392, Private Minute, Lord Trenchard to H. M. Howgrave-Graham, 5 July 1932.
60 PRO TNA MEPO 2/7442, anonymous memo headed 'Summary of applications for facilities to make films depicting Police work, etc.', undated (possibly 1938, or early 1939).
61 Ibid.
62 PRO TNA MEPO 2/8393, Parliamentary Question asked by Captain Alec Cunningham-Reid on 11 February 1937, dossier prepared 4 February 1937.
63 PRO TNA MEPO 2/8393, H. M. Howgrave-Graham to Commissioner Philip Game, Minute 4, 9 February 1937.
64 HC Deb 11 February 1937 vol. 320 cc. 571–2.

3

A reassuring necessity: Mediating images of law and order in the Second World War

Between 1940 and 1947, a wholesale shift away from the reticent attitude adopted during the interwar years within the Metropolitan Police (hereafter 'Met') towards the British film industry took place. The policy of withholding information and access from the written and visual press fostered by the successive Met Commissionerships of William Horwood (1920–8), Viscount Byng (1928–31) and Lord Trenchard (1931–5) was continued by Philip Game upon his accession to the post of Commissioner in 1935, and has been outlined in the previous chapter. However, the impending certainty of war appeared to sway Commissioner Game's opinions regarding the British film industry and the PR potential offered by cinema. A memo produced anonymously, but presumably by Hamilton Howgrave-Graham, the Met Secretary (a rank equal in stature to that of Assistant Commissioner), in 1938, headed 'Summary of applications for facilities to make films depicting Police work, etc.', retrospectively summarized the justifications given between 1927 and 1938 for rejecting over a dozen prospective film projects.[1] However, the production of this memo in itself is evidence of someone within the Met pushing for a review into and a discussion of the potential of police-press collaborations, presumably in light of the need to foster a tradition of domestic propaganda to ensure that the people of Britain are 'on side' should the certainty of war become the actuality of conflict. As 1938 ticked into 1939, there emerged a desire within the Met to use cinema's propaganda potential, rather than restrict it.

This chapter focuses upon the period between 1940 and 1947, during which the Met began – possibly with the 1938 summary memo in mind – to acknowledge the potential of cinema as propaganda, with particular concentration upon four key events that took place within the Met during this period. These events – the making of the Ministry of Information-commissioned General Post Office (hereafter MOI; GPO) Film Unit short, *War and Order* (Charles Hasse), in 1940; the appointment of Percy Horne Fearnley as the first Public Information Officer (PIO) in December 1945; the subsequent production of a prestigious Rank documentary, *This Modern Age: Scotland Yard* (John C. Monck, Production Facilities [Film] Ltd), in mid-1946 and the making of the first film collaboration with an independent producer, Paul Barralet, in mid-1947 – demonstrated the refinement of two key processes by which the Met sought to mediate the visual image of its own machinery. The collaborative production processes of the three films in question make apparent the Met's desire to collapse the entertainment/propaganda opposition which proved so troublesome with their first collaborative film, *Scotland Yard 1921: For the King, the Law, the People* – the production of which is discussed in the previous chapter.

Impending war curtailed, rather than encouraged, a collaborative atmosphere between the Met and the press, particularly during the 'Phoney War' period immediately following the invasion of Poland. What it did, however, was allow the Ministry of Information (hereafter 'MOI') – then a fledgling, bureaucratically paralyzed department responsible for the dissemination of domestic and international propaganda – to develop its internal PR machinery, especially its Films Division.[2] It was through pressure applied by the MOI that the Met finally followed up *Scotland Yard 1921* in 1940 with a ten-minute short, *War and Order*. The tumultuous Phoney War period of the

MOI's Films Division led the *Documentary News Letter* to opine the following in an editorial:

> We earnestly hope that most of the Divisions will be found to be comparatively free at least of the inefficiency, muddleheadedness and bureaucratic stupidity of the Films Division. In ten months this Division has achieved a mere fraction of what it should have achieved. Its lack of imagination, no less than its abysmal failure to be even competent at its job, have been the despair of all persons in the film trade who sincerely want to place their expert abilities at the disposal of the national effort.[3]

Nicholas Pronay has attributed this 'muddleheadedness' to the sacrificial nature of the insecure government at the time, led by Prime Minister Neville Chamberlain. His summary of this period is comprehensive and is quoted at length below:

> At the outbreak of war, the Chamberlain government was a badly weakened, shaken and easily harrassable government. The 'man of peace' who claimed to have saved peace for our time, was very much on trial as war leader in the House and in the country alike ... The Ministry of Information immediately emerged at the outbreak of war as a potential source of embarrassment and political rows because it made a singular mess of the teething troubles of the new wartime Ministries, as they hatched from the incubators of pre-war contingency planning. Under the circumstances, it was inevitable that Chamberlain would not wish to put up a fight to protect it from its critics. On the contrary, he wished to accommodate as many of them as possible by sacrificing whichever official's head was being bayed for – even if the mess was *far* from being solely due to their own inadequacies. The carefully and intelligently chosen Head of the Films Division came to be one of the sacrificial victims when, for no fault of his own or even of his staff, the initial film coverage of the war proved to have left much to be desired.[4]

Pronay is clearly an admirer of the sacrificial lamb in question, Sir Joseph Ball, who possessed a wealth of personal relations with senior British film studio figures and held the personal confidence of the Prime Minister – a seemingly perfect candidate for the role of overseeing the production of cinematic propaganda during the Second World War. According to Pronay, Ball 'was replaced by a rank amateur without *any* political affiliations with a pleasant, well-liked personality: Kenneth Clark. The Films Division, not surprisingly, failed to produce anything at all under him (once again not altogether his fault, for he *was* learning fast, but due to a variety of circumstances beyond his control)'.[5] This is an overestimation of the lack of productivity within the Films Division during his reign; Clark was, along with Sir Kenneth Lee, Director-General of the MOI, responsible for forcing the Met to acknowledge the potential of cinema for domestic propaganda purposes. The film in question, *War and Order*, is not particularly significant in terms of its impact, nor is its significance related to its aesthetic qualities – it is in fact an unassuming, largely unheralded film save for a few mentions in the occasional film survey book.[6] The film's production processes, however, instigated certain collaborative relationships between a filmmaking body and the Met – *War and Order*, in short, was a catalyst for the post-war period of collaborative productivity between the British film industry and the Met Press Bureau. Without the film, produced in 1940 by the GPO Film Unit and commissioned by Kenneth Clark's Films Division, it is entirely feasible that the Met would have continued to reject the potential of film propaganda in strengthening consent for the rule of law.

In order to secure a film collaboration with the Met, the MOI had to break down the suspicion with which filmmakers were regarded within the Commissioner's Office. Whether the MOI were actually aware of the culture of reticence within the Met towards film producers is uncertain, and so it may have been just good fortune that the MOI chose to employ the GPO Film Unit – already a semi-official production body – in the production of *War and Order*.

Indeed, the GPO Film Unit was fully taken under the control of the MOI in April 1940, such was the governmental level of trust in their ability to produce effective, line-towing propaganda for domestic and international audiences.[7] A. E. Highet, Controller of Publicity within the GPO and responsible for its Film Unit, had an assistant, G. E. G. Forbes, who wrote in a letter to the Treasury in June 1939 that

> in time of emergency, it is desirable for the Government to have at its instant disposal a film-producing organisation of a kind to which the departments generally, and especially those concerned with defense [sic], can surely grant access to secret information and secret localities; and this condition cannot be fulfilled otherwise than by the continuous maintenance of a film-producing organisation directly staffed and controlled by the Government.[8]

The wishes of Highet and his assistant came to pass in April 1940. The Films Division's lack of productivity under Kenneth Clark led to him being promoted out of the division and being given the role of Controller of Home Publicity; he recalled that the Films Division, along with various other departments, was 'nominally' under his control, but 'except on points of principle, their directors had to run them in their own way'.[9] Clark's oft-discussed ineffectiveness during his short time as Head of the Films Division is somewhat unfair – he was the first bureaucrat in a position of power within the machinery of the government to 'formulate specific ideas for the use of films by the MOI'[10] in a policy paper presented to the MOI's Coordinating Committee in January 1940. It may have been his expertise in planning, coupled with his seeming inability to implement, that led to his promotion.

His replacement as Director of the Films Division, Jack Beddington, was a former Director of Publicity at the Shell Group, and was partly responsible for the documentary successes of the Shell Film Unit. Beddington oversaw a period of successful, profligate productivity within the MOI Films Division, but Kenneth Clark's organizational expertise is responsible for at least an element of this. Clark's first move upon his promotion was to implement the recommendations of his predecessor, A. E. Highet, and his assistant, by formally assimilating the GPO Film Unit within the MOI Films Division. Without this move, the successful period of productivity that followed may not have come to pass.

Through their new-found status as official government filmmakers answerable to the MOI, 'access to secret information and secret localities' was granted, particularly in the case of *War and Order*, the production and research of which involved unprecedented levels of access to the machinery of Scotland Yard. In short, the MOI was trusted with this level of access and, by extension, so too was the GPO Film Unit, at a time when the Met was governed by a Commissioner deeply sceptical of the film industry's PR potential.

3.1 Producing *War and Order*

Thomas Baird of the MOI Films Division wrote to Met Secretary Hamilton Howgrave-Graham on 18 July 1940, to confirm that the GPO Film Unit had been commissioned by the MOI to 'produce a film dealing with the war-time duties of the Police'.[11] The GPO Film Unit and the MOI, effectively bullied their way into gaining permission from the Met for the proposed production to go ahead – following the receipt of the letter from Thomas Baird, Howgrave-Graham minuted the following for the attention of Commissioner Game:

> A Mr. Hudson of the GPO Film Unit rang up one of my people the other day and said that they had been commissioned by the Ministry of Information to make a Police Film.
>
> I therefore got into touch with him and told him (1) that the British Council were already trying to obtain permission to do the

same thing, and (2) that of course no film could be made without the Commissioner's prior authority.

Now we receive [Baird's letter] from the Ministry of Information, which strikes me as just a bit cool. They don't seem to think that there is any question of asking permission, but merely propose to go ahead in their own sweet way.[12]

The British Council had already instructed the Colonial Film Unit to produce a film for export introducing the colonies to the role of Special Constable prior to the GPO's commission.

Baird's letter to Howgrave-Graham attempted to alleviate any anxieties the Met may have felt towards the prospect of duplication of material by guaranteeing no overlap between the two films in terms of subject matter or shooting schedule, and in fact the Colonial Film Unit project was shelved in favour of the MOI project. Howgrave-Graham, the writer of the untraversable 1927 guidelines discussing the minutiae by which collaborative film projects may be accepted by the Met,[13] may very well have felt anxious about the slippage of control away from the Met and towards the central government in cases of the production of propaganda, which was clearly taking place following the commencement of hostilities. Were it not for the fact that the 'request' (that looked far more like a governmental instruction) to collaborate on a film project with the GPO Film Unit came from a government department, the likelihood would be that the production of the proposed police film would not have taken place.

The GPO film, to be titled *War and Order*, was produced for domestic audiences as part of a series of twenty-four film shorts dealing with wartime national security and home defences. The film is the first in which a process of collaboration – not control – is utilized by the Met and without its success, it is highly unlikely that the Met would have embraced the film industry to the extent that they did in the sixteen years that followed. Without *War and Order*, and the collaborative processes established (somewhat accidentally) over the course of the film's production, there would have been no *The Blue Lamp* (Basil Dearden, 1949), *Street Corner* (Muriel Box, 1952) or *The Long Arm* (Charles Frend, 1957).

The film's existence is solely the result of pressure from the MOI. Indeed, Philip Game, echoing the attitude of Howgrave-Graham, admitted his reluctance to go ahead with the project in a letter to Sir Kenneth Lee of the MOI:

> Yes, I must confess I am very doubtful as to the possibility of making even one Police film of any value; the only concrete evidence we have is the complete failure of the only one ever attempted.[14]

He did, however, agree to accede to the wishes of the MOI Films Division despite his doubts and invited Harry Watt, the proposed director, and the producer Alberto Cavalcanti to 'have a look at the work at a Police Station and possibly also in the streets'.[15] This degree of openness towards a film project that was not directly under the Met's control was unprecedented, and represented a surprising about-face from Commissioner Philip Game who, in 1935, had rejected a prospective film collaboration by indicating that 'if and when we want an official film, we must go about it in our own way and have complete control'.[16]

Five days after Game's letter to the MOI grudgingly giving permission for the film to be shot, Harry Watt sent a four-page outline of the as-yet-untitled film to H. M. Howgrave-Graham. The delivery of the outline only five days after permission was given for the project to begin indicates the speed and productivity within the GPO Film Unit and it would appear that the Met's suspicions were allayed by the outline, as very little of the suggested content failed to find its way into the completed film.

Howgrave-Graham did, however, annotate the following sentences by underlining them and placing a question mark in the left margin:

With the coming of the Blitzkrieg, the police station became a focal point for many new home defence measures. The police had to house the rifles of and check up on the volunteers for the LDV.[17]

The introduction of the Local Defence Volunteers (soon to be renamed the Home Guard) was announced two months before Watt's letter containing the story outline. Howgrave-Graham, in a move repeated many times over the following 17 years, objected to the association of the British police with weaponry, despite the fact that LDV rifles *were* actually stored at key police stations throughout London. This vetting of the film outline provides an example of the shifting approach of the Met to public relations; instead of suppressing media images of the police, the Met were instead *mediating* those images. This point regarding the LDV did, however, find its way into the shooting script, and is discussed later in this chapter.

The progress of technology coupled with the unique circumstances of the war in 1940 (Dunkirk, the Blitz, the fall of France and the consequences of Chamberlain's appeasement policy) made the depiction of British control agencies on screen not only inevitable, but also a reassuring necessity. The mediation of images of these control agencies for propaganda purposes was therefore a requirement in order to maintain the image of police strength, preparedness, authority and the propagation of the myth of the unarmed British bobby against the reality of a depleted, ageing police force bereft of its drafted contingent.

'Reasonable facilities' for the film's production were granted on 30 July 1940, by the Commissioner on the basis of the outline provided by Harry Watt.[18] Provision for two visits – one to Hammersmith Police Station to observe the daily routines of police officers and one to Peel House to research training procedures – was afforded to Harry Watt, who visited over the following two days.[19] These choices of research locations were not arbitrary; Howgrave-Graham had sought the advice of the Assistant Commissioner of 'D' Branch, responsible for personnel recruitment and training, who assigned a Chief Inspector to Harry Watt for the Peel House visit and also recommended Hammersmith Station:

> In view of the purpose and wide publicity which this film may have we should insist on the use of a modern Station; Hammersmith seems to me most suitable, it is a Divisional H.Q., pretty busy with cars, horses and yard space.[20]

The speed with which the project progressed, and the effort contributed by the Met toward the production, may be explained by a private memo written by Howgrave-Graham to the Assistant Commissioner of 'D' Branch on 30 July. For the first time since the introduction of the 1927 principles, the power of cinema as a tool for propaganda was officially acknowledged by the Met – but under the cover of private correspondence. Howgrave-Graham noted, in an exchange of confidential minutes with his fellow Assistant Commissioner, that 'if this film is to be done, we must make sure it is a good one as it will be exhibited all over the country and possibly in America'[21]. With this in mind, *War and Order* must be placed alongside a series of other films supported by the MOI that were aimed at depicting the British wartime situation in such a way as to elicit a response from a still-neutral United States – *49th Parallel* (Michael Powell and Emeric Pressburger, Ortus, 1941) and *Britain Can Take It* (Humphrey Jennings and Harry Watt, GPO Film Unit, 1940) in particular.

A shooting script for *War and Order*, alongside a provisional non-diegetic commentary, was provided by Harry Watt for the perusal and amendment of Howgrave-Graham and the Met on 7 August 1940 – a mere seven days after the Met authorized the production of the film.[22] The shooting script was provided by the GPO Film Unit for vetting by the Met in order to ensure a degree of accuracy, but, in doing so, the vetting process offered the Met the opportunity to mediate the material, ensuring that the short film depicted *their* idealized view of the Met. The shooting script and accompanying commentary were seen and amended by several senior figures within the Met; Commissioner Philip Game provided a page of suggestions, and the shooting script itself is annotated by two different hands – presumably Game and Howgrave-Graham.

The first section of the film depicts a series of training scenarios, including a mocked-up courtroom scene in which a trainee policeman is taught correct procedures in giving evidence, a dummy road collision in which a lecturer demonstrates to a group of trainees legitimate paths of action and also a series of drills involving street contamination procedures in the aftermath of a gas attack. The training scenes were shot at the Met's training school on 27 August 1940 under the supervision of Chief Inspector Ralph, the most senior officer based at Peel House, where the Met's training school was then housed.[23] The scenes involving gas, where trainees enter a tent filled with gas twice – once with gas masks on and once without any protection – followed by shots depicting trainees practicing decontamination procedures, were particularly contentious. Philip Game highlighted his thoughts both on the script itself, scribbling 'too much emphasis on gas' in a margin, and in a private memo to Howgrave-Graham, where he queried whether the Met were actually responsible for street decontamination.[24] It is unclear whether these concerns were passed on to Harry Watt, who by then had been designated the role of the producer in the making of *War and Order*, before filming commenced; however, during the shoot, Chief Inspector Ralph pointed out that police only decontaminate their own premises.

This account provides one of many examples of the Met mediating the filmic text for accuracy – a process that is central to the collaborative enterprise. Mediation for image management involves the Met constructing and encouraging the propagation of an ideological notion of British law enforcement and is the key process of control utilized in collaborative productions to maintain and buffer the legitimacy of the rule of law. Early examples of this process, which failed in the production of *Scotland Yard 1921* but was honed in the late 1940s, can be seen in the production of *War and Order*. The presence of this process is prevalent in the documents that detail the collaboration between the GPO Film Unit and the Met. In the case of *War and Order*, instances of mediation for image management can be seen in the censorship of Harry Watt's shooting script by Philip Game and Hamilton Howgrave-Graham, particularly in scenes in which firearms are associated with police practices.

Shot fifty-five of the shooting script, intended to depict Met trainees engaging in revolver practice, was objected to by Howgrave-Graham and Game. Howgrave-Graham chose to mark the shot with a red cross, with 'omit' written next to the cross, while Commissioner Game's minuted critique of *War and Order*'s shooting script notes, in response to shot fifty-five, 'I should like this cut out'.[25] This statement is anachronistic when considered alongside Game's other objections: seven of his eight comments suggest corrections or query certain depictions of police practices – such as street decontamination – proposing methods by which Harry Watt could allay the Met's concerns. This comment, however, forcefully shapes the film's depiction of the Met by maintaining the myth of the unarmed British bobby and is a much-iterated example of mediation for image management utilized by the Met. This provides a pertinent example of the Met-censoring filmic depictions of its own machinery and is quite surprising given the quasi-official nature of the filmmakers. A later correction by Game is indicative of a level of self-awareness of this process of control; correcting a shot that depicts the unloading of Local Defence Volunteer rifles in the yard of Hammersmith Station he writes, 'I do not think we housed [*sic*] L.D.V. rifles, but Ralph (Chief

Inspector of Peel House) will know. I don't want to indicate that we have rifles in Stations for our own use.'[26]

This example is particularly resonant once one is aware of the traditional working practices of the GPO Film Unit. Harry Watt, *War and Order*'s writer and producer, had visited Hammersmith Station and Peel House six days prior to handing Hamilton Howgrave-Graham a completed shooting script. Given the GPO's enthusiasm for 'authenticity' – for example, James Chapman has noted that 'it was an unwritten rule at the Film Unit that non-professional actors were preferable because they denoted 'real people' rather than fictional characters' – it seems likely that Watt had actually witnessed revolver practice. It is known that guns were assigned to various police stations across the Metropolitan Police District, but the GPO was effectively censored by the Met in order to prevent images of armed police reaching cinema audiences. Harry Watt acceded to the corrections and suggestions of the Commissioner and the Met Police Secretary; having had the Met's responses delivered by Hamilton Howgrave-Graham on 12 August 1940, Howgrave-Graham minuted that 'Mr. Watt ... accepted them all quite readily'.[27]

Filming commenced at Hammersmith Police Station on 22 August 1940, with further location filming at Peel House on 27 August 1940. Meticulous police reports were filed for both days of filming by Superintendent Archer of Hammersmith and Chief Inspector Ralph of Peel House. Both policemen were the most senior officers at their respective stations, and their assignments to supervise the location filming of *War and Order* again indicates both the prestige in which the film was held by the Met, and also the distrust still permeating the Commissioner's Office when dealing with cinema. Judging from their reports, it seems that they were assigned the duty of overseeing the filming process, while simultaneously correcting any issues in the filmmakers' understanding of the procedures depicted in the film. These interventions usually took the form of very minor mediations for accuracy regarding, for example, methods of fitting police uniforms and the order in which vehicles are despatched in emergency situations. Both reports were addressed to the Met Secretary, Hamilton Howgrave-Graham.

Following the shoot, the non-diegetic voiceover commentary was subjected to the same stringent mediation as the shooting script, but very little was amended by the Met, with the exception of several mediations for the purposes of accuracy. This may very well have been because, following the previous mediation processes surrounding the story outline, the shooting script and the actual filming, the GPO Film Unit was becoming aware of and acquiescent to the Met's intention to produce a hegemonic construction of its own image. As a gesture of goodwill, eighty police officers were invited to the MOI's base at Malet Street, Bloomsbury, to preview the film in the Films Division's theatre, sitting alongside newspaper critics, a week prior to the film's release on 27 January 1941.

The production of *War and Order* provides the earliest example of two control processes used by the Met when collaborating with film interests. Mediation for accuracy has been described in some detail above in order to provide an example of this typical process, which was repeated on every collaborative film project. As a process of control, it is of less interest than mediation for image management, in which the text itself is manipulated to maintain the hegemony of the rule of law, curtailing the film industry's ability to criticize and hold to account the activities of the Met. It is here where propaganda processes lie within the production of the film text, and it is also in this specific mediating process that the Met begins to fulfil the role of producer of visual culture, usurping the studio's appointed producer by maintaining control of the material conditions for the production. In the case of *War and Order*, this maintenance of control can be seen by analyzing the roles of Philip Game and Hamilton Howgrave-Graham; they acted as gatekeepers to the required materials and facilities for the production of the film, such as Hammersmith Police Station, Peel House and the series of police advisors used by Harry Watt in the course of his pre-production research. Game and Howgrave-Graham then exercised their censorial control over the content of the film, mediating the text for image-management by insisting on the removal of all references to firearms, again providing an example of the dominance of the Met in their collaborations with filmmakers. However, the Met were uneasy partners in this collaboration; *War and Order* would not have been made without the authoritative presence of the MOI persuading the Met that the production should take place, and the Met did not actively seek the production of a film project on which to collaborate.

3.2 'Such a step might appear on the surface to be revolutionary': Harold Scott, Percy Fearnley and the New Jerusalem of post-war policing

The year 1945 brought with it a revolution of approach within the Met, the central focus of which was split between the Commissioner's Office and the Press Bureau. A series of changes instigated an attitudinal shift within the Press Bureau, whereby the Bureau began to actively fulfil the role of producer in relation to collaborative film projects. Harold Scott, a professional civil servant, was appointed the successor to Philip Game as Met Commissioner on 1 June 1945 and was the first non-military appointment to the role. When summoned by the then-Home Secretary, Herbert Morrison, in 1944 to discuss Scott's suitability for the role of Commissioner, Scott recalled that Morrison 'wished to emphasize the civilian nature of the police force and thought that in the changed conditions of a post-war world the work of the Commissioner would call rather for experience of administration in a big civil department than experience in the military field'.[28] Scott certainly possessed this level of experience; during the Second World War, he had worked as a civil servant at the Ministry of Home Security before moving to the Ministry of Aircraft Production as Permanent Secretary, and had previously headed the Prison Commission.

The unusual appointment of Harold Scott as Met Commissioner heralded a remarkable period of openness at the Met towards the written and visual media. Scott writes, in his memoirs:

> One of my first acts was to get approval for the appointment of a Public Information Officer. There was already a small press bureau at Scotland Yard which gave out a limited amount of information on police matters, but its members had no experience as journalists and I felt it was essential, if our relations with the press were to be put on a satisfactory basis, that the officer in charge of the bureau should be someone who knew the ways and the people of Fleet Street.[29]

Scott's recollection of the decision to empower the Press Bureau is telling; the police-press relationship had to be 'put on a satisfactory basis', but who was this new relationship meant to satisfy? Once again, as with the introduction of the Press Bureau in 1919, the terms of debate in 1945 centered around the need to control the depiction of the police in popular culture, but to have this control hidden under the guise of furthering transparency and accountability.

A seasoned Fleet Street journalist by the name of Percy Horne Fearnley was appointed to the role of PIO in November 1945. Fearnley possessed a wealth of experience as unconventional as Scott's in terms of his preparedness for working within the traditionally closed-door working environment of the Met, but his status as an outsider was key in his revolutionizing of the way in which the Met instigated public relations. Fearnley, it was reported, 'had many years' experience in newspaper work', and had also occupied roles within the War Office's Public Relations department and as press officer for the British Broadcasting Company. Fearnley's upbringing and background were atypical of Scotland Yard bureaucrats of the period; he was born on 19 September 1906, in Merthyr Tydfil, Wales, to a Leeds-born father and a Wolverhampton-born mother. One of seven children, Percy Fearnley grew up in a cramped Welsh terrace, and journalism clearly ran in the family; his father was Acting Editor of a local Welsh paper at the time of the 1911 Census and, I presume, it is through his father's occupation that Percy was introduced to journalism before moving on to work within governmental public relations.

After a few months in the role of PIO, Percy Fearnley began making use of his outsider status to push for greater powers for his public relations machine. In a private minute dated 10 July 1946, he suggested that he should be directly informed by telephone of the progress of high-profile murder investigations by the detectives heading up the cases, which would then lead to Fearnley visiting the crime scene while it is still under investigation to 'collect relevant facts, and issue these, with any other background information, in the Press Room later'.[30] This, he believed, would remove the need for the press to foster illicit channels of information sourcing:

> Such a step might appear on the surface to be revolutionary, but has much to commend it. In all murder cases speed counts as far as the Press are concerned. In the three recent cases we have been hours behind the event. Indeed, the 'News Chronicle' were 'covering' the Belgravia murder six or seven hours before we received official intimation and, as a result, secured a first edition 'beat' on the whole of Fleet Street (and for which they paid, so I am credibly informed, £10 to their informer).[31]

His inability to successfully control the flow of information to the press was a crucial stumbling block in his attempt to establish the Press Bureau as a credible source of information to Fleet Street, and his resolve to know everything, in real time, in order to feed a mediated form of this information directly to the press as quickly as possible, was his solution to this problem.

His desire to implement a closer relationship with the press was not wholly motiveless; Fearnley was mindful of the forthcoming Met recruitment drive and the need to make use of the press to maximize the effectiveness of this campaign:

> If we go to the Press at present and ask them to help us in this recruiting campaign they will retort 'You always come to us when you want help and expect us to give it you, but when we want your help you seldom reciprocate'.[32]

The proposal was rejected; with typical short-sightedness, the Assistant Commissioner responsible for the CID, Ronald Howe, thought that the presence of an untrained investigator at a major crime scene would prove a nuisance. However, Fearnley's intention to control and improve public relations mechanisms within the Met revolved around his ability to be the sole source of information to the written and visual media within the Met; he commented in retaliation to the Assistant Commissioner's rejection of his proposal that

> it is for me … to make decisions as to whether publicity of one kind or another is good or bad public relations. If this is not so the whole foundations of my appointment crumple beneath me … [This is not the case] at present. Information is being given to the Press by persons who are not authorized to do so. I and the Press Bureau are being frequently overlooked … and when questions are subsequently asked as to how the Press got certain information, I am expected to know. I can only surmise.[33]

The failed attempt to introduce a public relations methodology whereby the *appearance* of transparency is fostered by the carefully controlled release of mediated information caused Percy Fearnley to produce the following frustrated outburst:

> The Press tell me my appointment (from the C.I.D. point of view) is the most unpopular in Scotland Yard [and] that if I try to make public relations function properly here and see that all information goes through proper channels I shall make myself even more unpopular. If the Press are well informed on this point (and they often are) my unpopularity is already assured so I might as well forestall anything else that may come along by saying in the strongest possible terms that public relations will not work in this Force until the department authorised to operate it gets more support and co-operation from inside and there is far less talking to the Press outside. My present position, and that of the Press Bureau, is ludicrous.[34]

Fearnley's unapologetic push for the Press Bureau to be managed *his* way, regardless of the hostile reception his ideas received from the Assistant Commissioners, may be his attempt to take advantage, and an element of power, away from the Met Secretary; as I have discussed in the previous chapter and also in the case of *War and Order*'s production, Hamilton Howgrave-Graham possessed a considerable amount of control over police-press relations until Fearnley's appointment as PIO, but Howgrave-Graham retired in early 1946 after twenty years in the role. His successor, Richard Jackson, was a barrister and had formerly worked in the Directorate of Public Prosecutions. Jackson's appointment, at a time when Harold Scott and Percy Fearnley were attempting to reorganize the internal and external communications policies of the Met, may have been perceived as the ideal time for Fearnley to take from the Secretary some responsibilities previously held by Howgrave-Graham prior to his retirement.

Fearnley's outburst reads ominously as a veiled threat to resign, and his minute is not followed up by either Richard Jackson or any of the Assistant Commissioners, but Fearnley was still occupying the position of PIO two months later when he was again pushing for greater powers, this time in dealing with the film industry:

> I think we should 'vet' all film scripts submitted to us and also invite other film Companies to get into the habit of submitting their scripts before commencing shooting. By so doing, we can ensure to some degree, that the Police are not held up to ridicule on the cinema screen, as they so often have been ... My view is that one of our biggest tasks here is not to bring the Press into line (because it is coming into line slowly but surely), but to bring film Companies into line; and if we can do this, we shall have done a tremendous job which will redound to the credit of the Police in this country around the world.[35]

Fearnley, here, sought to implement the same level of control over visual depictions of the Met as he tried, and failed, to implement over the flow of information from the Met to the written media. In his dealings with Wardour Street, Fearnley was far more successful than he was with Fleet Street – a situation that was not directly his fault. Despite his status as an experienced Fleet Street hand, the higher echelons of the Met were not as willing to provide him with the requisite power over Fleet Street information channels as they were with his aspirations to control cinematic images of the Met. Fearnley made no attempt to hide his intentions in dealing with the film industry in internal communications with Robert Jackson and Harold Scott; in order to 'bring film Companies into line', he sought to implement a system whereby the Met Press Bureau occupied the role of producer of the filmic text, mediating the film text from the earliest stages of production. Fearnley believed that 'ridicule' of the Met would be eradicated, or at least lessened, if the Met *appeared* to be more open towards the film industry, offering advice in the form of specialist police personnel, or facilities such as location shooting at police stations or the loan of uniforms and vehicles.

One other reason why he may have had more success in controlling the flow of information given to film companies than to newspapers may involve the differing value of newsworthiness to both forms of media. With newspapers, immediacy is key to maintaining and improving circulation, and the fostering of internal police sources by journalists to circumvent legitimate channels of information represented by the Press Bureau would involve the payment of sources financially or in kind by Fleet Street crime reporters.[36] This arrangement, of course, was beneficial to some individuals within the Met but, as a collective, the continuance of this arrangement was detrimental to the cause of public relations; so long as the status quo was maintained, the Press Bureau could not successfully manage the flow of information to the press. However, the film industry, in its dealings with the Met, placed more value on expertise, experience and the ability to 'open doors' than the ability to provide newsworthy, salacious information. Film industry 'sources' would, of necessity given the audience's predilection for a realist aesthetic fostered by the wartime documentary movement, need to be legitimate in order to provide 'filmworthiness', and so Met insiders would be unable to take advantage of illicit revenue streams from the British film industry to the extent that they were benefitting from their Fleet Street handlers.

3.3 Producing police narratives: *This Modern Age: Scotland Yard* and *The Girl from Scotland Yard*

After less than a month in the role of PIO, Fearnley was already attempting to co-opt the film industry into the production of police narratives with his newly empowered Press Bureau. The two years immediately following Fearnley's appointment represented a teething period whereby Fearnley indulged in a series of relatively low-key film experiments in order to establish a process of collaboration where he retained a significant amount of control. These experiments were interesting in their own right, and the two productions that emerged from this period – *This Modern Age: Scotland Yard* (John C. Monck,

1946) and *The Girl from Scotland Yard* (Paul Barralet, 1947) – help to shed light upon the institutional reasoning behind the Met's larger, full-length collaborations that follow.

The production of *This Modern Age: Scotland Yard* began to be a topic for discussion within the Press Bureau a mere nineteen days after *The Times* reported the appointment of Percy Fearnley to the post of PIO. Following a review of the Press Bureau's files, Fearnley commented:

> I have now had an opportunity of looking through the files of film facilities granted by Scotland Yard in recent years. From them I cannot find any indication of the granting of any facilities to make full length films of the history and activities of the Metropolitan Police.[37]

The immediacy with which Fearnley decided to make use of the film industry pre-empts his stated objective to 'bring the film industry into line' by nine months, and makes clear his aspirations to accommodate the British film industry within a post-war Met domestic propaganda push as soon as possible. The Press Bureau had received two applications from filmmakers for assistance in the making of police films at this point: one from Harold Baim's Federated Film Corporation and one from G. Ivan Smith to produce a documentary to form part of a series of supporting features aimed at competing with the US *March of Time* series for a newly formed Rank subsidiary, Production Facilities (Film) Ltd – or Piffle, as it came to be known by its employees.[38] Judging by Baim's track record and the stated objectives of Piffle, neither of these were going to provide the full-length film collaboration Fearnley clearly desired; Harold Baim produced anything he could – travelogues, variety skits, ghost stories – providing it was cheap and met with the criteria set out to qualify for a circuit booking as a British film short, or supporting feature, and G. Ivan Smith wished to produce a series of topical twenty-minute documentary features.[39]

It is worth pointing out the obvious here: filmmakers could depict the police without the support of the police. It was not a legal prerequisite, or even an unspoken gentleman's agreement, to approach a police body for endorsement before embarking on a police film, and so a rejection from the Press Bureau to a prospective film producer did not necessarily mean the end of the project. However, the mysterious nature of the machinery of the Met, identified by the Assistant Commissioner of 'B' Branch in September 1946 as 'the aura of secrecy and glamour which surrounds Scotland Yard',[40] meant that any filmmaker who could obtain collaborative permission to shoot within the Yard's environs and therefore claim to show *the real Scotland Yard* could make a cheap, and a hugely successful, supporting feature. Failure to receive this authorization from the Press Bureau would mean if the production was to go ahead, the film would become just another police 'B' feature with nothing new to offer in a saturated market.[41]

The proposal from Harold Baim was not taken up by Fearnley, and does not seem to have been taken up independently by Federated. This, of course, was a sensible decision – J. Arthur Rank had financially backed Piffle extensively, and Fearnley could be assured that their supporting-feature series was a prestige production. The extent to which Rank had bankrolled the production of the documentary series that would eventually be known as *This Modern Age* is surprising given the climate of exhibition in the post-war era. Leo Enticknap has identified audience and exhibitor preference for the two-feature cinema programme in this period, noting that in 1948, only 6 per cent of cinemas played a main feature supported by a programme of shorts.[42] Enticknap suggests, then, that the series may have been initiated by Rank 'to appease his critics' in the wake of controversies surrounding the monopolistic tendencies of his vertically integrated organization:

> Both the documentary movement and left-wing elements within the pre-1945 coalition government had taken an anti-Rank position in the monopoly debate. In particular, the Palache Report

noted the limited opportunities available to producers without access to Rank-owned studio space and exhibition outlets. By capitalising on the cultural kudos of the British 'realist' cinema and offering a forum for political and social debates in a mainstream setting, Rank could claim to be practising responsible capitalism by fulfilling a public service obligation.[43]

In fact, there was a dire shortage of quota B films (hence Rank began producing its own at Highbury) and the cheaply made shorts were generally of low quality. So Rank needed good, versatile programmers. These factors, coupled with Rank's bankrolling capabilities and their possible desire to assuage critics with the *This Modern Age* project, may have assisted Fearnley in his decision to support the proposed Scotland Yard film.

However, the decision to accept G. Ivan Smith's proposal was not taken solely by Percy Fearnley. Hamilton Howgrave-Graham, entering the final two or three weeks before his retirement, sought the advice of Ronald Howe, at that time the Assistant Commissioner of 'C' Branch (responsible for the CID) just before Christmas 1945. He suggested to Howe that

> It would be good to have your observations (a) because you know a lot of the film people + (b) because much of the work of the proposed film would fall upon your people.[44]

How Howe came to befriend members of the British film industry is unclear, but what is apparent from this exchange is that he and certain film interests – specifically those involving J. Arthur Rank – were very well-connected. Howe received a letter from a solicitor, G. I. Woodham Smith, on New Year's Day 1946, presumably in response to an enquiry he made at the behest of Howgrave-Graham regarding the Piffle project. Woodham Smith and Howe were well acquainted – from him, we learn amusingly that Howe enjoyed being called 'Ronnie', and had a sense of humour – and Woodham Smith was also a director of Rank's film conglomerate. Woodham Smith appealed to his friend 'Ronnie' Howe's vanity, in a somewhat tongue-in-cheek manner:

> Ivan Smith is connected with a new monthly feature tentatively called 'Progress Parade' which will be on the same lines as the American 'March of Time'. Its [sic] a Rank group enterprise and I may add, although I don't want to frighten you, I am on the Board of the company which will produce it.
>
> Arthur Rank will be most grateful to you, and to the organisation you direct, for any help you can give. I can see no reason myself why the Assistant Commissioner should not play a leading part himself and thus demonstrate that the good looking cop is not a mere film fiction.[45]

Howe recommended that the collaboration between Piffle and the Press Bureau should go ahead and, on the basis of Howe's recommendation and Howgrave-Graham's new-found enthusiasm for the film industry (possibly because of the fact that his retirement was imminent and that Percy Fearnley had taken on some of his media duties), Harold Scott agreed to the commencement of the first collaboration between the Met and a studio wholly controlled independently by the government.

The speed with which the GPO Film Unit wrote the outlines, treatments, shooting script and commentary for *War and Order* contrasts sharply with Piffle's turnaround time for *This Modern Age: Scotland Yard*. A meeting was scheduled with Ronald Howe, Robert Jackson (in one of his first duties as Met Secretary), Percy Fearnley, G. Ivan Smith and *This Modern Age*'s producer, Sergei Nolbandov, on 17 January 1946, at which the production was provisionally agreed, subject to the submission of the script to the Met 'for approval' and subject to the Commissioner's own opinion of the completed film.[46] However, Piffle did not provide a treatment until 25 April – an astonishing wait of four months. In comparison, it took Harry Watt seven days from the Met authorizing the production of *War and Order* until their receipt of a shooting script, and the provision of a shooting script tends to indicate that the production is further down the line than the treatment stage. The treatment was produced following two research visits undertaken by G. Ivan Smith, the scriptwriter Percy Hoskins (crime reporter of the *Daily Express*), and *This Modern Age: Scotland Yard*'s director, John Monck. Fearnley had scheduled visits to the Criminal Record Office, Fingerprints and Photographic Departments, along with further tours of the Information Room and Saville Row Police Station – the latter conducted by Assistant Commissioner Ronald Howe. Interestingly, the director was involved in the research trips; the director of *War and Order*, Charles Hasse, was not as heavily involved in the research as Monck was, with Harry Watt solely responsible for researching and writing the GPO Film Unit production.

The film makes use of a voiceover commentary to emphasize the danger of the black market, and how British citizens subject to a system of rationing may 'unintentionally' be supporting organized criminal activity. From an original idea that the film should solely revolve around the black market, the film developed into a story designed to display the activity of as many departments within the Scotland Yard as possible. It is not clear whether this move was at the suggestion of the Press Bureau, in order to depict the Met as an agency of strength and depth, or the idea of Piffle who wished to create a behind-closed-doors prestige documentary in order to instigate a positive critical response. Regardless, the idea to develop the story from a tale of racketeering to a police procedural involving a warehouse robbery and murder may have been mutually beneficial; despite the Met's involvement in putting a scene of murder on screen, the overall effect as deterrent seemed, for the Press Bureau at least, to outweigh the possible criticisms that might be levelled at the Met for involvement in a 'sordid' film (see the early sections of Chapter 3 for a full discussion of British black-market film controversies in the late

1940s). Fearnley was happy with the treatment: 'This film,' he noted, 'should be exceptionally good and help the Police considerably'.[47]

Beginning with shots of groceries displaying a series of signs – 'No Oranges', 'No Biscuits', 'No Offal' – the film demonstrates the temptations of the black market in London, before displaying the various agencies within the Scotland Yard tasked with suppressing the subversive potential of racketeering, including the Printing Bureau, the Criminal Record Office, the Flying Squad, the Fingerprint Department and the Information Room, as well as demonstrating the methods of communication between these various departments. The film provides a thin-end-of-the-wedge argument for the threat of the black market, suggesting that the young *palais* attendee supplementing her wardrobe with under-the-counter stockings is inadvertently supporting a complex network of violent criminals and that, while the black market remains prosperous, shortages will continue. By displaying the Met within this context, the film also promotes the omnipresence of the process of crime detection; the departments depicted interlink with the Area Wireless Cars, Flying Squad and Women Police seamlessly through the feted 'Hue-and-Cry' communications procedure, which presents a reassuring narrative of the inevitability of punishment.

The mediation process within Scotland Yard had altered considerably since the production of *War and Order* five years previously. As I have discussed earlier in this chapter, the mediation stage of *War and Order* placed primary responsibilities upon the offices of the Commissioner and Secretary, who then vetted the treatment and commentary for the film and suggested alterations for the purposes of accuracy and image management. However, responsibility in this case was delegated to Percy Fearnley, with technical input from Ronald Howe. Very little mediation for image management was suggested by either Fearnley or Howe; alterations were made by Howe and Fearnley for the purposes of accuracy, including amending code numbers for police cars. Fearnley cleverly avoided the need for the Home Office to be consulted on the film's production, citing the inevitable delays such consultation would cause to the film:

> I have deleted references to provincial forces because, if these remain, the Home Office will have to see the script, and this will only cause still further delay in making a start.[48]

However, by doing this, Fearnley also ensured that he would retain ultimate control of the mediation process, establishing his position as the gatekeeper of publicity and public relations within the Met. Fearnley was clearly suspicious of the Home Office, and the Central Office of Information (a body that, through rebranding, constituted the former Ministry of Information), as this was not the only occasion that Fearnley sought to exclude the Home Office from the production of public relations material for the Met. In October 1946, Fearnley contracted the celebrated graphic design artist Abram Games to develop a poster for a Met recruitment campaign. In justifying the expense of employing Games, Fearnley notes that

> The Central Office of Information could produce the poster for us, but going through their channels would delay matters considerably, and I am afraid the approach to them would have to go through the Home Office.[49]

This may explain why, despite the presence of a dedicated film production arm answerable to the government at his disposal, Fearnley chose not to collaboratively produce a single film with the COI – they were too slow, too bureaucratic, and too close to the Home Office for Fearnley's liking.

Further amendments suggested by Fearnley over the course of *This Modern Age: Scotland Yard*'s production included reducing the visibility of certain individuals within the employ of Scotland Yard – specifically Superintendent Fred Cherrill (the renowned fingerprint expert) and Divisional Detective Inspector Jones of the CID. Cherrill

A Reassuring Necessity   83

and Jones feature prominently in the film, but Fearnley refused the filmmakers' permission to name them directly in the non-diegetic commentary. Instead, they were referred to by their role within Scotland Yard but, as the latter quote of the two reproduced below demonstrates, more prominent individuals within the structure of Scotland Yard were allowed to be named:

> The Supt. ~~Cherrill~~, who is in charge of Scotland Yard's Fingerprint Department, is recognised as a world authority on his subject.[50] (Additions and crossings-out in original, by the hand of the Public Information Officer.)
>
> At Scotland Yard next morning Assistant Commissioner Howe of the C.I.D. holds a conference to review progress. With him are ~~the heads of the Scotland Yard Departments~~ [his deputies, Mr Hugh Young + Mr Percy Worth + the C.I.D. Supt. of the District] whose help ~~Jones~~ [the Divisional Detective Inspector] needs on this case.[51] (Additions and crossings-out in original, by the hand of the Public Information Officer.)

What is particularly interesting about these amendments is the emphasis placed on authority within the Met. As I have earlier mentioned, 'the aura of secrecy and glamour which surrounds Scotland Yard'[52] would be flagged up by the Assistant Commissioner of 'B' branch as a preservational requirement a few months after *This Modern Age: Scotland Yard* had finished shooting. It is apparent from the above, however, that Percy Fearnley was already aware of public intrigue surrounding Scotland Yard, and he chose to maintain this image by limiting the public faces of the Met to an elite few at the top of the Scotland Yard hierarchy. Fred Cherrill's celebrity would become established upon the publication of his autobiography in 1954, but, having been directly involved in a series of high-profile murder cases and having revolutionized the role of fingerprint identification within Britain, he was already a glamorous, press friendly figure.[53] Fearnley, however, sought to maintain the secrecy of Scotland Yard by presenting only the highest levels of management as the public faces of the Met, allowing only the Commissioner, his four Assistant Commissioners and the Deputy Assistant Commissioners to be named figures within the Met.

Fearnley raised concerns over the role that Divisional Detective Inspector (DDI) Jones was to play in the proposed film. Expressing the view that 'Police are Police first and not professional actors', Fearnley sought to have G. Ivan Smith appoint an actor in Jones' place.[54] The main point of concern involving the issue of DDI Jones' role in the film's production was one of outside perception, however:

> To allow the DDI to take this part in the film would mean that a considerable amount of his time would be occupied in posing for film shots ... and it would almost certainly lead to adverse comments from the Press and the public about police wasting time as film actors.[55]

Fearnley was, to an extent, overruled by Ronald Howe, DDI Jones' senior supervisor, and Jones did indeed play a central role within *This Modern Age: Scotland Yard*. However, a compromise of sorts was reached between Piffle and the Press Bureau; G. Ivan Smith had originally proposed that diegetic sound be recorded, but instead all filming was taken silently with a voiceover added in post-production. Filming was mainly based at Savile Row Police Station, with brief sequences shot in the Information Room and Police Laboratory. The shoot itself took a piecemeal form; unlike the concentrated two days of filming for *War and Order*, Rank's new company followed a shooting schedule that was spread over June and July of 1946, which caused a considerable amount of disruption to the day-to-day work of the police sections within which the filming took place. However, no police reports were filed by the liaison officers assigned by Percy Fearnley to oversee the filming process. This seems to indicate a level of trust upon the part of the Met towards the filmmakers; with

War and Order, meticulous confidential reports were filed by the senior officers at the police stations and training colleges involved in the shoot, but this was not deemed necessary for *This Modern Age: Scotland Yard*.

The final sequence was filmed at the Commissioner's Office on 1 August 1946. This sequence, which actually constitutes the opening prologue of the film, depicts Harold Scott seated in his office, delivering a direct-to-camera address. His address – which was written by Scott and the Press Bureau, and redrafted six times until it fit the needs of both the Met and Piffle – acknowledged the prevalence of the black market in early post-war Britain and also, unusually, the financial rewards of black marketeering. Scott, by acknowledging the inherent temptations of circumventing rationing, makes clear his confidence in *This Modern Age: Scotland Yard* as a discouragement to crime and a successful propaganda tool. Following his address, in which he states that 'the bulk of crime is sordid, commonplace, and – in normal times – poorly rewarded. Nowadays with the Black Market it is rather different', the film delivers a propagandist treatise on the inevitability of detection, stressing the surveillance machinery within the Met.

The film's editing process was speedy, particularly in comparison with the prolonged shooting process. Despite the mediation processes employed by the Met at various points of the production, the final film still needed to receive the Met's official approval before its release. A private screening of the film's rough cut was arranged for 14 August 1946, with Harold Scott, Ronald Howe, Met Secretary R. L. Jackson and Percy Fearnley all present amongst others. Two representatives of the Home Office were also present, despite Percy Fearnley's previous attempts to remove the Home Office from *This Modern Age: Scotland Yard*'s production processes. Fearnley's concerns regarding possible delays arising from Home Office intervention proved well-founded; the Home Office officials raised two objections regarding the accuracy of the voiceover, which was re-recorded at their direction.[56]

This caused a delay of two weeks to the press screening of the film while these objections were addressed, and is indicative of Percy Fearnley's doubts as to the efficiency of the PR operation within the Home Office; Fearnley would again attempt to circumvent the Home Office in the productions of *The Girl from Scotland Yard* and *The Blue Lamp* – a move that, in the case of the latter film, would cause significant controversy.

A press screening in the 200-capacity Gaumont-British Theatre at Rank's headquarters in Wardour Street was held on 27 September 1946. The screening also incorporated the first entry into the *This Modern Age* series, *Homes for All* (John Monck, 1946). Leo Enticknap has explored the ways in which *Homes for All* 'presents a forceful case for the government's planning policy'[57] which is surprising given J. Arthur Rank's strained relationship with Clement Attlee's post-war Labour government. Despite this, it was the second of the two *This Modern Age* entries on the bill, *Scotland Yard*, that drew the attention of the Press. *The Times* reported on the press screening, without referring to *Homes for All*:

> Scotland Yard is now adopting every method of enlisting public cooperation in the war on crime. Its latest departure is to provide actors for a film, which will be shown throughout the country, giving an inside picture of the methods by which criminals are brought to justice.[58]

The fact that the collaboration between the Met Press Bureau and the producers of *This Modern Age* was deemed newsworthy (and indeed it was – the photo desk at the Associated Press had, in June, unsuccessfully approached the Press Bureau with a view to obtaining 'a very nice little series [of photographs] for publication in the home and world press' of the filmmakers at work[59]) is indicative of how out of the ordinary the Yard's acceptance of the film industry was considered. Percy Fearnley was clearly enamoured with the film industry; without waiting to gauge the responses of critics and audiences to *This Modern Age: Scotland Yard*, Fearnley assented to the production of a similar film of supporting-feature length, to be produced and directed by the small independent producer, Paul Barralet.

3.4 'I agree Police *"Girl"* is too frightful for the title': *The Girl From Scotland Yard* and the Metropolitan Women Police

Barralet had proposed a 'short film on Policewomen' in a letter to Percy Fearnley, dated 18 September 1946.[60] In the same letter, Barralet stressed his experience in propaganda production during the war:

> We would add that our Company has been producing films of this nature for a number of years and during the war we were engaged in making instructional pictures for the Admiralty and War Office.[61]

This is not the weighty resume that it may at first seem. Chibnall and Macfarlane have noted that, 'as the end of the war came in sight after D-Day, almost every branch of the fighting and supporting services had a documentary tribute paid'.[62] These 'tributes' required the efforts of dozens of 'B' film units in operation during the period, one of which included Paul Barralet's B. S. Productions. B. S. Productions was a small, largely inconsequential outfit formed by Barralet and Granville Squiers; their output was limited to a series of Government training films (presumably the 'instructional pictures' mentioned in Barralet's letter) and actuality films, including 1943's *Pinnacle of Fame* (Paul Barralet, 1943), 'a film about Madame Tussaud's waxworks, that made full use of the notorious Chamber of Horrors'.[63] By stressing his experiences in government-commissioned instructional films, Barralet signposted his willingness to accede to the hegemonic narrative if Fearnley were to agree to collaborate on this project.

Despite this, Barralet's experiences in the film industry have more in common with the one-man supporting-feature factory Harold Baim than the prestigious careers of the Met's previous collaborators, including Sergei Nolbandov, Alberto Cavalcanti and G. Ivan Smith. Given the lack of prestige Barralet's career brought to the project, it is therefore surprising that Percy Fearnley gained unanimous agreement from his Met peers to green-light the proposed film.

Fearnley's confidence in dealing with the British film industry was clearly bolstered by his experiences in the production of *This Modern Age: Scotland Yard* and, in pitching Barralet's proposal to the Assistant Commissioners responsible for 'A' Branch (Alexander Robertson, whose responsibilities included uniformed policing and the Women Police) and 'D' Branch (Philip Margetson, responsible for personnel and training), Fearnley was unequivocally positive:

> Ever since the need arose for increased publicity for the Women Police to bolster up recruiting, we have been trying to get something on the cinema screens on these lines. The request from Paul Barralet Productions is a heaven-sent opportunity, and I do not think we should miss it.[64]

Despite the fact that Barralet approached Fearnley, it is clear from this minuted response that Fearnley had been actively seeking to produce a film based around the activities of the Women Police even before *This Modern Age: Scotland Yard* had been released. Cost proved to be the main reason against in-house production; Fearnley had mentioned that 'if we were to produce a film on these lines ourselves, it would cost at least £2000, and distributing it afterwards probably even more than that'.[65] Fearnley was aware of the budgetary strain placed upon the producer, then, but he was also aware of the air of intrigue surrounding Scotland Yard, and the proposal from a small-time British producer allowed Fearnley to manipulate Barralet's film to such an extent that the product represents the first example of the Met

Press Bureau fulfilling the role of a producer of a filmic text. Barralet acted as financier and directed the film himself but, as I will discuss, Percy Fearnley retained power over the schedule of production. This relationship allowed the Met to control its own image in the film whilst also distancing its organization from the financial liabilities of the film's production – an ideal relationship, then, to put into practice the processes of control that had been slowly developed over the course of the previous six years.

Assistant Commissioner Alexander Robertson sought the opinion of Superintendent Dorothy Peto, the most senior female police officer in Britain at the time. Her response makes apparent the depth of her experience within the Met; she attained the position of Commander in 1930, and was, along with Sofia Stanley, one of the first official members of the Women's Patrols in 1919:

> Our weakest point [in previous dealings with newsreel producers] is usually the presentation of our actual work; we tend to show the woman constable interviewing the stranded girl and nothing else. Perhaps we could think out something more on the lines of the recent C.I.D. film, including the not infrequent incident [sic] of the Woman Constable engaged on an enquiry or escort, and breaking off to arrest an offender whom she sees committing a theft as she goes along – or an absconder whom she identifies from general appearance, etc.[66]

As Peto was writing before the press screening of *This Modern Age: Scotland Yard*, which is certainly 'the recent C.I.D. film' to which she refers, it must be assumed that she was present at the August screening of the rough cut to a select few within the Met's hierarchy, which is understandable given her position as a veteran of the force. Her support of Barralet's proposal, therefore, is indicative of the positive reception of *This Modern Age: Scotland Yard* among those within the Met who had seen the film; after all, the depiction of the CID in the Piffle documentary was something that other Met departments aspired to replicate. Dorothy Peto's suggestions regarding the narrative content proved influential, and helped to shape the treatment, which will be discussed in some depth later in the chapter.

Peto also had the opportunity to exert her influence during the research visits. These were scheduled for 27 September 1946, just a week after the original letter from Paul Barralet, and involved visits to Peel House, the Women Police quarters situated at Pembridge Hall and West End Central Station to provide first-hand opportunities for Barralet's representative to see the work of the women police.[67] Peto herself led the visits, and reported that Barralet's associate 'saw recruits in training at Peel House, and applicants being tested for sight, + weighed + measured at Beak St'.[68] Dorothy Peto's influence looms large over the completed film; all of these activities are found in the film, along with the locations mentioned.

Following the visit, Paul Barralet forwarded a synopsis of the suggested script to the Met Press Bureau on 3 October 1946, with the working title *Police Girl*, with an attached note signalling his willingness to adhere to the wishes of the Press Bureau's liaison officers:

> We should like to say that in its present form it is only intended to convey the theme of our story and any suggestions you may care to offer will be most welcome.
>
> A list of necessary facilities is attached to the script and we are of the opinion that the picture can be made in a very short time, without upsetting your normal routine. We understand, however, that we should not be allowed to commence for five weeks, when the new uniforms will be available.[69]

In the list of facilities required, Barralet requests that the 'right authority' within the Met reads the suggested non-diegetic commentary, 'and add any suggestions for the improvement of the picture'.[70] Barralet's acquiescence was without precedence in terms of the previous collaborations between the Met and the British film industry. The synopsis itself is very vague, consisting of three pages in which the proposed plot of *Police Girl* is discussed in the briefest detail. This, along with Barralet's obvious willingness to accept any proposals regarding narrative content put forward by the Met, meant that very little attention was paid to the synopsis by the Press Bureau; as a planning document, it was not taken as seriously as the synopses for *War and Order* or *This Modern Age: Scotland Yard*. Very minor mediations for accuracy were made within the body of the synopsis by the hand of Dorothy Peto; Fearnley did not make any amendments or suggestions, choosing instead to rely upon the experience of Peto. Peto did, however, make a significant mediation; the second word of the title has been crossed out on the front page of the synopsis and her successor to the role of Superintendent of Women Police, Elizabeth Bather, later noted that 'we simply cannot have it called *Police Girl*!!'.[71]

Percy Fearnley and the Press Bureau occupied a facilitative role during the production of Paul Barralet's film, unlocking materials held by the Met – advisors such as Dorothy Peto, locations including Women Police living quarters, and actresses sourced from the ranks of the Women Police – necessary for the production of the film. Fearnley, in this instance, appeared confident enough in the abilities of his expert advisors to maintain control over the content of the film to delegate his role as principal point of contact for the mediation process. Equally, Commissioner Harold Scott allowed Fearnley almost complete freedom to coordinate this public relations exercise with the film industry; there is no evidence to suggest that Harold Scott even saw the files relating to the production of Paul Barralet's film. Scott did not minute the file, and the file was never officially presented to Scott through any acknowledged channel.

Fearnley's freedom to act as an unacknowledged producer of the film is evidenced by the delay caused to the film by the late arrival of Women Police uniforms. While Barralet had provided the Press Bureau with a synopsis of the proposed film in early October 1946, the shooting stage did not begin until 14 April 1947. This six-month delay was caused by Fearnley, who forbade Paul Barralet from beginning filming until new, more flattering uniforms for the Women Police Branch had been designed, produced and delivered.[72] While uniforms were expected to be delivered in February 1947, the fuel shortages of early 1947 were causing concern for Superintendent Elizabeth Bather, Dorothy Peto's successor following her retirement:

> I must warn you that the present electricity out is likely to cause another serious delay in the production of the new uniform. It is quite impossible now to give any date for its issue which is very disappointing but completely beyond our control.[73]

Despite these delays, Percy Fearnley and Elizabeth Bather ensured that Paul Barralet was engaged in the casting of the film, even though the film was yet without a treatment or script. Superintendent Bather had drawn up a shortlist of Women Police to undergo screen tests at 'some studio in Central London'[74]:

> If it is not too many I would suggest testing 2 WP. Inspectors, 3 WP. Sgts + 6 WPCs to select 1 Inspector + 1 Sgt who will be needed for subsidiary parts + 2 WPCs – the 'lead' + another.[75]

Not only did the Met possess the power to agree in principle to the collaboration in the first instance but, through the Women Police and the Press Bureau, they maintained the power to cast and costume the production. However, their ability as an organization to override Paul Barralet was ultimately displayed upon the delivery of the first draft of the script. Elizabeth Bather noted, in minuted correspondence with Percy Fearnley:

> Yesterday I + two of my WP. Inspectors went through the proposed script with Mr Barralet's representative Mr Collin. As a result of our discussion a new script will be prepared + will be submitted for approval next week.[76]

It is worth noting here that, despite the delays and amendments enforced upon Paul Barralet, no correspondence from his production company is extant in the production file from the period between September 1946 and March 1947. I would tentatively suggest that this indicates his willingness to accommodate the impositions placed upon his production by the Met; he did not petition or appeal against any of the suggestions made or delays caused by the Met, instead choosing to accept his subordinate position to the Met representatives with whom he was required to collaborate. The Met communicated with Barralet verbally, usually face-to-face but sometimes telephonically, and very few of these conversations were minuted in any detail within the production file. The lack of minutes indicate that these conversations and meetings usually passed without incident – there was clearly very little to communicate to the Met bureaucracy.

Paul Barralet promptly returned a second treatment to the Press Bureau exactly a week after the meeting between Superintendent Bather and Peter Collin. The treatment was greeted with an enthusiastic response; Percy Fearnley noted that it was 'much better than the first', and that the rewritten draft provided the 'foundation for a good film'.[77] Despite Fearnley's positive reception of the rewritten treatment, Superintendent Bather still found that a degree of mediation was necessary. The treatment was still titled *Police Girl*, much to the consternation of Bather, but no alternative was forthcoming from the Met; Bather crossed the second word of the title out in red pencil, possibly in the hope that the producer and Fearnley may pay a little more attention than the last time. Interestingly, it is Elizabeth Bather rather than Percy Fearnley who mediates the treatment for Paul Barralet's as-yet-untitled film; she makes a series of small amendments for accuracy, and three interesting examples of mediation for image management.

The treatment is indicative of Paul Barralet's previous two strands of work in the supporting feature industry; his acquiescence is symptomatic of a film producer who has previously produced government-training films, but some of the content of the treatment demonstrates an exploitative tendency on the behalf of the author. Elizabeth Bather had also noticed this, amending one part of the treatment as below:

> Back in the classroom recruits are intrigued by a lecture in progress on instruments and weapons used by criminals. ~~An interesting collection of genuine articles are shown and explained by the instructor.~~[78]

This is a particularly interesting amendment, as it demonstrates the progress made by the Met since 1938 in implementing a public relations strategy. In that year, the then-Met Secretary, Hamilton Howgrave-Graham, naively suggested that 'the only subjects which occur to me as suitable for [cinematic] treatment ... are (1) publicity for Information Room and wireless organisation, and (2) vulnerability of certain types of flat and jerry built houses and also of Yale locks; advantages of mortice locks.'[79] Of course, any filmmaker who followed the second subject would be demonstrating the methods by which criminals took advantage of domestic security weaknesses, but Howgrave-Graham does not acknowledge this. Nine years later, a filmmaker suggested producing exactly the subject specified by Howgrave-Graham, but the Met's cinematic literacy has developed from interwar levels of confusion and ignorance, as demonstrated by Bather's amendment. However, Paul Barralet ignored Bather's amendment; in the completed film, there is indeed a scene in which a police lecturer demonstrates the processes of crime, including the use of a jemmy on a door and the methods by which pickpockets operate.

The second and third examples of mediation for image management are further examples of the Met's control over this project. The treatment follows the career of WPC Dorothy Shepherd. Shepherd was cast from Elizabeth Bather's suggested pool of six

Women Police Constables, and successfully passed a screen test with Paul Barralet and Peter Collin to take part in the film. At the midpoint of the treatment, the author had written the following scene:

> W.P.C. Shepherd again on patrol. She notices a girl aged no more than 16 enter a cafe. Knowing that the cafe has an unsavoury reputation, she goes in herself to investigate. Ordering a cup of tea she sits down and takes a further look at the young girl who is now attempting to resist the attentions of a drunken man. An older woman, rather flashily dressed, and painted up, enters from the back of the cafe and W.P.C. Shepherd notices that the young girl is obviously under the influence of this undesirable character. In addition, she recognises the older woman as a person wanted by the Police. She gets up and questions them both and escorts them to the Police Station.[80]

There are a series of subtextual references here, and these were not missed by Elizabeth Bather. Without explanation or invitation, Bather rewrote the scene, paper-clipping her typewritten amendment over the above paragraph, through which she had drawn a large 'X'. Bather's rewrite subtly removes the scene's potential bias towards exploitative content:

> W.P.C. Shepherd again on patrol. She notices a girl who looks no more than 16 enter a cafe and join a flashily dressed and heavily made up older woman. She enters the cafe and speaks to the pair who are sitting at a table with two men. She recognises the older woman as a person wanted by the Police. She asks them both to accompany her outside and there she questions them. She decides to take them both to the Police Station.[81]

Of course, the original draft of the treatment carries connotations of prostitution through the references to the 'unsavoury reputation' of the cafe, the 'attentions of a drunken man' within, and the 'painted up' and 'undesirable' older lady (read brothel madam) under whose influence the young girl lies. By removing these references and moving the focus of the scene from the young runaway at risk of falling into prostitution and towards the assertive young W.P.C., Elizabeth Bather redirected the treatment away from salacity.

The third significant mediation was made in order to prevent Paul Barralet's film from being *too* accurate. Bather had passed the treatment to her superior, Assistant Commissioner Robertson, for his recommendations prior to Bather articulating her input. Robertson responded with the following:

> I agree *Police 'Girl'* is too frightful for the title [and] I am inclined to wonder that from a recruiting propaganda point of view whether the last 'scene' is altogether appropriate. Isn't there too much of this drinking in pubs and clubs in it? Rather discouraging to any parent with a decent daughter aspiring to become a W.R.C.![82]

Robertson's comments echo Percy Fearnley's original statement regarding the proposal to produce a film with Paul Barralet; the 'heaven-sent' aspects of the production derive from the free publicity Barralet's film will generate for the Women Police recruitment drive – a film in which the sleek, modern Women Police uniform would be showcased. However, Barralet's treatment included a finale that exposed his background in salacious supporting-feature programming. What is remarkable about this finale is that it is firmly grounded in reality.

The treatment's author concludes his narrative with Dorothy Shepherd, having been promoted to the position of Detective, shadowing a group of three 'suspected Black Marketeers ... probably armed'.[83] After gathering intelligence that the group frequents a pub, Dorothy becomes a regular customer herself in an attempt to gain their confidence. After making the 'Black Marketeers' acquaintance, Dorothy is invited to a private party at 'a gambling and illicit drinking club' and judges that the time is right to request backup in making an arrest. However, there is only one telephone in the property, and in reaching it she must avoid arousing the suspicion of the gang leader, who 'is plying her with drinks':

> Eventually she persuades him into the room where the telephone is situated. She finishes her drink; the gangleader goes out to obtain refills and whilst he is absent she dials 999 and manages to pass the necessary information to Scotland Yard.[84]

Scotland Yard then sent detectives to the address and 'at a given signal both front and back doors are broken down and the police rush in', arresting the gang.[85]

Assistant Commissioner Robertson's objection revolved around the fact that the scene depicts Women Police consuming large amounts of alcohol, portraying this as part of everyday life and duty for prospective recruits. His colleague, Assistant Commissioner Arthur Young, agreed with his objection, noting that

> we use Police women keeping observation in Clubs and Public Houses with a view to detecting crime, and I do not want to over emphasize the work they are doing because it will give too much away.[86]

The mediation of this scene, then, did not derive from the scene's potentially salacious qualities, but from the fact that the processes of detection were too accurate, and threatened to undermine the investigative tactics employed by the Met.

Elizabeth Bather is directly responsible for the unwelcome accuracy of this scene; upon reading the original draft, Bather handwrote the following at the top of a suggested amendment to this scene:

> This is the story of a real incident in which W.P. Insp Yates was the Police Officer. We discussed it with Mr Collin but he didn't get it quite right so I've re-written it.[87]

Bather's mediations added a sense of documentary authenticity to the treatment; drawing upon the experiences of her staff, the final scene exists as an adaptation of a real arrest, heightening the level of accuracy. This caused the objection from her superiors that the final scene 'gave too much away' in terms of procedure utilized by the Women Police in the process of arrest.

This scene was altered considerably before filming; the film concludes with a scene in which Dorothy Shepherd, in plain clothes, attempts to track down a stolen car. Upon overhearing in a pub that a used-car dealer of ill repute frequents the Bluebird Cafe, Dorothy maintains an undercover presence there and pretends to have won an amount of money with which she plans to buy a car. The used-car dealer is attired in the uniform of the black market; duck's-arse haircut, wide-lapelled suit, pencil moustache and a loud, large tie. The spiv shows the undercover policewoman the car and, from the chassis number, Dorothy identifies the car as stolen. Dorothy calls the Information Room of Scotland Yard, who circulate her location to the CID. A car chase ensues, with the spiv driving Dorothy who, undercover, had requested a 'quick spin' in the car. The CID officers then arrest the man by blocking his car with their vehicles. It is a thrilling and more glamorous conclusion to the narrative than the one suggested by Elizabeth Bather. The uses of cinematic shorthand in this scene – most notably in the presence of the spiv and the car chase – firmly situate the film within the conventions of the British crime thriller genre. However, by the time of the film's release, the prevalence of films depicting the activities of the British black market was causing much cause for concern for the Met. By replacing scenes in which Women Police officers were seen drinking undercover on the grounds of secrecy and decency, the Met were in fact moving the film away from its police documentary predecessors and instead pandering to the zeitgeist.

Propaganda during the Second World War portrayed racketeers as virtual fifth columnists, undermining the social idealism of the period. The racketeers, by diverting rations and creating an illicit black market, increased the prices of goods. As rations decreased due to their illegal interception and distribution, people were forced to do business with the black market in order to accommodate their needs. One such example of inflation caused to basic consumer goods due to such a diversion was reported by *The Birmingham Mail*:

> Combs and articles of small haberdashery have been cornered by black market operators, who are using market traders as a medium of supply to the public ... As a result of the racket, the public are being forced to pay fantastic prices for essential articles in short supply, and for which the Board of Trade had fixed maximum prices.[88]

Whilst large numbers were driven to the black market through necessity – or, at the very least, through dissatisfaction with the rationing system and clothing shortages – it nevertheless carried a social stigma. Through local press reportage and national propaganda, it was driven home that the black market was undermining the war effort, and this argument was largely accepted. However, by the time of Paul Barralet's film, an attitudinal shift towards the black market had taken place. As the reason for rationing altered in the post-war period, so too did attitudes towards the black market; under-the-counter salesmanship undermined the shared-sacrifice ethic of British citizens in wartime, but in peace, the salvation of sterling seemed a poor cause to fight after the defeat of Nazism:

> During ... 1946 and 1947, the post-war economic difficulties were coming to a head. The fuel shortage paralysed many industries. Bread rationing in July 1946 symbolised for many the misery of austerity. 'The war has been over twelve months,' one Birkenhead baker complained, 'and now we have come down to rationing the people's staple food.'[89]

The black market was no longer seen as counter-productive by British citizens, argues Smithies, but instead provided a means of rebellion against the top-down governmental Labour strategy seen as overly bureaucratic and restrictive by a society that felt cheated out of a victory celebration.

For David Hughes, Clement Attlee's Labour Party had simply misjudged the mood of the British people:

> Never had a bureaucracy so absurdly flaunted its total failure to comprehend the spirit of the times, which was low and resentful, or to indulge, even in small measures, the desperate moods and requirements of the people. So, really, almost everyone participated; it was a sort of pale hangdog spivvery in back kitchens and at the rear of shops.[90]

Everyone, then, was at it, simply because 'this was the time when a jungle of petty restrictions reminiscent of the medieval sumptuary laws positively invited evasion;'[91] the perceived absurdity of the bureaucratic, all-powerful state allowed for the black market to be seen as a vehicle for the individual to claim back his or her right to choose. The black market of this period did not solely cater for the working-classes; the middle class, similarly as enraptured with the idea of 'fight[ing] against being state-ridden,'[92] also made use of it. Dorothy Shepherd enacts a middle-class black-market patron in the cafe scene; despite the austere nature of early-postwar Britain, her undercover character's disposable income is accepted on merit by the spiv without arousing suspicion.

David Kynaston provides further evidence of this black-market consumer base by making use of middle-class diarists' comments from the period;[93] what previously may have carried a social stigma was, by 1946, a source of anti-establishment expression. The figure of the spiv embodied this sentiment:

> With his trilby hat, loud racecourse clothes, padded shoulders and narrow waist, his quick-fire retailing of nylons from a cardboard suitcase at the kerbside, the spiv was a hero of austerity folklore. No

one threatened to flog or shoot him. Instead, he was impersonated on the music-hall stage by such comedians as Frankie Howerd, Sid Field and Arthur English. Cartoonists relished his distinctive appearance. It had been possible to hate such a man whilst Germany was the enemy. As public antagonism turned against bureaucrats, snoops and politicians, the spiv was a licensed jester at the government's expense, 'Flash Harry' or 'Jack the Lad'.[94]

Not only were the cartoonists and comedians enamoured with this 'anti-austerity'[95] folk hero; a tongue-in-cheek union – the Spiv's Union – was created, with subscribers receiving a periodical funny paper, the *Spiv's Gazette*, replete with tips on how to live a life of spivvery. British crime films of the period were dominated with portrayals of the spiv figure, from Stewart Grainger's portrayal of Ted Purvis in *Waterloo Road*, *Noose*'s (Edmond T. Gréville, ABPC, 1948) Bar Gorman (Nigel Patrick), and through to Sidney Tafler's Morry in *Wide Boy* (Ken Hughes, Merton Park Studios, 1952). As becomes clear in Paul Barralet's collaboration with the Met, the spiv injected colour into a drab, austere society. David Hughes notes that 'it was the spiv who stood for London, set the tone of her recovery from war, and was regarded with that blend of affection and mistrust which the English reserve for anyone who seems to symbolize the way things are going'.[96] The post-war black market, then, was reinforced by public support and patronage, and so it is surprising that the Met chose to acknowledge the allure of the black market so candidly in *This Modern Age: Scotland Yard* (as a means of avoiding the limitations of 'No Oranges', 'No Biscuits', 'No Offal' in legitimate outlets) and in Paul Barralet's film.

Despite the candid portrayal of the black market, the script for Paul Barralet's film – still prospectively titled *Police Girl* – was passed by the Met on 2 April 1947. After taking on board the suggestions of Bather and her senior officers, Fearnley submitted the Met's suggestions to Paul Barralet on this date, and Barralet responded with a shooting schedule for Met locations on 11 April 1947. The Met provided Paul Barralet with access to West End Central and Peel House police stations, the Information Room, the Receiver's Store (to shoot scenes in which recruits are measured for their newly designed uniforms), Hendon Police College and Women Police accommodation at Pembridge Hall. The number of locations used in this instance dwarfs the three previous collaborative projects, and so the lack of Met documentation regarding the shooting of the film is surprising:

> Shooting commenced April 14th, 1947. Shooting concluded May 30th, 1947.[97]

The above was written by the hand of Percy Fearnley, and is a remarkably brief record of a period in which an independent producer occupied Met property in the process of recording a film. Long gone are the detailed, confidential daily reports filed during the production of *War and Order* under Philip Game's Commissionership, and it seems that the success of *This Modern Age: Scotland Yard* allowed Percy Fearnley complete freedom in the implementation of cinematic PR opportunities within the Met, as evidenced by the lack of input from Commissioner Harold Scott in the production of Paul Barralet's as-yet-untitled film.

Paul Barralet addressed a letter to Percy Fearnley on 3 June 1947, regarding the success of the shoot.[98] In it, he expressed his gratitude to WPC Shepherd and also to Elizabeth Bather 'whose hard work on our behalf is greatly appreciated'.[99] Fearnley responded via an internal minute:

> I don't suppose we shall ever make a film more easily than this one, because there was one hundred per cent co-operation on all sides, and, just as important, mutual understanding of each other's problems.[100]

He also wrote to Paul Barralet to express his thanks:

Making this film with you has been a pleasure. That it proceeded smoothly, almost without a hitch, was due just as much to your understanding of our problems and obvious desire to help us overcome them, as to any help we were able to give. We hope that the final results will be just as satisfactory – to us as well as to you.[101]

Both of these records of appreciation indicate the level at which the Press Bureau's processes of control were operating; for Fearnley, Paul Barralet's willingness to be guided by the Met in the production of the film represented the zenith of his post-war film collaborations.

This atmosphere of collaborative amiability continued throughout June; a rough cut of the film, without commentary, was screened on 24 June 1947, and two minor reshoots were requested by the Met. These were accepted by Paul Barralet, and another rough cut was screened for Assistant Commissioner Alexander Robertson, Percy Fearnley and Commissioner Harold Scott three weeks later. During this screening, a new title was suggested:

The Commissioner expressed the view that the film was excellent and A.C.A. [Robertson] thought we would have difficulty in finding a better title than the one chosen – 'The Girl From Scotland Yard'.[102]

Elizabeth Bather disagreed:

I would like to point out that I have not seen this file nor has the film been discussed with me since the 24th June. I was given no opportunity by P.I.O. to see the final showing on 14th July nor has he discussed the title with me.

In minute 13 I objected to the then proposed title 'Police Girl'. The word 'girl' is cheap and anathema to any decent woman's organisation. Throughout [the production] I have again and again raised the question of the title. I would certainly never have agreed to the present title 'The Girl From Scotland Yard'. I do feel that when A.C.A. approved this title he assumed that I had been consulted and I respectfully request that he may be approached to re consider his decision on his return from leave.

'Women of Scotland Yard' was one of the titles suggested and I think, although not perfect, it would be quite satisfactory.[103] The dispute surrounding the title reached the Commissioner's Office, and Elizabeth Bather's objection was maintained.[104] Percy Fearnley – who clearly preferred *The Girl from Scotland Yard* from a marketing point of view – was tasked with discussing with Paul Barralet the possibility of changing the title:

> I discussed title with the Company who stated that unanimous advice of film renters, after seeing film, was that 'Women of Scotland Yard' as a title would damn the film from an exhibition point of view.[105]

Anxious to ensure that the film reached the largest audience possible, Harold Scott ruled against Elizabeth Bather, and the film was finally given a title eleven months after the project was first proposed by Paul Barralet. The choice of title demonstrates the Press Bureau's shrewdness in dealing with the British film industry; Percy Fearnley and Harold Scott would presumably have been aware of the nuances of using *The Girl from Scotland Yard* as a title, and would have also understood Elizabeth Bather's objection, but their developed awareness of film exploitation allowed them both to justify the use of the somewhat patronizing title.

While *The Girl from Scotland Yard*'s title was being disputed, the Met had been sent a typescript of the suggested voiceover commentary, written by Paul Barralet. Unlike *War and Order* and *This Modern Age: Scotland Yard*, *The Girl from Scotland Yard* was not totally reliant upon a non-diegetic soundtrack but, in keeping with documentary convention of the period, large swathes of the film were recorded without synchronized sound. The commentary was subject to the same stringent mediation as the treatment; it was handed to Elizabeth Bather, Alexander Robertson, and Percy Fearnley, and a series of mediations for accuracy were suggested in a letter to Paul Barralet dated 5 August 1947.

The voiceover typescript is mundane, grammatically and syntactically weak and, at times, ignorant of previous mediations made by the Met to the film's visual elements:

> Sometimes prisoners try to get tough, but woe betide the wrongdoer who fondly imagines a Police Girl cannot cope with such a sitation [*sic*].[106]
>
> Within a few weeks Dorothy has become a fully qualified officer of the law, with all its responsibilities. The job has it's [*sic*] compensations and it isn't everyone who meets such a good looking horse as this.[107]

The two examples above are indicative of the quality of the proposed voiceover. The Met's representatives enthusiastically indulged in amendments, providing Paul Barralet with three pages' worth of changes to be made. The majority of these amendments involved mediating the commentary for accuracy; however, the Met suggested replacing 'police girl' for 'policewoman' on four occasions, and the Met also suggested that the following be inserted at a fairly arbitrary point:

> Sometimes Dorothy's duties will take her on the beat as they have done this afternoon but at others she will be out in plain clothes on enquiries, or on any of the many other police duties. It is very seldom that a woman officer does a whole tour of duty on the beat, and in this respect, therefore, she gets more variety in her daily work than her male counterpart.[108]

While the Met were happy with the majority of the content of the commentary and script, this alteration betrays the propagandist imperative behind their agreement to collaborate on this project. Fearnley gambled by allowing a second-feature, second-rate production unit access to Scotland Yard in the hope that he would be repaid by their acquiescence. It was a gamble that paid off; the mediation suggested above was incorporated verbatim into the final film, and further demonstrates the ways in which the Met manipulated *The Girl from Scotland Yard* into becoming a recruitment tool for the Women Police.

The film in its completed form, with the mediated commentary and the reshot material, was screened for Commissioner Harold Scott, Percy Fearnley and Elizabeth Bather on 28 August 1947.[109] This version of the film obviously met with their approval, as a preview screening was held a fortnight later for seventy-five Met employees, some of whom has been directly involved in the making of the film.[110] The second screening seems to have been accorded similar gravitas to the press screening of *This Modern Age: Scotland Yard*, with one crucial exception; while the Met provided a speaker (Assistant Commissioner Robertson) to address the gathered audience, and Peter Collin represented Paul Barralet Productions, the press had not been invited. As such, no press response to *The Girl from Scotland Yard* was formulated, which itself is an anomaly given the Met's enthusiastic response to the film.

On 15 September 1947, Woman Police Inspector S. Hill was appointed to 'carry out a recruiting and publicity campaign to stimulate interest in the work of Women Police'.[111] This outreach took the form of a series of lectures delivered to branches of organizations as diverse as the National Federation of Soroptimist Clubs of Great Britain, the Women's Institute and the Women's Section of the British Legion. In all, WPI Hill delivered over eighty lectures across the Met district and further afield over the course of fifteen months in order to boost recruitment to the Women Police service. However, her progress in delivering the outreach material was stunted by the unavailability of a 16mm touring print of *The Girl from Scotland Yard*; the film's release was delayed until September 1948, possibly due to difficulties in finding a distributor.[112] Percy Fearnley wrote to Elizabeth Bather on 3 April 1948 – nineteen months after Paul

Barralet first suggested the collaboration – to inform her that the film had been picked up by a distributor and was on the verge of being scheduled for release:

> At long last things are moving and our patience is on the point of being rewarded![113]

However, it took another five months for the film to be released. Between August 1947 and September 1948, extant documentation suggests that the Met had very little to do with the production; there is a distinct lack of correspondence between the distributor, producer and the Met in the Public Record Office during this period, which suggests that the delay was not the fault of the Met or the Home Office. Paul Barralet Productions were unwilling to produce a 16mm print of the film for the Metropolitan Police Film Library until *The Girl from Scotland Yard* was on general release in September 1948.[114] Upon its release, three copies of the film were provided, gratis, by the production company for educational purposes within the Met, and its popularity as an educational tool for new police recruits is indicated by the renting database of the Met Police Film Library; by the time an audit of the Library was held in March 1958, *The Girl from Scotland Yard* had been exhibited within the Met and other forces 157 times, making it the second most popular educational film held in the Library, behind *The Blue Lamp*'s 161 screenings. While the film seems to have not received much critical or box-office acclaim, the Press Bureau were clearly happy with the finished product's potential as a recruitment stimulus; the first six screenings of *The Girl from Scotland Yard* within the Met were held by W. P. I. Hill on her outreach tour, as she reported:

> It was unfortunate that a copy of 'The Girl From Scotland Yard' only became available in September 1948. I found this ideal for showing in Youth Clubs and to the senior girls in High Schools and

Grammar Schools, and it was shown on six occasions with great success.[115]

The Girl from Scotland Yard, then, represents a key turning point in attitudes towards the film industry expressed by the Met. While previous collaborative projects – *War and Order* and *This Modern Age: Scotland Yard* – attempted to experiment with cinema's potential for domestic propaganda, *The Girl from Scotland Yard* was the first film in which the Met actively occupied an authorial position. In the midst of a drive to increase Women Police recruits, which incorporated commissioning a Women Police Inspector to engage in dozens of outreach lectures alongside a sleek redesign of the Women Police uniform, Percy Fearnley granted permission for a pliable 'B'-movie producer to research, write and direct a film involving the Women Police Service. By withholding key resources – including the locations – until such time as the new uniform was available, and enforcing rewrites suggested by internal Met advisors, Percy Fearnley usurped Paul Barralet's role as producer of *The Girl from Scotland Yard*. The processes of control employed by the Met in making *The Girl from Scotland Yard* proved successful; the final product occupies the position of propaganda authored by an influential control agency, but the film masks this authorship through its appearance of having been produced by an independent filmmaker. Simply put, audience members would have no idea they had watched a state-authored propaganda film as they left the cinema. Having honed the processes of control inherent in the collaborative enterprise between the Met and the British film industry in the production of *The Girl from Scotland Yard*, Fearnley and his Press Bureau now chose to apply their skills in cultural production to a far more ambitious medium – a long-gestating collaboration between Gainsborough Studios and Ealing Studios that would become *The Blue Lamp*.

Notes

1. Public Record Office, The National Archives (hereafter PRO TNA), MEPO 2/7442, anonymous memo headed 'Summary of applications for facilities to make films depicting Police work, etc.', undated (probably 1938).
2. See James Chapman, *The British At War: Cinema, State and Propaganda, 1939–45* (London: I. B. Tauris, 2000) for an authoritative account of the work of the MOI Films Division.
3. Anon., 'Go To It!', *Documentary News Letter*, July 1940, p. 3.
4. Nicholas Pronay, '"The Land Of Promise": The Projection of Peace Aims in Britain', in K. R. M. Shortt (ed.), *Film and Radio Propaganda in World War II* (Tennessee: University of Tennessee Press, 1983), p. 56.
5. Ibid., p. 57.
6. Robert Murphy discusses the prevalence of the black market in his seminal book, *Realism and Tinsel*. Noting that 'very little' of the black market was seen on British cinema screens, he continues by situating *War and Order* briefly as a film that 'sought to reassure the public' at a time of police shortages and salacious headlines. Robert Murphy, *Realism and Tinsel* (London and New York: Routledge, 1992), p. 147.
7. See Chapman, *The British at War*, p. 28.
8. Paul Swann, *The Hollywood Feature Film in Postwar* Britain (London and Sydney: Croom Helm, 1987), p. 83.
9. Chapman, *The British at War*, p. 28.
10. Ibid., p. 27.
11. Public Record Office, The National Archives (hereafter PRO TNA), MEPO 2/6964, Thomas Baird, Ministry of Information Films Division, to H. M. Howgrave-Graham, Secretary of the Metropolitan Police, 18 July 1940.
12. PRO TNA MEPO 2/6964, Minute 1, H. M. Howgrave-Graham to Sir Philip Game, Commissioner of Police of the Metropolis, 19 July 1940.
13. PRO TNA MEPO 2/2259, Memo from H. M. Howgrave-Graham, to 'S. of S.' (presumably the Under-Secretary of State for the Home Office), 23 February 1929.
14. PRO TNA MEPO 2/6964, Philip Game to Sir Kenneth Lee, Ministry of Information, 24 July 1940.

15 Ibid.
16 PRO TNA MEPO 2/7392, Lord Trenchard, Commissioner of Police of the Metropolis, to R. R. Scott, Permanent Under-Secretary at the Home Office, 7 May 1932.
17 PRO TNA MEPO 2/6964, Harry Watt, GPO Film Unit, to H. M. Howgrave-Graham, 29 July 1940.
18 PRO TNA MEPO 2/6964, Minute 8, H. M. Howgrave-Graham, 30 July 1940.
19 Ibid.
20 PRO TNA MEPO 2/6964, Minute 9, Assistant Commissioner of 'D' Branch, Metropolitan Police, 31 July 1940.
21 PRO TNA MEPO 2/6964, Minute 8, H. M. Howgrave-Graham, 30 July 1940.
22 PRO TNA MEPO 2/6964, 'The Police in War' Shooting Script, Harry Watt, 7 August 1940.
23 PRO TNA MEPO 2/6964, Metropolitan Police Report filed at Hammersmith Station, Chief Inspector H. Ralph, 27 August 1940.
24 PRO TNA MEPO 2/6964, 'The Police in War' Shooting Script, Harry Watt, 7 August 1940, p. 4; PRO TNA MEPO 2/6964, Minute 14, Philip Game, 9 August 1940.
25 Ibid.
26 Ibid.
27 Ibid.
28 Harold Scott, *Scotland Yard* (London: Mayflower, 1970), pp. 7–8.
29 Ibid., pp. 37–8.
30 PRO TNA MEPO 2/9352, Minute 1, Percy H. Fearnley, Metropolitan Police Public Information Officer, 3 July 1946.
31 Ibid.
32 PRO TNA MEPO 2/9352, Minute 5, Percy H. Fearnley, 10 July 1946.
33 Ibid.
34 Ibid.
35 PRO TNA MEPO 2/7849, Minute 1, Percy Fearnley, 10 September 1946.
36 The following file contains an account, submitted by Percy Fearnley, of just one such instance of this: PRO TNA MEPO 2/9352, Minute 1, Percy H. Fearnley, 3 July 1946.
37 PRO TNA MEPO 2/6979, Minute 2, Percy Fearnley, 19 December 1945.

38 Geoffrey Macnab has remarked that 'Production Facilities (Films) Ltd [was] quickly abridged to 'Piffle' by producers who regarded it as a tiresome nuisance'. Geoffrey Macnab, *J. Arthur Rank and the British Film Industry* (Abingdon: Routledge, 1993), p. 104.
39 Chibnall and McFarlane's comprehensive survey of 'B' film production is peppered with references to projects undertaken by Harold Baim, the majority of which appear exploitative, cheap and to represent the nadir of supporting-feature filmmaking. Steve Chibnall and Brian McFarlane, *The British 'B' Film* (London: Palgrave, 2009), pp. 14–15, 23–30, 118.
40 PRO TNA MEPO 2/7849, Sir Alker Tripp, Assistant Commissioner 'B' Branch, Minute 4, 16 September 1946.
41 Chibnall and McFarlane have noted that 'if there was one perennial theme in the post-war 'B' film, it was the activities of Scotland Yard.' An interesting account of the production of Yard-tinged 'B' films follows the quote. See Chibnall and McFarlane, *British 'B' Film*, pp. 219–40.
42 Leo Enticknap, '*This Modern Age* and the British Non-Fiction Film', in Justine Ashby and Andrew Higson (ed.), *British Cinema, Past and Present* (London and New York: Routledge, 2000), pp. 207–20.
43 Ibid., p. 213.
44 PRO TNA MEPO 2/6979, H. M. Howgrave-Graham to Ronald Howe, Assistant Commissioner 'C' Branch, Minute 3, 20 December 1945.
45 PRO TNA MEPO 2/6979, G. I. Woodham-Smith to Ronald Howe, 1 January 1946.
46 PRO TNA MEPO 2/6979, Percy Fearnley, Public Information Officer, to G. Ivan Smith, 19 January 1946.
47 MEPO 2/6979, Percy Fearnley to Commissioner, Minute 19, 29 April 1946.
48 Ibid.
49 PRO TNA MEPO 2/7576, Minute 2, 30 October 1946.
50 PRO TNA MEPO 2/6979, First Draft Shooting Script, p. 5.
51 Ibid., p. 8.
52 PRO TNA MEPO 2/7849, Alker Tripp, Assistant Commissioner, 'B' Branch, Minute 4, 16 September 1946.
53 Fred Cherrill, *Cherrill of the Yard* (London: Harper and Collins, 1954).
54 PRO TNA MEPO 2/6979, Percy Fearnley to Commissioner, Minute 19, 29 April 1946.

55 Ibid.
56 PRO TNA MEPO 2/6979, R. H. Jackson, Minute 48, 20 August 1946.
57 Enticknap, 'This Modern Age': British Screen Journalism in Transition, 1945-51', pp. 24-7.
58 The Times, 'Scotland Yard Film', 28 September 1946.
59 PRO TNA MEPO 2/6979, John F. Paterson, Associated Press to Fearnley, 3 June 1946.
60 PRO TNA MEPO 2/7850, Paul Barralet to Fearnley, 18 September 1946.
61 Ibid.
62 Chibnall and Macfarlane, British 'B' Film, p. 13.
63 Ibid.
64 PRO TNA MEPO 2/7850, Minute 1, Percy Fearnley to Philip Margetson, Assistant Commissioner, 'A' Branch, 19 September 1946.
65 Ibid.
66 PRO TNA MEPO 2/7850, Dorothy Peto, Commander of A4 Branch, to Percy Fearnley, Minute 3, 20 September 1946.
67 Ibid.
68 PRO TNA MEPO 2/7850, Peto to Fearnley, Minute 9, 30 September 1946.
69 PRO TNA MEPO 2/7850, Barralet to Fearnley, 3 October 1946.
70 PRO TNA MEPO 2/7850, 'Synopsis of Suggested Script of *Police Girl*', page headed 'Notes'. Undated.
71 PRO TNA MEPO 2/7850, Bather to Percy Fearnley, 19 February 1947.
72 'Mr. Collins [sic], of Paul Barralet Productions, informed by telephone that, in view of the fact that the new uniforms would not be available until February or March, little useful purpose would be served by pursuing the matter at present'. PRO TNA MEPO 2/7850, Percy Fearnley, Minute 11, 17 December 1946. Fearnley later calls the film a 'facility', which he notes has been 'hanging fire for several months pending the issue of the new uniform to the Women Police'. PRO TNA MEPO 2/7850, Percy Fearnley, Minute 12, 5 February 1947.
73 PRO TNA MEPO 2/7850, Bather to Fearnley, Minute 13, 19 February 1947.
74 PRO TNA MEPO 2/7850, Percy Fearnley to A4, Minute 12, 5 February 1947.

75 PRO TNA MEPO 2/7850, Bather to Fearnley, Minute 13, 19 February 1947.
76 PRO TNA MEPO 2/7850, Bather to Fearnley, Minute 14, 13 March 1947.
77 PRO TNA MEPO 2/7850, Percy Fearnley to Met Secretary, Minute 16, 20 March 1947.
78 PRO TNA MEPO 2/7850, *Police Girl: Second Treatment*, p. 3. The authorship of this treatment is a subject of conjecture; Paul Barralet is credited as writer, producer and director, but I suspect that Peter Collin wrote the treatment. Evidence for this lies in a later example of Bather's mediation for image management; in an amendment discussing the treatment's depiction of a real event, she notes that 'we discussed it with Mr Collin but he didn't get it quite right so I've re-written it'.
79 PRO TNA MEPO 2/7442, anonymous memo headed 'Summary of applications for facilities to make films depicting Police work, etc.', undated (possibly 1938, or early 1939).
80 PRO TNA MEPO 2/7850, *Police Girl: Second Treatment*, p. 5.
81 Ibid., Amendment.
82 PRO TNA MEPO 2/7850, Assistant Commissioner 'A', Alexander Robertson, to Met Secretary, 26 March 1947, Minute 19.
83 PRO TNA MEPO 2/7850, *Police Girl: Second Treatment,* p. 7 (original).
84 Ibid. All quotes in previous paragraph also derive from the same source.
85 Ibid.
86 PRO TNA MEPO 2/7850, Arthur Young, Assistant Commissioner, 'D' Branch to Met Secretary, Minute 20, 28 March 1947.
87 PRO TNA MEPO 2/7850, Supt Bather's amendment to p. 7, *Police Girl: Second Treatment*, undated.
88 Anon., 'Black Market', *The Birmingham Mail*, 13 September 1945, p. 3.
89 Smithies, *The Black Economy*, p. 90.
90 David Hughes, 'The Spivs', in Michael Sissons and Philip French (eds), *Age of Austerity: 1945–1951* (London: Hodder and Stoughton, 1963), p. 95.
91 Harry Hopkins, *The New Look: A Social History of the Forties and Fifties in Britain* (London: Martin Secker & Walburg, 1963), p. 97.
92 David Kynaston, *Austerity Britain 1945–51* (London: Bloomsbury, 2007), p. 171.

93 Ibid.
94 Donald Thomas, *An Underworld at War: Spivs, Deserters, Racketeers and Civilians in the Second World War* (London: John Murray, 2003), p. 356.
95 Ibid.
96 David Hughes, 'The Spivs', p. 89.
97 PRO TNA MEPO 2/7850, Minute 25, Percy Fearnley, 29 August 1947.
98 PRO TNA MEPO 2/7850, Barralet to Percy Fearnley, 3 June 1947.
99 Ibid.
100 PRO TNA MEPO 2/7850, Minute 28, Percy Fearnley, 9 June 1947.
101 PRO TNA MEPO 2/7850, Percy Fearnley to Paul Barralet, 9 June 1947.
102 PRO TNA MEPO 2/7850, Minute 38, Percy Fearnley, 15 July 1947.
103 PRO TNA MEPO 2/7850, Elizabeth Bather to Major Sir Philip Margetson, Assistant Commissioner 'A' Branch, 30 July 1947.
104 PRO TNA MEPO 2/7850, Minute 45, G. Peel to Percy Fearnley, 11 August 1947.
105 PRO TNA MEPO 2/7850, Percy Fearnley, 14 August 1947.
106 PRO TNA MEPO 2/7850, Paul Barralet, Voiceover Reel 2, p. 1.
107 Ibid., Reel 3 p. 2.
108 PRO TNA MEPO 2/7850, G. R. Peel to Paul Barralet, 5 August 1947.
109 PRO TNA MEPO 2/7850, Minute 51.
110 PRO TNA MEPO 2/7850, Minute 52.
111 PRO TNA MEPO 2/7950, W. P. I. S. Hill to Elizabeth Bather, 'Women Police Recruiting and Publicity Campaign', 15 December 1948.
112 Sherwood Films were eventually tasked with distributing the film. PRO TNA MEPO 2/7850, Minute 57, Percy Fearnley, 3 April 1948.
113 PRO TNA MEPO 2/7850, Percy Fearnley to Elizabeth Bather, 3 April 1948.
114 PRO TNA MEPO 2/7850, Percy Fearnley, Minute 53, 16 September 1947.
115 PRO TNA MEPO 2/7950, W.P.I. Hill to Supt A4, 15 December 1948.

4

The police as producer: Percy Fearnley, the Metropolitan Police Press Bureau and the Making of *The Blue Lamp*

Between the releases of *This Modern Age: Scotland Yard* (John C. Monck, Rank Organisation, 1946) and *The Blue Lamp* (Basil Dearden, Ealing Studios, 1949), a series of British crime films were released without the collaboration of the Metropolitan Police (hereafter 'Met'). These films tended to highlight the weaknesses of the police by using the criminal as the central focus of their narratives. In this chapter, I argue that the critical hostility to these films forced the Met into the collaborative production of *The Blue Lamp* with Gainsborough Studios at first, before the project was passed to Michael Balcon's Ealing Studios. The film's production was expedient and an example of the power of the Met's Press Bureau at this point in time; the project represents the zenith of police collaborations with the British film industry due to the balance finally achieved between the transparency/control dichotomy upon which the Press Bureau was founded in 1919.

> *The Blue Lamp* benefitted from the critical hostility which greeted its predecessors, as evidenced by the failure of *Night and the City* (Jules Dassin, Twentieth-Century Fox, 1950) at the box office in comparison with *The Blue Lamp*:[*Night and the City*] fared badly at the box-office and, as hostile criticism had not harmed the commercial prospects of earlier spiv films, this indicates that public tastes were changing, an impression reinforced by the huge success afforded Dearden and Relph's *The Blue Lamp*.[1]

This shift in public tastes is indicated, according to Robert Murphy, by *The Blue Lamp*'s success; the film – unlike its spiv-film predecessors – demonstrates the police's strengths, grounding the representatives of law and order firmly within the communities within which they serve.

However, this shift was not due to *The Blue Lamp* itself, but rather the ideological impetus of the film's narrative. This impetus was not included at the filmmaker's behest, but it was instead an inclusion of the Met Press Bureau. The success of this shift of narrative focus away from the criminal and to the institutions of law and order correlates with wider changes within British society. Robert Reiner notes that

> The all-important final factor which facilitated the legitimation of the police was not an aspect of police policy, but the changing social, economic and political context. The working class, the main structurally rooted source of opposition to the police, gradually, unevenly and incompletely came to be incorporated as citizens into the political institutions of British society.[2]

For Reiner, it is the transitional nature of British society in this period that causes the police force to be perceived as a useful instrument of the state. Quite literally, the working classes became 'incorporated' into the police force. Reiner's identification of 'context' as the principal drive behind this change is vague, and fails to address the extent to which these 'contexts' were in fact created by the institution of law and order. This 'incorporation' was arrived at by such ideological interjections as *The Blue Lamp*; through the collaborative process of production, the Met sought to strengthen consensus for the legitimacy of the police's role within British society. The film's success, then, is not symptomatic of a 'changing social, economic and political context', but it is instead – at least partially – the cause.

The evolution of this ideological process can be traced through the Met's incursion into film authorship in this period with *This Modern Age: Scotland Yard*, *The Girl from Scotland Yard* (Paul Barralet,

Paul Barralet Production, 1947) and *The Blue Lamp* (Basil Dearden, Ealing Studios, 1950). *The Blue Lamp* in particular dominates the cultural landscape of Britain in the early 1950s; Aldgate and Richards suggest that

> it is impossible to overestimate the importance of *The Blue Lamp* either at the time or subsequently. It was the top British moneymaker of 1950 ... [i]t also established an image of the police force which persisted for over a decade.[3]

The Met sought to bolster the legitimacy of the police force through *The Blue Lamp*, which acted as an 'animated recruitment poster'[4] for the police and depicted their benevolence and social standing within the community.

This chapter analyses the collaborative relationship between the Press Bureau and the two studios involved in producing *The Blue Lamp*, which represents the first feature-length fiction film produced with significant input from the Met Press Bureau. The Met's role in the production of *The Blue Lamp* extended beyond the facilitative. Building upon the effective processes of manipulation and control employed in *The Girl from Scotland Yard*, the Met Press Bureau maintained an authorial presence in the production of *The Blue Lamp*, fulfilling a role akin to that of a producer by maintaining control of the material conditions required for the production of culture. The film is the result of a trade-off between the entertainment directives of both Ealing and Gainsborough Studios, and the propagandistic prerogatives of the Met Commissioner, Harold Scott and his Public Information Officer, Percy Fearnley. The bias, however, leans more heavily towards a subtle form of propaganda masked as entertainment, and this outcome is the product of the Press Bureau's influence over the film.

As I have demonstrated in previous chapters, Harold Scott's appointment as Commissioner in 1945 instigated fundamental changes to public relations (hereafter PR) machinery within the

Met. Scott, the first Commissioner without a military background, appointed Percy Fearnley, a seasoned journalist, to the role of Public Information Officer, who immediately began to push for greater powers for his Press Bureau to collaborate with the British film industry. This lobbying resulted in the production of two supporting features, *This Modern Age: Scotland Yard* and *The Girl from Scotland Yard*. By 1948, however, the Met had still not collaborated on a feature-length fiction film.

4.1 'Sordid, Squalid, sadistic and altogether unpleasant': British Crime Cinema before *The Blue Lamp*

In the meantime, a series of British crime films featuring the black market were dominating British studio releases. The critical reception of these films pressured the Met into producing a feature-length response. *Brighton Rock* (John Boulting, ABPC, 1947), *Dancing With Crime* (John Paddy Carstairs, Coronet Films, 1947), *Dear Murderer* (Arthur Crabtree, Gainsborough, 1947), *Good-Time Girl* (David MacDonald, Gainsborough Pictures, 1947), *It Always Rains on Sunday* (Robert Hamer, Ealing Studios, 1947), *Night Beat* (Harold Huth, British Lion, 1948), *No Orchids for Miss Blandish* (St. John Legh Clowes, Tudor-Alliance, 1948), *Noose* (Edmond T. Gréville, APBC, 1948) and *They Made Me a Fugitive* (Alberto Cavalcanti, Warner Bros., 1947) were all released in the period between Paul Barralet's letter proposing the production of *The Girl from Scotland Yard* and its eventual release two years later.

James Chapman has noted that

> the underworld cycle, which peaked around 1947–48, represents a significant production trend in post-war British cinema. In 1945,

1946 and 1947 there were, respectively, only 40, 39 and 48 'long' films registered by British producers with the Board of Trade, rising to 68 in 1948, 77 in 1949 and 74 in 1950. It has been calculated that between 1946 and 1950 there were two dozen films 'in which underworld-based crime is a central activity' and a further 44 which contained some element of criminal activity.[5]

The 'underworld cycle' of films to which Chapman refers has previously been identified by Robert Murphy as the 'spiv cycle'.[6] It is these films, according to Chapman and Murphy, that contribute to the rise in British feature production during the late 1940s. These films, Murphy argues, are defined by their response to the changing pattern of crime – namely, the rise of the black market in the face of rationing – in Britain in the Second World War and the late 1940s.[7] The many academics who have analyzed this cycle of postwar British crime cinema tend to agree with Murphy's conclusions. Peter Wollen's contribution, 'Riff-Raff Realism', appropriates many of the conclusions of Murphy's work (and the title of his 1986 chapter) and argues that the spiv cycle

> presented a mutation in the traditional crime film in response to the changing pattern of crime that grew up in wartime as a result of state regulation of the economy[8]

and Tim Pulleine has concluded that the spiv films embody both disillusion with the postwar age of austerity and a desire to escape from 'that era's chafing restraints'.[9]

The spiv cycle of postwar British crime cinema exists as a response to the unique sociopolitical circumstances of Britain in the age of austerity. The communities of early post-war Britain embraced the rebellious, 'Rabelaisian' figure of the spiv and reacted negatively to the puritanical representatives of the state, evidenced by attitudes towards the police force.[10] Robert Murphy sums up the general ambivalence towards the police in the immediate post-war period:

To the middle classes the policeman was a social inferior whose usefulness in preventing burglaries had to be balanced against his nuisance value with regard to motoring offences. Among working-class people the police were generally regarded with suspicion, in the rougher areas with fear and derision.[11]

The effectiveness of the police, and their place in British society, is a key discourse interrogated within the crime films of the late 1940s. The fact that the spiv cycle seemed to undermine the legitimacy of the police by depicting the prevalence of the underworld led to the films being received with vitriolic hostility by contemporaneous reviewers. For example, Jack Davies, writing in *The Sunday Express* of *Brighton Rock*, complained that the film

> cannot be classed as entertainment because the subject matter with which it is concerned is sordid, squalid, sadistic and altogether unpleasant.[12]

Joan Lester's contextualization of *Brighton Rock* is equally telling, and indicative of the gathering of a panic over crime films reaching British audiences:

> Crime doesn't pay and crooks never prosper – at least after the last reel but one. That is the law of the cinema. The scruples of such bodies as the U.S. Hays Office censorship [sic] are satisfied if the screen impresses upon the young that the more obvious forms of vice are not the royal road to lifelong wealth and success. But that has not prevented producers from depicting crimes as exciting and the criminal as glamorous. Such falsifications of life are far more dangerous.[13]

Despite, or perhaps because of, the critical outrage over these crime films, they seemed to perform well in the cinemas that did manage to programme them. *Brighton Rock,* for instance, proved to be the fourth most successful film released into ABC cinemas in the financial year 1947–8, amassing box office receipts of £190, 147 from 350 bookings.

Admittedly, *Noose* and *Night Beat* in the following financial year failed to live up to *Brighton Rock*'s returns, but both were well booked. *Noose* received 335 first-feature bookings on the ABC circuit against *Night Beat*'s 324, and both amassed above-average returns for the period.[14] While the middle-class critics sharpened their knives before the release of a British crime film, filmgoers weren't influenced by their ideologically inflected diatribes of the harmful effects of depictions of crime upon the pliant masses.

Regardless of the underlying causes of this critical hostility, the releases of *No Orchids for Miss Blandish* and *Good-Time Girl* in April 1948 elevated journalistic concern about British crime cinema to the level of a moral panic. Brian McFarlane writes of *No Orchids* that

> not until Michael Powell's *Peeping Tom* a dozen years later was the British critical fraternity of the time stirred to such a frenzy of disapproval by a film.[15]

McFarlane surveys the critical response to *No Orchids*, and his findings are similar to Chapman's hypotheses regarding the root cause of the outrage caused by post-war British crime cinema:

> These are films that parade what the national psyche preferred to repress, and which the more prestigious arms of the British film industry usually treated with a decent reserve.[16]

The fact that British cinema screens were erupting with previously repressed images of violence and criminality, and that these images were produced by British filmmakers, seemed to be the root of this outrage among newspaper writers.

The prevalence of British crime film releases in this period, and the producers' remarkable ability to get such material past the censors, has been attributed to instability at the British Board of Film Censors (BBFC); between 1946 and 1948, over half of their examiners and management tendered their resignations, with new appointments taking their place.¹⁷ This liberalization of attitude towards topical, controversial depictions of crime in the post-war period from the reincarnate BBFC drew short shrift from newspaper critics and politicians, as a moral panic over violence in British cinema gathered pace resulting, in the month following the release of *No Orchids for Miss Blandish* and *Good-Time Girl*, in the BBFC Secretary, Sidney Harris, stating that

> the continued choice of stories of a brutal and sadistic nature, with their dependant [sic] incidents, can no longer be regarded as acceptable to large sections of the public ... The Board will not, therefore, in future be able to grant its certificate to any film in which the story depends in any marked degree on the violent or sadistic behaviour of the characters or to allow in any film any incident in which there is recourse to needless violence.¹⁸

Brian McFarlane and James Chapman have both stated the significance of the *No Orchids for Miss Blandish* controversy in the BBFC's decision, following pressure from the Home Office, to be more stringent in their approach to British crime cinema.¹⁹ However, *Good-Time Girl* played as important a part in the controversy; James C. Robertson has indicated that a 'lengthy delay for the film at the [BBFC], between July and September 1947, and an even longer delay before its premiere at the end of April 1948' was caused by Home Office concerns over levels of violence in the film.²⁰ However, these concerns were raised in private correspondence between the Ministry of Health, the Home Office and three independent petitioners due to a *Picture Post* article of 3 May 1947, which brought the government's attention to the film's production.²¹

4.2 The scriptwriter and the commissioner's Daughter: *The Blue Lamp*'s tentative beginnings

On 30 April 1948, the *Evening News* reviewed *Good-Time Girl*, labelling it 'another rough melodrama of a kind which only gets British films a bad name'.[22] After almost a year of press controversies beginning with the *Picture Post* article featuring the production of *Good-Time Girl*, and taking in the releases of *They Made Me a Fugitive, Brighton Rock, Night Beat, No Orchids for Miss Blandish* and, finally, the actual release of *Good-Time Girl*, the British film industry seemed ready to respond to this outcry from the press and the political establishment. On 6 May 1948, scriptwriter Jan Read wrote to Sir Harold Scott, proposing a feature-length film about the Met. He wrote that

> We should not want to make another film like *Night Beat*, which as it seems to us, used the police as an excuse for yet another cops and robbers story about spivs and the East End. Our idea is to make something much more genuinely about the police force and policemen.[23]

Jan Read was keen to distinguish his proposed film from the moral panic-inducing British crime film cycle, identifying his potential project against the 'spivs and the East End' narratives so prevalent. It is ironic, therefore, that he fails to mention *Good-Time Girl*, which was produced by Gainsborough Studios, who were Jan Read's employers. Read's proposed idea would have been produced by Sydney Box – *Good-Time Girl*'s producer – and the final product, which of course would become *The Blue Lamp*, would be based upon an original treatment by Read and his colleague, Ted Willis. Willis had co-written the screenplay for *Good-Time Girl*.

The parallels between the two projects do not end at the production personnel. Read suggested in his introductory letter to Harold Scott that Gainsborough was, at the time of writing, 'engaged ... on a series of entertainment pictures based on contemporary sociological themes'.[24] As examples, he lists *Holiday Camp* (Ken Annakin, 1947) and *Easy Money* (Bernard Knowles, 1948), which respectively look at working-class leisure pursuits and the football pools in a populist manner. Jan Read refrained from bracketing *Good-Time Girl* within this series of sociologically aware Gainsborough entertainment films, but nevertheless, both productions were instigated with similar motivations. For instance, research for *Good-Time Girl* and *The Blue Lamp* both began with visits to the state institutions the producers intended to depict in the film. On 22 May 1947, a Home Office civil servant minuted the following in the response to the *Picture Post* article regarding *Good-Time Girl*'s production:

> It appears that last autumn Gainsborough Pictures were afforded facilities, through Public Relations Branch in consultation with D. 1. Division, to visit a Senior Girls' Approved School and that their representatives also visited Aylesbury Girls' Borstal.[25]

James C. Robertson has also unearthed another visit, noting that 'on 12 June 1946 Gainsborough wrote to the Home Office to request facilities for three of its scriptwriters to visit Holloway Prison for women'.[26] These three research visits formed the basis, along with the true story of a 1944 murder (the 'Cleft Chin' case), for *Good-Time Girl*.[27] Similarly, within a fortnight of Read's proposal, Harold Scott and Percy Fearnley met with him and scheduled an unprecedented series of research visits between 15 and 22 June 1948, including trips in Area Wireless Cars, tours of two police stations, and visits to the Criminal Record Office and the Finger Print Department. The level of access granted to Read, an employee of the independent British entertainment industry, indicates the extent to which PR machinery had developed at the Met; the Press Bureau, under the guidance of Percy Fearnley, had begun to realize the potential of police-press collaborations, and *The Blue Lamp* would indeed go on to represent the collaborative process at its most ideologically powerful.

One possible reason for the Met's willingness to collaborate with Gainsborough on this project may lie with Jan Read himself; in his introductory letter to Harold Scott, Read makes it clear that he is an old family friend of Harold Scott, and enquires as to the whereabouts of his daughter, Daphne:

> My father tells me that Daphne is in London now. I haven't seen her since going to America and should so much like to look her up. Could you tell me where I can get in touch with her?²⁸

Read's personal relationship with Sir Harold Scott and his family may have guaranteed that the *Good-Time Girl* controversy did not prejudice the Met in accepting Gainsborough's proposal for a film based around the police, despite the similarities between the two projects from the outset.

In July 1948, Read wrote to Harold Scott, informing him that a 'skeleton story' had been worked out, informed by his series of research visits:

> When [the story] is a little further towards completion I will look forward to submitting it to you and Mr. Fearnley for your comments and advice. After talking with so many policemen of all ranks I do feel that we can incorporate in our story points which will both encourage recruitment and aid public co-operation with the Service.²⁹

In response, Percy Fearnley sent Jan Read a dossier that would prove crucial to *The Blue Lamp*'s development.³⁰ Prepared by Inspector Robert Fabian, the dossier was an account of the murder of Alec De Antiquis, a have-a-go hero who was killed in London while trying to prevent a group of revolver-wielding young robbers from escaping the scene of a botched robbery of a jewellers in Charlotte Street. Jan Read greeted this dossier with interest, noting that it 'makes very fascinating reading and will be most useful to me'.³¹ Commentators have previously identified the incorporation of the Antiquis murder into *The Blue Lamp*'s narrative, but it is through the production of this file, sent to Read by Percy Fearnley and authored by Robert Fabian, that the case found its way into the film. The tracing of Dirk

Bogarde's spivvy juvenile delinquent, Tom Riley, through his raincoat, the failure of an identification parade to pick out the right man, and the discovery of the murder weapon by a young child, along with the murder of the central protagonist, P. C. George Dixon (Jack Warner), while trying to disarm the young perpetrator of a botched robbery are all key narrative points that can be traced back to the Antiquis case. Jan Read readily acknowledged the influence of the Antiquis dossier in his treatment for *The Blue Lamp*. After outlining the scene in which the identification parade fails to incriminate Tom Riley, Read cuts away from the narrative and writes the following:

> NOTE: This may appear strange, but in this particular I am following what actually happened in the Antiquis case.[32]

The incorporation of the Antiquis case into *The Blue Lamp*'s narrative provides another point of comparison with *Good-Time Girl*'s use of key elements of the 'Cleft Chin' murder; the two films have far more in common than may initially be apparent.

From this point, the production of what would become *The Blue Lamp* progressed apace. There was hope within the Met Press Bureau that the film would 'begin shooting at the beginning of November' 1948, but this hope proved misplaced.[33] A treatment was submitted to the Met Press Bureau on 21 September 1948, which indicated that the project was some way from reaching the shooting stage. The treatment, which was headed 'The Blue Lamp', was authored by Jan Read and prefaced with a defence of his narrative choices. This defence is significant, as is the reaction to it by the Met, as both provide evidence of the Met's level of control over *The Blue Lamp*:

> The film has been written so that it can be shot among the streets and in the houses, shops and Police Stations of Greater London ... As I see it, the action will centre around Leman Street Police Station. The newer stations, such as Hammersmith, are lighter and more commodious, but lack atmosphere and associations. One

has the feeling about Leman Street that its various rooms – the overcrowded office with its shiny Victorian furniture and shabby linoleum, the sanitary-tiled parade room, the winding gas-lit stairs, the policewoman's room with its rickety gas-fire, the rabbit-warren of a detective's office – have been the setting for innumerable human tragedies. It will be much easier to get over a sense of comradeship in such crowded surroundings than in a concrete glass expanse. There will be plenty of opportunities to show modern police equipment at Scotland Yard itself.[34]

This was poorly received by Percy Fearnley, who wrote that 'if this film is going to help recruiting in any way it should not be shot at Leman Street Police Station, but at one of our newer Stations, even if by so doing we lack atmosphere and associations'.[35] As a compromise, it was later agreed that the police station sequences of the film would not be shot on location:

It has now been decided, in order to save time and lessen inconvenience to the Police, to play the majority of the scenes in the studio and shoot there.

Fearnley ended this minute with his belief that, as a result of building the stages, 'shooting will probably not begin until the early Spring'.[36]

Despite the fact that Leman Street proved a dead end, Read's willingness to take a risk by locating his story within more atmospheric confines, instead of opting for the easy propaganda route, is indicative of his attitude towards the project – throughout *The Blue Lamp*'s pre-production, Read consistently opts for narrative choices that the interwar Met Press Bureau most certainly would have rejected. The fact that Read's choices were largely accepted, including his decision to include the death of a policeman at the mid-point of his treatment, is testament to the foresight of Harold Scott and Percy Fearnley, who gambled their professional reputations on *The Blue Lamp* in the hope that the film would have the desired propagandist effect.

Secondary sources assessing the production of *The Blue Lamp* have propagated a series of myths about this stage of the film's collaborative processes. These myths tend to underestimate the contribution of Jan Read in the production of *The Blue Lamp* by instead stressing the contribution of Ted Willis or the Ealing scriptwriter-auteur, T. E. B. Clarke. Charles Barr, for example, credits the 'creation of PC George Dixon' to Ted Willis and omits any mention of Gainsborough Studios in his lengthy textual analysis of *The Blue Lamp* which, tellingly, is included in his chapter dedicated to T. E. B. Clarke.[37] In looking at the influence of relationships forged during *The Blue Lamp*'s production, Barr notes that 'the significant collaboration is that of [Basil] Dearden and [T. E. B.] Clarke', despite the fact that the film was shaped, in detail, by Jan Read and Ted Willis of Gainsborough Studios in collaboration with Percy Fearnley and Harold Scott before Dearden and Clarke were employed to work on the project.[38] Jan Read's treatment, submitted on 21 September 1948, almost entirely details the key plot points that propel *The Blue Lamp*'s narrative; contrary to Charles Barr, for example, the treatment provides evidence that P. C. George Dixon was Read's creation – not only in name, but also in personality:

> Dixon painstakingly brings back Andy's attention to the job in hand, and to his disgust, seems much more concerned with the shepherding of schoolchildren across the road, in keeping an eye on street traders and in pointing out the geography of public houses and amusement arcades, than in the investigation going on around them...
>
> In response to Dixon's good humoured can't-have-this-there-here attitude, ruffled tempers subside as if by magic.[39]

George Dixon is also referred to as 'large and placid' by Read. These character traits, transferred in full to the final film, are identified as crucial to the success of *The Blue Lamp* by Sue Harper and Vincent

Porter.[40] Without the characterization established by Jan Read, George Dixon would not have had the same degree of influence over the film. His death takes place at the hands of Tom Riley at the midpoint of Jan Read's treatment:

> Tom is just at the door of the box, when Dixon appears in the foyer blowing his whistle. As the policeman advances on him with drawn staff, Tom loses his head. He draws a revolver and shoots twice at point blank range. Dixon crumples and falls on the terrazzo floor.[41]

Read also introduces Diana Lewis (Peggy Evans) and her family, and fleshes out key plot points, including her use of a stolen compact after being accompanied to the police station to talk to a women police sergeant, her impoverished background and incessantly arguing family, and her access to the cashier's desk at a cinema. Another plot point suggested by Jan Read that finds its way into the finished film includes the method of discovery of the weapon used to shoot Dixon:

> [Andy's] attention is attracted by a circle of children bending over a small boy with something in his hand. Andy goes across to investigate. Gently asking his way through the centre of the group he persuades the child to show him what it is in his hand. Unwillingly, the child gives up a rusty revolver.[42]

Jan Read's treatment, then, is the first instance in which these key plot points are presented to the Met Press Bureau who, of necessity given their role as gatekeepers of the required materials for the film's production, are consulted at every significant step of *The Blue Lamp*'s production.

Regardless, there were aspects of this treatment that were improved by the input of, first, Ted Willis, and then T. E. B. Clarke. For example, the character of Andy in Read's treatment is ambitious, reckless on occasion and prone to losing his temper. After reacting to a group of youths who were making 'derisive remarks about the flat-footed copper', Andy is reprimanded by his sergeant:[43]

At Dixon's house that evening, Andy talks the affair over with the older man, saying that he feels that he has been most unfairly treated, that he is getting nowhere in the Force and ought to resign. Dixon tells him not to be such a fool.[44]

Also, Dixon's wife is younger than her husband, and they have two living children. After Dixon's death, Read treatment hints at the possibility of Andy marrying Dixon's widow:

> In view of the nearness of Dixon's death, this scene must obviously be handled very carefully. If the audience is left thinking that Andy will probably marry the widow later, they will in some way be satisfied without the tragedy's being lessened.[45]

The treatment was well received by the Met Commissioner, Harold Scott, who instructed Percy Fearnley that 'we should let them include the murder of a policeman' – a brave, and unprecedented, step by a Commissioner in dealing with a collaborative film production:[46]

> Indeed, he thinks the treatment is so good that we should let Gainsborough pretty well have their way, subject, of course, to our keeping them correct on police procedure.[47]

Fearnley disagreed with Harold Scott – four weeks earlier, Fearnley had minuted that the treatment 'will appear very slow, which in fact I think it is. The subsequent shooting script, with the dialogue and the commentary, may make the story run very much more quickly.'[48] Fearnley tabled a series of suggested mediations for Jan Read to consider; however, these mediations were not for the purposes of accuracy, as directed by the Commissioner. Instead, his mediations concern image management. As well as mentioning that shooting the film at Leman Street would harm the film's use as a recruiting tool, Fearnley also suggests that Detective Inspector Cherry's character should 'be a man of between 40–45, and not 55 … [t]he younger we can make the Detective Inspector the better it will be from a recruiting angle'.⁴⁹ Jan Read, in another of his asides, suggested the following in his treatment:

> I'm all for putting some straight punches into this commentary. They will make the picture seem more important. Housing and pay are constant themes when policemen talk and might advantageously be introduced into conversations in the film.⁵⁰

Fearnley, however, suggested that 'references in the commentary or the dialogue to such things might be extremely dangerous'.⁵¹ Fearnley's mediations were all incorporated into the final film: the film was not shot at the Leman Street police station; Bernard Lee, aged forty-one in 1949, was cast as Detective Inspector Cherry; and, aside from a brief exchange prior to Dixon offering his spare room to Andy (Jimmy Hanley), themes involving housing and pay were omitted from the dialogue and commentary of the final film.

One additional suggestion was made by the Assistant Commissioner of 'A' Branch:

> I appreciate the necessity to hold the interest of the audience but, even so, would have thought that sufficient interest and excitement could have been raised without the murder of a policeman ... [I]n a film that is made with the full co-operation of the Commissioner I feel that the murder of a policeman is rather undesirable and ... not altogether in good taste.⁵²

This suggestion by the Assistant Commissioner bears similarity with the approach taken in the interwar period, prior to the empowerment of the Met Press Bureau. Notions of taste and popular culture, here, prevent the Assistant Commissioner from seeing the propaganda potential of a crime film produced under the jurisdiction of the Met that elicits public sympathy by depicting the murder of an everyman police officer and re-establishes the working-class welcome of the rule of law. The 'brilliance of [*The Blue Lamp*'s] propaganda' is achieved by the characterization, and subsequent murder, of George Dixon.⁵³

Through constructing George Dixon as a point of identification for the audience and then having that point of identification eradicated by Tom Riley, the embodiment of the postwar phenomenon of juvenile delinquency, *The Blue Lamp* co-opted the working classes into the fight against disorganized crime. Harold Scott recognized this, and so the murder of George Dixon remained despite the Assistant Commissioner's protestations.[54] Percy Fearnley met with Ted Willis and Jan Read in early November 1948, to pass on his mediations, and a series of research visits were arranged for Ted Willis to attend in that month in preparation for scripting the dialogue and commentary for *The Blue Lamp*.[55]

4.3 'P.C. 99 ... might be dealing with sheep dipping': The Home Office suggest a crime film

During the production of *This Modern Age: Scotland Yard* in 1946, Percy Fearnley had made concerted efforts to avoid having to involve the Home Office or the Central Office of Information (hereafter COI) in the production of the film, despite the fact that the COI was the successor to the Ministry of Information Films Division and, as I have outlined in the two preceding chapters, the Films Division were effectively a government agency responsible for the production of state-authored propaganda films. In justifying the reason behind his commissioning of the graphic designer Abram Games to produce a recruitment poster in 1946, Fearnley argued that approaching the COI 'would delay matters considerably, and I am afraid the approach to them would have to go through the Home Office'.[56] Home Office civil servants delayed the release of *This Modern Age: Scotland Yard* by two weeks,[57] despite Fearnley's earlier attempt to avoid their input by omitting any references in the film to provincial police forces 'because, if these remain, the Home Office will have to see the script, and this will only cause still further delay in making a start'.[58] During the production of *The Blue Lamp*, Fearnley and Scott had attempted to avoid any input from the Home Office or COI by simply not mentioning to either body that the Met were involved in the production of a feature film. However, the Home Office and the COI were discussing the possibility of producing a film about the police at the same time as *The Blue Lamp*'s treatment was being circulated in Scotland Yard. A private memo between two Home Office civil servants outlined the proposal:

> There was some discussion about this time last year of the desirability of including a police film in the Home Office programme of films which was sent to the C.O.I. In the end a general film about the police, with the dual object of educating the public about their work and value to the community and of interesting potential recruits, was included in the programme, but ... no action was taken. This year C.O.I.'s interest is much more lively and they are very keen on the project.[59]

As a result of this expression of interest from the COI, a three-page memo, headed 'Films On The Police', was drawn up by two Public Relations Officers based at the Home Office – Mr. Baker and Mr. George Griffiths. This memo summarized previous film activity involving the police and suggested potential themes 'which can with advantage be brought out in films on the service'.[60] Griffiths and Baker believed that previous collaborations between the police and the British film industry 'have portrayed important aspects of Police work but have pandered to the public by producing excitement in the aspect of a criminal who had to be chased and is inevitably captured. The truth is, of course, that exciting chases do not come the way of an ordinary Police officer very often'.[61] Griffiths and Baker sought to remedy this by producing a film that demonstrated the everyday work of the police:

> The film should aim at lessening the feeling of resentment that some people have when the law catches up with them by showing

that there is a need for most laws (e.g. that rear lamps on cycles save the lives of cyclists) and that by seeing these laws are obeyed the Police are looking after the interests of the majority of the people.[62]

The memo concludes with a suggestion for the police film that demonstrates the activities of a selection of police constables with the badge number '99' in one day, across a variety of different constabularies:

P.C. 99 in the Blankshire Constabulary might be dealing with sheep dipping.

P.C. 99 in X City might be dealing with an accumulation of found property.

P.C. 99 in Y County might be one of a party searching for a lost child on a desolate tract of countryside (giving an opportunity of showing the usefulness of a heliocopter [sic]).

P.C. 99 in a London Division might be helping to inspect the cycles of school children.[63]

As riveting as these themes do indeed sound, these suggestions indicate how advanced the PR machinery of the Met Press Bureau was in 1948, in comparison to the Home Office. The project proposed by Griffiths and Baker is reminiscent of the memo authored by the then Met Secretary, Hamilton Howgrave-Graham, in 1938, in which he suggested that the only way the film industry could benefit the Met in a collaborative production would be by producing a film that highlights the 'vulnerability of certain types of flat and jerry built houses and also of Yale locks; advantages of mortice locks'.[64] While previous collaborations between the Met and the film industry may have 'pandered to the public by producing excitement' instead of soberly depicting the work of the police with a morose gravity, the Met Press Bureau were clearly more attuned to the basic concepts of propaganda and film production than the Home Office – excitement and entertainment sell cinema seats and, by disguising propaganda as entertainment, the processes of control employed in a collaborative project could be utilized to greater impact.

Following the production of the 'Films on the Police' memo, Griffiths and Baker arranged for a consultation to be held at the Home Office regarding the possibility of the COI producing an official film on the activities of the police. The consultation took place on 15 November 1948, and Met Commissioner Harold Scott and Sir Frank Newsam, Permanent Under-Secretary of State to the Home Office, were both among those invited to the meeting, which took place at the same time as Ted Willis was meeting the CID Superintendent and a Met District Commander in preparation for writing the script for *The Blue Lamp*.[65] At the consultation, Scott 'mentioned in passing' to Frank Newsam that the Met were collaborating with Gainsborough Studios on the production of *The Blue Lamp*, and agreed (reluctantly, presumably) to let the Home Office have a copy of the draft treatment which had been sent to the Met two months previously.[66]

The fact that the Met had agreed to undertake this project without consulting the Home Office had irked the latter's PR officers considerably, for two reasons. George Griffiths believed that 'there should be consultation between [the New Scotland Yard] Publicity Officer and H.O. Public Relations, especially in matters of national rather than Metropolitan interest … and, in my opinion, it is a project that lies in the national, and not in the local, sphere of publicity responsibility'.[67] Secondly, Griffiths was concerned that *The Blue Lamp* – a film that he deemed, based on the treatment, 'rather a cheap and flimsy effort' – would undermine the COI project:

> We are now threatened with serious complications as a result of the Yard's procedure, because this commercial film may endanger, possibly even ruin, the official project. It cannot be right that publicity action by the Yard should be in a position to defeat the central Department's handling of a national theme.[68]

The Met Press Bureau, then, had exceeded its remit in the eyes of the Home Office, to which the wider Met hierarchy was accountable. While the Met Press Bureau's remit included publicity matters of direct interest to the Met district, generating publicity of national significance was the responsibility of the Home Office. It is therefore surprising that, in light of the ill-advised suggestions included in the 'Films On The Police' memo, the Home Office's publicity machine had failed to grasp the significance of entertainment as propaganda as successfully as the Met Press Bureau.

George Griffiths doubted the outcome of a collaboration with Gainsborough, or indeed any film producer working within the commercial sector, and drew upon the controversy caused by *Good-Time Girl* to demonstrate how employing processes of control to manipulate a commercial production would, in his opinion, be counter-productive:

There are, I think, two ways of dealing with the situation in which we find ourselves:-

(1) that H.O. should explore with Gainsborough the possibility of getting them so to shape their commercial production as to make an official film unnecessary;
(2) that [New Scotland Yard] should confine facilities to a scale so restricted as to ensure that the police sequences do not prejudice the official film.

Gainsborough are a firm of high standing with immense resources (including stars), but they have the reputation of being dominated by Box Office considerations ('Good Time Girl'!) and it is very doubtful whether we could get a successful collaboration with them on a film about crime and Police. Nevertheless, I think we ought to have a shot at it.[69]

The subtext of this internal correspondence is reminiscent of the Met Press Bureau's attitude towards the production processes of *Scotland*

Yard 1921: For the King, the Law, the People (Edmund Distin-Maddick, Topical Film Company, 1921) and *Secrets of Scotland Yard* (Frederick White, The Frederick White Company, 1921). *Scotland Yard 1921* was also referred to privately as 'the Official Film'⁷⁰, and was commissioned and controlled by the Met, whereas *Secrets of Scotland Yard* was a commercial production produced without Met involvement. The Met's heavy-handed approach to suppressing the latter, coupled with the commercial failure of the former, led the Met to believe that there was no value in accommodating the commercial sector in the production of a film depicting crime and the police force. This attitude prevailed until Percy Fearnley's appointment as Public Information Officer in 1945. It is remarkable that, after the successes of the British documentary producers in the Second World War, attitudes reminiscent of the Met's PR reticence of the early 1920s were still prevalent amongst Home Office PR staff in 1948.

Sir Frank Newsam did not altogether agree with Griffiths' negative reaction to the treatment of *The Blue Lamp*, noting that

> the proposed treatment of the film is certainly not so unsatisfactory as to make it desirable for the Home Office to suggest to Scotland Yard that no official co-operation should be given to the makers of the film.⁷¹

While this is hardly a ringing endorsement, it proved vital to the ongoing production; the Home Office could have forced the Met to withdraw their collaborative consent, and Newsam's opinion ensured that the project could continue. However, he agreed with Griffiths that the Home Office should have a degree of input into the film's production.⁷² As a result, Newsam wrote to Harold Scott on behalf of the Home Secretary, James Chuter Ede, in early January 1949. In the letter, Newsam scolded Scott, noting that 'the Home Secretary feels that he should have been consulted on this at a much earlier date', and invoked Home Office authority to take control of *The Blue Lamp*'s production:[73]

> We have ... decided to defer our official film for another year, and in the meantime to see whether it is possible to do anything to improve the Gainsborough film from the national point of view, although I fully appreciate that at this late stage it will not be easy to see that any aspect other than the Metropolitan is properly dealt with ... [W]e should bring in the four Chief Constables [of the provincial forces] with whom we had already begun consultations, and see whether they have any useful suggestions to make.[74]

Three days after Newsam's letter was written, Harold Scott issued a response. Scott defended his decision to collaborate on the production of *The Blue Lamp* by stating that a 'refusal to assist would not necessarily have prevented the film being made' and, by ensuring that the Met maintain an influential, quasi-authorial presence in the film's production, his decision to collaborate with Gainsborough Studios would ensure that the film does not include 'undesirable inaccuracies and sensationalism'.[75] Scott's justifications were numerous and telling – just as he readily admitted a year later in an interview with the *Daily Mirror* that the Met were 'hoping to win recruits from this film. It shows the Yard as it really is, and is a miracle of casting'[76], he similarly defended the Met's collaborative presence in the film's production against Home Office intrusion:

> It seemed to me that the results of our giving this assistance would be to secure excellent publicity for recruiting and to bring home to the public the need for their co-operation in a way not possible through any other medium and without the expenditure of a penny of public money.[77]

As a result of Harold Scott's defence of *The Blue Lamp*, the Home Office backed down, and decided against including the input of the four provincial Chief Constables who had already been consulted;

Newsam grudgingly conceded to Harold Scott that, 'if the suggestion that the four provincial chief constables should be brought into the discussion of "The Blue Lamp" at this stage embarrasses you, we do not wish to pursue the matter further'.[78] Scott had queried whether *The Blue Lamp* fell within the national interest, noting that the previous film collaborations involving the Met were not subject to Home Office intervention, and Frank Newsam rescinded his instruction that the film be 'shaped' according to the wishes of the Home Office. He did, however, warn Scott about blindsiding the Home Office in the production of any future collaborations:

> I hope, however, that you will be able to ensure that we are brought in at an early stage in any future venture of this kind involving official co-operation on your part and the provision of police facilities, so that it can be decided whether any particular project would best be dealt with on a national rather than on a purely Metropolitan basis.[79]

4.4 The Met lose control: J. Arthur Rank and the *Ad-Valorem* tax

While Harold Scott and Percy Fearnley were busy attempting to prevent *The Blue Lamp*'s production from falling into the grasp of the Home Office and Sir Frank Newsam, they were also mediating the first draft of *The Blue Lamp*'s script, which had been delivered by Jan Read and Ted Willis on 19 December 1948. Read himself admitted that the script was far from finished:

> We shall be very grateful for any comments and suggestions that we can incorporate in a further script so as to improve it. You will, of course, bear in mind that this is our first effort at a complete draft, and we realise ourselves that a good deal of further work will be necessary.[80]

With Read's willingness to incorporate any suggestions made by the Met in the final shooting script in mind, Percy Fearnley gave copies of the script to three on-the-ground police superintendents in order to vet the script's dialogue and police procedures. The script had clearly impressed Fearnley; in a letter to one of the superintendents, he commented that, 'as things are progressing I think we are going to get a really good film on the Police'.[81] The three superintendents offered less than half a page of amendments combined, and these amendments concerned minor mediations for accuracy. All of these amendments were put to Jan Read and Ted Willis in a meeting with Percy Fearnley held on 31 December 1948; Fearnley asked the scriptwriters 'to incorporate the suggestions submitted … They agreed to do so.'[82] At this meeting, it became clear that the script had not only impressed the higher echelons of the Met, but Sir Michael Balcon – head of Ealing Studios – had also become quite interested in the project:

> Mr. Read mentioned that Sir Michael Balcom [sic] had seen the script and now wished to take over the production of the film at Ealing Studios, where they hoped to go into production at the beginning of May. Willis would continue with the script until completed and then Ealing Studios would take over all matters before production. Sir Michael Balcom [sic] might wish to discuss the film with the Commissioner.[83]

Michael Balcon was able to suggest that *The Blue Lamp*'s production should be relocated from Gainsborough to Ealing because of the desperate situation the British film industry was in at this point in time. 1947's worldwide dollar shortage was acutely felt by Britain, whose economic dependency on the $4,300 million loan from America, granted in 1945, had prevented the growth of national export industries, and it led to the Exchequer attempting to cut down on luxury foreign imports in an attempt to prevent the loss of British sterling to foreign shores. The financial wastage through importation was reaching a critical level of self-indulgence; Geoffrey Macnab, for example, has cited Paul Swann's estimation that 'the amount spent by the British on American films and tobacco exceeded the sum total of the country's exports to the USA'.[84]

The Labour government sought to move the British economy away from its dependency upon the rapidly decreasing Anglo-American loan and rectify the problem of the British addiction to American imports. On 6 August 1947, the cash-strapped British government imposed a 75 per cent tax upon the import of American films for exhibition in British cinemas in an attempt to strengthen the pound and encourage a British production drive for both home and export markets. This newly introduced tax duty lay alongside the pre-existing exhibition quota, which stipulated that British exhibitors must devote a significant percentage of their screenings to indigenous productions. The Motion Picture Association of America (hereafter MPAA) promptly responded by enforcing a boycott of the British marketplace. Eric Johnston, head of the MPAA, was quoted as saying that 'if the British do not want American pictures, that is one thing; if they do, they should not expect to get a dollar's worth of film for 25 cents'.[85] In fact, after costs and the *ad valorem* tax were taken into consideration, US studios were only recouping 4 per cent of British box-office receipts.[86] Whilst the tax is now perceived by cultural historians as having a detrimental impact upon the British film industry on the whole, it nevertheless was greeted with optimism at the time by both film producers and the British public.[87]

The tax, and subsequent embargo, proved surprisingly popular. A Gallup poll posed the following question in September 1947: 'If the tax on USA films means that we get no more American films after a few months, should the tax remain?', and 58 per cent of respondents said that the tax should be kept.[88] The key to taking advantage of the opportunity offered by a Hollywood embargo on exporting films to Britain lay with J. Arthur Rank. 'Unlike any previous British producer,

Rank, with assets in excess of $200 million, had an organization as large as the American "Big Five", and these assets included Gainsborough Studios, Ealing Studios and two of the three largest exhibition chains in Britain – Odeon Cinemas and Gaumont-British.[89] J. Arthur Rank sought to exploit the new opportunity afforded by the embargo while it was still in place by increasing production of British films for exhibition in his Gaumont and Odeon chains, and it was expected that others would soon follow suit.[90]

When Harold Wilson repealed the tax duty in March 1948, the Rank Organisation's investment in increased British production, intended to replace the reruns that dominated British screens during the embargo, was placed in jeopardy by the reintroduction of American imports. Geoffrey Macnab has discussed the effects of Harold Wilson's decision to repeal the tax duty:

> The Anglo-American dispute had lasted for barely more than six months. During this period, neither had the Hollywood embargo had the chance to bite ... and nor had the British been given the time and protection to exploit the pictures made in the great production drive ... [B]y caving in so peremptorily, [Wilson] denied the British industry its one chance to stand on its own feet, without being buttressed by Hollywood.[91]

The embargo had started to encourage American studios to invest in existing British filmmaking interests – a situation welcomed by Harold Wilson, as he admitted in a 1981 *Screen* interview.[92] This overseas investment was further encouraged by Harold Wilson's next step; aware that his truce with the MPAA would effectively bankrupt the Rank Organisation, Wilson sought to protect British film production by implementing an increase in the exhibition quota to 45 per cent. Rank's desperate enthusiasm for the increased quota, based upon his failed gamble during the embargo, led him into a disagreement with independent exhibitors, who were reluctant to devote their screen time to British films when the American films were more profitable. Rank stated that he is 'going to have statistics prepared to see that defaulters under the Quota are brought to book', whilst a conglomerate of independent exhibitors queried how the 45 per cent quota could possibly be met without significant expansion and investment in studio space.[93] Harold Wilson was fully aware that the quota was unworkable unless the American studios found a way around the legislation, whereas J. Arthur Rank idealistically went about fervently constructing a challenge to Hollywood's dominance without heeding the warnings of the independent exhibitors. A conglomerate of Scottish independent cinema proprietors issued the following reproach to Rank's idealism:

> Mr. Rank is not the British Government. He is not even a member of the Government. He is only a private citizen, and dictatorial statements such as his may be in order in other countries, but not in Britain.
>
> If our present Government had any sense of their own dignity they would have rapped Mr. Rank's knuckles to remind him that he is not at present dictator of Britain.
>
> The present Government have gone on record as being opposed to monopolies. Now, by the Quota they have fixed, they have established one of the tightest and most dangerous monopolies it is possible to conceive.[94]

The independent exhibitors had underestimated the youthful ambition of Harold Wilson. With the full permission of the Board of Trade, American companies began acquiring larger shares in British production companies, exporting technicians, cast members and crew to Britain and subsequently filming runaway productions here in order to avoid the terms of the quota by releasing films as Anglo-American co-productions. However, the influx of American money into British filmmaking interests effectively destroyed any chance of building the British industry up to a level where it could challenge Hollywood. Rank's circuits posted significant losses as audiences proved less patriotic than he envisaged, and the major Hollywood studios began making inroads into British production, including the purchase of a significant stake in Rank Organization's main British rival, the Associated British Picture Corporation (ABPC).

This situation had left the Rank empire in 'deep financial trouble':

> In October 1948, Rank told the shareholders of Odeon Theatres Ltd. that the company had £13.6 million in bank loans and overdrafts, and a year later the figure had risen to £16.3 million.[95]

As a result of this financial situation, Rank tasked his managing director, John Davis, with 'sort[ing] out the company's collapsing financial empire':[96]

> He concentrated production at Pinewood, closing down the Gainsborough Studios at Shepherd's Bush and Islington and the Two Cities studio at Denham. Sydney Box, who ran Gainsborough, was sent on a year's holiday.[97]

This arrangement gave further power to Michael Balcon and the production company he ran, Ealing Studios. While Ealing was nominally under the control of the Rank Organisation, it was not fully subsumed into its machinery; Harper and Porter summarized the relationship between Rank and Balcon as follows:

> When Balcon became a powerful presence on the Palache Committee, Rank bought him off by offering a deal which seemed too good to refuse; he would cover half Ealing's production costs, in return for world-wide distribution rights.[98]

This context, interestingly, is not apparent in the extant correspondence between the Met, Gainsborough and Michael Balcon. What becomes clear, though, is that the Met Press Bureau did not want the project to transfer to Ealing. Jan Read mentioned to Percy Fearnley in the meeting held on 31 December 1948, that Balcon was keen to transfer the film's locale from the East End of London to the Paddington district, 'and PIO suggested that such a step might not be advisable in view of the work which had been put in already by [police personnel based in the East End], and that in any case the dialogue in the film was definitely that of the East End'.[99] Read requested that Fearnley write him a letter to that effect, so that he could pass Fearnley's opinions on to Michael Balcon – this move, of course, is indicative of Read attempting to keep hold of a project that was rapidly slipping out of his control. It also indicates the strength of Fearnley's working relationship with Jan Read and Ted Willis; Fearnley had minuted that 'if this film is going to help recruiting in any way it should not be shot at Leman Street Police Station' less than three months before his conversation with Read about Balcon's wish that the location for *The Blue Lamp* be changed.[100] Now, at Read's behest, Fearnley was prepared to write the following:

> In view of the work which has already been put into this film at Leman Street, we feel that to transfer the location to Paddington might adversely affect it… Moreover, the Police at Leman Street have become very keenly interested in the film and are looking forward to assisting in some way in its production.[101]

This letter and Harold Scott's letter to Frank Newsam fending off Home Office interest in the project were both sent on the same day – 7 January 1949. A project that had seemingly followed a smooth path, at least from the Met's perspective, was slowly beginning to unravel amid a series of unwelcome intrusions from both the state and other elements within the British film industry.

Balcon wrote to Percy Fearnley directly on 12 January 1949, presumably after meeting with Jan Read and having been shown the letter from Fearnley to Read. While Balcon had perceived the commercial potential of the project, he was not willing to put the script as it stood into production, and so he informed Fearnley of the appointment of T. E. B. Clarke to the role of script supervisor. He also saw fit to meet with Fearnley, possibly with a view to assuaging some of his doubts about the project's transfer:

> As we have had no opportunity of personal contact on THE BLUE LAMP as yet, I am wondering if you could possibly find time to come down and lunch with me at Ealing, when I can introduce you to the Director, Associate Producer and Writers who will now be working on the subject. I feel it would be a great convenience if we could all meet in this way at the outset so that we could exchange views on the story.[102]

Balcon's letter demonstrates the position of power Fearnley occupied in the production of *The Blue Lamp*; as I have mentioned earlier in this chapter, academics have credited the impact of *The Blue Lamp* to the Dearden/Relph director/producer partnership, or the film has been categorized within the oeuvre of T. E. B. Clarke. However, Dearden, Relph, Clarke and Fearnley were invited to this meeting, indicating the significance of Fearnley's input in the collaborative processes inherent in the film's production. Regardless of Fearnley's prior doubts about *The Blue Lamp*'s production being taken over by Ealing, it is clear that, over the course of this meeting, Balcon, Clarke, Dearden and Relph convinced Fearnley to back the project in its new locale. Fearnley's past allegiances to Willis and Read were forgotten, and Fearnley instead had found fit to schedule a series of research visits for T. E. B. Clarke 'to enable him to get police atmosphere' before he embarked upon his task 'to change the script a little'.[103]

4.5 'This guinea pig film': The script and the shoot

Between the delivery of the first script in December 1948 and the submission of T. E. B. Clarke's amended script in May 1949, *The Blue*

Lamp went through five drafts in total. The structure of the story remained largely intact throughout the redrafting process; Jan Read's treatment, based on the Antiquis dossier authored by Robert Fabian, provided the backbone for the story, but T. E. B. Clarke's contribution can be seen in the overhaul of dialogue in his final draft. Clarke emphasized the father-son relationship between the two police constables, Mitchell and Dixon. In the draft submitted by Willis and Read, Dixon has a dog, and lives with his daughter, Mary. Mary and Andy Keith (to be changed to 'Mitchell' in Clarke's draft) develop a relationship after Andy is taken in as a lodger in Dixon's house, and the relationship is strengthened by the death of Dixon. Clarke, in order to further strengthen Andy's position within the film as a surrogate son to Dixon, omits the dog from the script and also removes the character of Dixon's daughter, instead replacing her with M. – Dixon's wife (played in the final film by Gladys Henson). The first draft script also situates Inspector Cherry (Bernard Lee) far more centrally within the text; he provides the voiceover, and occupies a prominent role during the investigation of Dixon's murder. In Clarke's final draft, Cherry is a peripheral, archetypal detective figure, with little to contribute to the film.

Clarke replaced the first draft's focus upon the detective's office with the camaraderie of the policeman's mess hall, sidelining Cherry and scenes at Scotland Yard and substituting them with Taffy's policeman's choir, communal darts matches and scenes involving lost dogs, Campbell Singer's desk sergeant and the practices of the '"mature" underworld'.[104] Clarke also replaced the first draft's rather clichéd finale. In it, Riley – who had been identified by the landlady of a lodging-house where he had taken refuge from the manhunt – was to be chased on foot through suburban back gardens and bombsites before being confronted by Andy:

> [Tom] backs against a railing, his hand reaching for his gun. He gets the gun out. Andy advances towards him. Tom raises the gun. Andy halts for a split second and then hurls his cape – or truncheon – at Tom. Tom ducks and Andy dives on him. In a moment it is all over.

Deprived of his gun, Tom puts up no fight but lies on the ground, whimpering and gibbering – a disgusting sight.[105]

This ending – reminiscent of Pinkie's (Richard Attenborough) demise in *Brighton Rock* – is immediately followed by Andy providing directions to a passer-by before the film closes. This scene is retained in T. E. B. Clarke's final script; Clarke uses it to mirror the introductory sequence in which Dixon gives directions on the same street as Andy. While T. E. B. Clarke's dialogue does add a great deal to the first draft script authored by Read and Willis, there are several key scenes that are transported verbatim from the initial script into the final version. These scenes include Dixon's death. In the script submitted by Read and Willis, the scene is as follows:

> Suddenly Dixon comes running into the cinema, followed by a man who has obviously warned him. Tom, one hand full of money turns quickly, and the little group, including Dixon, stop quickly. A thrill runs through them.
>
> **CROWD:** He's got a gun ... Watch out
> **SPUD:** Come on – let's get out of this
> **TOM (in high-pitched voice):** Get back – all of you – get back. You too, copper
>
> The crowd fall back but Dixon comes slowly forward.
>
> **DIXON:** Drop that and don't be a damned fool ... drop it.
> **TOM:** I'll drop you ... get back – this thing works –
>
> He commences to back out with Spud, while Dixon walks steadily towards him. Tom is getting more and more panicky.
>
> **TOM:** Get back ... (almost screaming) Get back, I tell you ... get back.
>
> Dixon steps quickly forward. He starts to blow his whistle. Tom fires at him twice at close range. Pushing aside one or two people he and Spud rush for the car. Dixon falls on the terrazzo floor.[106]

T. E. B. Clarke's script stages this scene as follows:

SPUD (urgently to Tom): Come on!

He goes out to the waiting car.

TOM: Just coming.

He grabs a last handful of notes and hurries from the pay-box.

Suddenly DIXON comes running into the cinema, followed at some little distance by LARRY and JUNE, both very nervous but reluctant to miss the excitement. TOM comes face to face with DIXON – points the revolver at him.

TOM (tightly): Keep back!

DIXON takes in the situation then moves slightly forward.

DIXON (quietly): Drop that and don't be a fool ... Drop it.

TOM (his voice rising): I'll drop you. Get back – this thing works.

DIXON continues to advance steadily towards him.

TOM (almost screaming): Get back ... Get back, I say!

But DIXON comes on. TOM fires twice at close range.[107]

From the comparison of the two drafts above, it is clear that this scene – so crucial to *The Blue Lamp*'s propaganda potential – was authored by Jan Read and Ted Willis, and *paraphrased* by T. E. B. Clarke.

The extant documents preserved in the National Archives regarding the production of *The Blue Lamp*, the analysis of which forms the basis of this chapter, demonstrate that the contribution of Read and Willis to the film was crucial to the final production. Their contribution and their willingness to collaborate with the Met Press Bureau, guaranteed the film's production and, despite the Met's misgivings about the project transferring to Ealing Studios, the work of Read and Willis had progressed the project to such a stage that the

Met agreed to concede an element of their control over the project to Michael Balcon.

One particular concession made by the Met involved T. E. B. Clarke's version of the final sequence, which involved a scene in the White City greyhound stadium. This scene – a version of which was included in the finished film – was suggested by T. E. B. Clarke in the fourth draft of the script, which was received by the Met in early May 1949, and circulated to the Assistant Commissioners of 'A', 'C' and 'D' Branch by Percy Fearnley on 11 May.[108] Fearnley noted the following in a covering letter to the three Assistant Commissioners:

> On the whole the script seems a reasonable [sic] good effort – in fact in parts it is brilliant – but there are still a number of weaknesses which we are now trying to strengthen. I do not think you need concern yourself with the climax in White City Stadium. This is not true to life, and we are having still further discussions with Ealing Studios about this scene.[109]

In a private minute to the Met Secretary two days later, Fearnley commented that 'we are still working on the police dialogue and the climax (the latter is wrong)'.[110] As the fourth draft of the script does not survive, the cause of Fearnley's consternation is unclear – it is neither directly mentioned in the extant correspondence, nor in the minutes in the Met file relating to *The Blue Lamp*'s production. Interestingly, pages ninety-two to ninety-six of Basil Dearden's personal copy of the final shooting script (fifth draft) are pink.[111] These pages comprise the final sequences of the film, including the White City scene – scenes written on pink paper, as opposed to the standard blue, indicate that their inclusion is the result of last-minute amendments, so it would seem that Fearnley was able to push through an amendment to satisfy his objections to the White City sequence.

Several other amendments were also requested by Fearnley over the course of *The Blue Lamp*'s shoot. Fearnley's presence during the filming process and his ability to successfully petition Michael Balcon, Basil Dearden and Michael Relph, provide further examples of his position as producer of the text:

> I have discussed with Michael Relph and Basil Dearden the ... [a]rrival of Police at Masie's flat [and] P. C. Mitchell being followed by school-children when taking Queenie to the Police Station.
>
> On [the former] I told them and Sir Michael Balcon that the Police Sargeant in the R/T car was badly cast, and not properly attired, and that I thought the sequence should be re-shot. This scene is being re-cast and will be re-shot in the studio.
>
> On [the latter] I said I thought the sequence should be shortened because in its present form I felt it tended to ridicule the Police. They did not entirely agree but said they would attempt to shorten it.[112]

Fearnley was able to make this judgement of the material filmed over the course of the shoot because he, along with Harold Scott and the Met Secretary, R. L. Jackson, were invited at several points to Ealing, where they observed studio sequences being filmed and rough-cut footage was screened for them – all this while being chaperoned by Michael Balcon.[113]

Chief Superintendent Elizabeth Bather, Britain's most senior policewoman and the supervising officer of the Metropolitan Women Police, had suggested a series of mediations 'in order that the women may be included so that the public will appreciate that they are an integral part of the Force'.[114] As soon as Fearnley received Bather's suggestions, he wrote the following to Michael Relph:

> We had been wondering whether it would be possible to include one or two more shots about the activities of the Women Police in 'The Blue Lamp', and we should like to put forward the following suggestions, some of which you may find yourself able to act upon:-

(1) A. 11. The commentary to include "men and women whose experience"
(2) A. 17 or A. 24. Include a Woman Police Officer.
(3) A. 29. Include Women Police in the canteen.
(4) C. 20–24. Include Women Police in one shot.[115]

There is no reply on file from Relph, although the file held by the National Archives does seem to be missing material on the film's production and release from this point onwards. However, some of these mediations can be seen in the completed film. For instance, scene A. 29 – the first canteen scene immediately following the charging of the drunken man singing at the station desk – includes a scene within which two tables of policewomen can be seen.

Fearnley was also monitoring the shooting process via the Met officer appointed as the official on-set liaison between Fearnley and Ealing, Inspector Leonard Pearcey. Fearnley had agreed to second Pearcey, an instructor at Hendon Police College, to Dearden and Relph in order 'to advise the Director on procedure, deportment, etc'.[116] Pearcey was also submitting confidential police reports on his activities for the attention of his Sub-Divisional Inspector, who would then forward Pearcey's information on to the Press Bureau. The first of Pearcey's reports provides a summary of the shooting process:

> On Tuesday 21st June, 1949, I commenced my duties as liaison officer with the [sic] Ealing Studios on the making of the film 'The Blue Lamp' ... At the moment and for about the next two or three weeks filming of outside shots is taking place. This necessitates my attendance daily at various places in the Paddington District. It is almost impossible to know in advance exactly when and where the various film shots will be taken owing to weather conditions and other factors influencing time of takes etc.[117]

Pearcey's statement underestimated the duration of the shoot; Michael Relph's shooting schedule details location shooting taking place between 20 June and 22 July, with second-unit photography (directed by Alexander Mackendrick) running parallel between 26 June and 3 July.[118] The shoot did not actually finish until 14 September. The delay was caused by Percy Fearnley, who took exception to three scenes and ordered them to be reshot. However, Michael Relph had scheduled the shoot to finish just before Ealing Studios was shut for a summer holiday break for its staff for the majority of August, and so Fearnley's reshoots had to wait until the Ealing staff had returned. In a handwritten note, Fearnley outlined the reshooting schedule, and the reasons behind each of his objections:

> Sequences remaining to be shot after Ealing Studios holiday break are:
>
> (1) Aug 30. Pedestrian crossing in Harrow Road with Jimmy Hanley. Retake because motorist was cautioned while car was astride crossing.
> (2) Sept 1. Identification Parade at Paddington Green station because of recasting.
> (3) Sept 4. Final crash of Riley's car at Stowe Road. A radio car with crew will be required for this shot.[119]

Despite Fearnley requesting the reshooting of certain scenes, he later noted that the filming process 'went through without any untoward incident or mishap'.[120]

Although Fearnley asserted that the shooting progressed smoothly, he was required to push through a series of last-minute corrections, as detailed above. In order to do this, he was required to maintain a supervisory position over the shoot itself. His influential position was strengthened by the quantity of materials loaned to Ealing by the Met; a 'flat-bottomed boat ... with its normal crew',[121] 'an Area Wireless Car and crew (3 P.Cs.)',[122] 'an Officer to advise the Director of the film on police procedure' (Inspector Pearcey),[123] police uniforms,[124] and locations including the Information Room, the Commissioner's Office and Paddington Green Police Station[125] were all provided for the shoot by the Met. Paddington Green was only used as an external location; in a meeting on 4 May 1949, between Fearnley, CID representatives and a party of Ealing employees including Michael Relph and Basil Dearden, Fearnley 'pointed out that all the scenes in Paddington Green Police Station would be shot in the studio on sets built from still photographs, but ... there would be shooting outside Paddington Green Police Station'.[126]

Ealing did, however, have to pay for these provisions. Payment proved to be a point of negotiation, which culminated in Ealing recompensing the Met for the wages of the personnel required, and the cost price of purchasing additional resources. In sparing these materials and personnel at a time of manpower shortage within the Met, the driving trio within the Met for *The Blue Lamp*'s production (Harold Scott, Percy Fearnley and R. L. Jackson) demonstrated the importance with which the project was regarded internally. The importance of the project was referenced directly in correspondence between Percy Fearnley and the Met Receiver, prior to the Receiver invoicing Ealing Studios for the Met resources used during the production of *The Blue Lamp*. Fearnley seemed, from this correspondence, intent on building a working relationship with Ealing, and pleads their case:

> In assessing all charges, however, I think it should be borne in mind that 'The Blue Lamp' is going to be the first film ever to go on the British screen which depicts a Police Officer as he really is, and may prove to be of tremendous propaganda value.[127]

After taking Fearnley's plea for clemency into account, the receiver raised an invoice of £14. 10s. 11d. (approximately £1,000 in 2014). Ealing instead offered to pay only direct charges for materials and, in lieu of subsistence and advisory fees, offered to provide the Met with the following:

> Ealing Studios have promised to

(1) Present us, free of charge, with a 16mm copy of 'The Blue Lamp'.
(2) Arrange two (or three, if necessary), free screenings for the Force.
(3) Arrange, if the appropriate organisations agree, a charity premiere, the proceeds of which would be devoted to Metropolitan Police Charities named by us.
(4) Prepare publicity material to enable us to arrange recruiting (or other) exhibits in cinema foyers when the film is shown to the public.[128]

Fearnley was clearly delighted with both the shooting process and the potential of the final production, noting in the same minute that 'we are going to receive from the film, and from Ealing Studios, far more than any charges we may decide to make'.[129]

Fearnley was not alone in expressing this sentiment; after viewing the final rough cut on 11 November 1949, the Commissioner, along with his Assistant Commissioners, the Met Secretary, Percy Fearnley and the Home Office PR representative, S. J. Baker (who had previously tried to wrest control of *The Blue Lamp* away from the Met), discussed the film at length with Michael Balcon and 'agreed no changes necessary'.[130] *The Blue Lamp* did not, however, signal the end of Percy Fearnley's ambition to utilize the medium of cinema for the dissemination of police entertainment-as-propaganda; after a series of press screenings and previews for the film, Fearnley was called upon by Assistant Commissioner Arthur Young to defend his decision to allocate liaison officers to the project. His response reveals his plans to continue to implement his PR strategy through cinema:

> A Police Officer was loaned to Ealing Studios for 7 ½ weeks. He was not fully employed in an advisory capacity during the whole of that time, because, for instance, some of the scenes shot were merely of the criminal actors ... A better plan might be for us to call on the Police for assistance when we want an Officer for a particular day, or couple of days, for any particular scene. Such occasions, it should

be borne in mind, will become more rare in the future because we have profitted substantially from the errors and omissions of this, shall I call it, 'guinea pig' feature film ... What was done this time can be done next time with greater efficiency.[131]

4.6 'Though very occasionally they may get killed, nothing else can ever conceivably go wrong with them': The critical reception of *The Blue Lamp*

The Blue Lamp was premiered at the Odeon Theatre, Leicester Square, on 19 January 1950. Two press screenings preceded this, at the same venue on 10 January and also at Gaumont-British's trade theatre on Wardour St on 13 January.[132] In all, over 500 free tickets were given to Met personnel to see the film at one of these three screenings. The premiere was a prestigious affair, with Prime Minister Clement Attlee and Chancellor, Stafford Cripps, both in attendance – indicative, of course, of the level of faith the political establishment had in the film.

While the extant material regarding *The Blue Lamp* housed either in press archives or in the Public Record Office fails to indicate Attlee's opinion of the film, it is safe to assume that Attlee was pleased with the principle of independent British film producers being afforded facilities by the Met. In October 1938, Attlee – then an opposition MP – was contacted by the Progressive Film Company after Christopher Brunel, the son of Adrian and Progressive's key filmmaker, had been refused a press pass by the then-Commissioner, Philip Game. Attlee wrote to the Conservative Home Secretary, Samuel Hoare, supporting Christopher Brunel and accusing Hoare and the Met Commissioner of encouraging a monopoly of official newsreel access shared between the prominent film producers of the time.[133] Attlee, then, was keen to encourage further cinematic access to bodies such at the Met, and so his appearance at the premiere was understandable.

The Met was keen to collaborate with the film's distributors in exploiting the PR potential of the film upon its release across the country. This keenness manifested itself via a police presence in *The Blue Lamp*'s exploitation. For instance, the Piccadilly branch of the Simpson's department store hosted an exhibition curated by the Met to coincide with the film's release. Titled 'Inside Scotland Yard: The Secrets Behind *The Blue Lamp*', the exhibition featured 'many exhibits released for the first time from the famous Yard Crime Museum [including] material from the Charles Peace, Jack the Ripper and Crippen cases ... [and] Himmler's death mask.'[134] *Kinematograph Weekly* reported on this with great enthusiasm, with the late-February provincial release of the film in mind:

> The Simpson Store, the Metropolitan Police, and Ealing Studios co-operated with the publicity department of the [Cinema Managers Association] to put on this most successful tie-up for the premiere run at the Odeon, Leicester Square.
>
> Arrangements have already been made for replica exhibitions in the provinces when the film is released ... Showmen are assured of police co-operation wherever the film is to be shown.[135]

The Met were also keen to announce their guiding hand in the film's production; the *Evening Standard* commented that 'the Yard backed the picture with full co-operation: policemen actually took part in it'[136], for instance, and the fact that the Met were involved in the film seemed to be a key selling point for the film. The following review from the *Sunday Pictorial* evidences this:

> This is no ordinary thriller. It is the first 'fiction' film ever made with the wholehearted co-operation of the Metropolitan Police. Every shot was vetted at Scotland Yard because it was the wish of the Police Commissioner, Sir Harold Scott, as well as Ealing Studios, that 'The Blue Lamp' should be a true picture of London's police at work. And it is. I guarantee that everyone who sees this film will look at the next policeman he meets with new respect.[137]

The *Daily Mirror* adopted a similar stance, commenting in their positive review that 'Scotland Yard gave Ealing Studios facilities never before granted to motion picture producers';[138] *The Star* pointed out that the film was 'filmed with full co-operation of Scotland Yard ... every detail of the screenplay ... was passed by Yard experts'[139] and the *Yorkshire Post, Liverpool Post*, the *Scotsman* and the *Glasgow Herald* all remarked on the collaboration between Ealing and the Met.[140]

The press reception of the film focused upon the authenticity lent to the fictional narrative through the collaborative presence of the Met. However, for *The Police Review*, *The Blue Lamp* failed to reach the requisite level of accuracy – their anonymous reviewer laments the unlawfulness of Diana Lewis' arrest,[141] the fact that one police officer wears 'his trousers braced an inch and a half from his boots'[142] and also that 'life behind the scenes in this Police Station is rather jollier than some Policemen will have found it to be'.[143] However, the reviewer concedes that *The Blue Lamp* 'is the first time the Police of this country have been adequately presented on the screen', and continues by providing a balanced argument regarding the success of the film as 'a stimulus to recruiting' against the possibility that 'others might be incited to emulation by the sneering, confident lawlessness of the power-drunk little gunman'.[144] The reviewer concludes, using the word 'illusion' to incisively illustrate the processes of control employed by the Press Bureau in *The Blue Lamp*'s production:

> One effect it is bound to have on most people: once you have seen it you look at all Policemen with a new respect and affection, and are buoyed up by the illusion that, though very occasionally they may get killed, nothing else can ever conceivably go wrong with them.[145]

This provides the most insightful contemporary response to *The Blue Lamp*; Fearnley's presence throughout, as I hope to have demonstrated, allowed for the total mediation of the content of the film. The illusiveness of the film is the direct result of Fearnley's input, which succeeded in couching a propagandist message within the acceptable medicine of realist entertainment, and is also summed up by the *Daily Herald*'s response to the film:

> Now it's entertainment, now it's propaganda. The quickness of the hand deceives the eye.[146]

Fearnley was the only constant throughout the production process; he controlled the flow of production materials (advisors, props, costumes, locations, rough cuts, publicity and extras) in exchange for exerting authority over the content of the script. As such, the film is illusive: in order to demonstrate that policewomen play an integral part within the Met, a key scene is filmed with half of Paddington Green Police Station's Mess Hall filled with policewomen, despite the fact that policewomen had their own canteen; an incidental actor failed to resemble the physical requirements of a police officer closely enough, and so Fearnley ordered a reshoot; the original treatment incorporated themes of housing and pay, but Fearnley objected. Fearnley and the Met Press Bureau exerted an influence over *The Blue Lamp* akin to that of a producer, and were allowed to occupy this position by Gainsborough Studios and Ealing Studios, who were both eager to depict the first *real* fictional Scotland Yard. Fearnley is then able to create the illusion that 'nothing else can ever conceivably go wrong with them', furthering the legitimacy of the Met at a time when a post-war crime wave, coupled with low-police numbers, meant that the police were on the receiving end of a series of high-profile negative newspaper headlines. The final film, and the processes by which the final film was reached, are a triumph of the Met's control of the production of culture exerted through the Press Bureau; after years of experimentation with entertainment-as-propaganda, the Press Bureau had hit upon the right formula, and they sought to take this forward through further collaborations with the same key film interests involved in the production of *The Blue Lamp*.

Notes

1. Robert Murphy, *Realism and Tinsel: Cinema and Society in Britain 1939–49* (London: BFI, 1989), p. 164.
2. Robert Reiner, *The Politics of the Police*, 3rd edn (Oxford: OUP, 2000), p. 58.
3. Tony Aldgate and Jeffrey Richards, *Best of British: Cinema and Society from 1930 to the Present* (London: I. B. Tauris, 2009), pp. 125–6.
4. Steve Chibnall, 'The Teenage Trilogy: *The Blue Lamp, I Believe In You* and *Violent Playground*', in Alan Burton et al. (eds), *Liberal Directions: Basil Dearden and Post-war British Film Culture* (Wiltshire: Flicks Books, 1997), p. 137. See also Steve Chibnall and Brian Macfarlane, *The British 'B' Film* (London: BFI Palgrave, 2009), p. 220 for a discussion of *Scotland Yard* within the context of Sir Harold Scott's 'public relations offensive'.
5. James Chapman, '"Sordidness, Corruption and Violence almost Unrelieved": Critics, Censors and the Post-war British Crime Film', *Contemporary British History* (vol. 22, no. 2, June 2008), p. 182.
6. Robert Murphy, 'Riff-Raff: British Cinema and the Underworld', in Charles Barr (ed.), *All Our Yesterdays: 90 Years of British Cinema* (London: BFI, 1986), pp. 286–305; see also Robert Murphy, *Realism and Tinsel: Cinema and Society in Britain 1939–49* (London: BFI, 1989), pp. 147–67.
7. Ibid.
8. Peter Wollen, 'Riff-Raff Realism', *Sight & Sound* (vol. 8, no. 4, April 1998), p. 19.
9. Tim Pulleine, 'Spin A Dark Web' in Steve Chibnall and Robert Murphy (eds), *British Crime Cinema* (London: Routledge, 1999), p. 27.
10. Harry Hopkins observed that the 'baffling' co-existence of two opposing sides of British identity in the post-war period provides an example of 'the perennial dialogue between the Puritan vein in the British character and the older, underlying, Rabelaisian vein; to some extent also – and this, too, was no new process in our history – the one England had given birth to the other'. Harry Hopkins, *The New Look: A Social History of the Forties and Fifties in Britain* (London: Martin Secker & Walburg, 1963), p. 97.

11 Robert Murphy, 'Riff-Raff: British Cinema and the Underworld', in Charles Barr (ed.), *All Our Yesterdays: 90 Years of British Cinema* (London: BFI, 1986), p. 303.
12 Jack Davies, *Brighton Rock* film review, *The Sunday Express*, 11 January 1948.
13 Joan Lester, 'Bold Analysis of Spivery', *Reynolds News*, 4 January 1948.
14 Vincent Porter, 'The Robert Clark Account: Films released in Britain by Associated British Pictures, British Lion, MGM, and Warner Bros., 1946–1957', *Historical Journal of Film, Radio and Television* (vol. 20, no. 4, 2000), pp. 469–512.
15 Steve Chibnall and Brian McFarlane, *The British 'B' Film* (London: Palgrave, 2009), pp. 39–40.
16 Ibid., p. 48.
17 Chapman, Sordidness, Corruption, p. 187.
18 Ibid., p. 194.
19 Steve Chibnall has recently discussed this period of instability within the BBFC and covers the topic more comprehensively than I am able to, given the constraints of space. Steve Chibnall, 'From *The Snake Pit* to The *Garden of Eden*: A Time of Temptation', in Edward Lamberti (ed.), *Behind the Scenes at the BBFC: Film Classification from the Silver Screen to the Digital Age* (London: Palgrave, 2012), pp. 29–52.
20 James C. Robertson, '*Good Time Girl*, the BBFC and the Home Office: A Mystery Resolved', *Journal of British Cinema and Television* (vol. 3, no. 1, 2006), pp. 159–61.
21 Ibid. Robertson's insightful report into *Good-Time Girl*'s production is based on PRO TNA MH 102/1137, which was declassified in 2006. However, the following PRO TNA files shed further light on *Good-Time Girl*'s production: MH 102/1137, MH 102/1138, MH 102/1140, MH 102/1141, MH 102/1142. As *Good-Time Girl* does not provide the central focus of this chapter, however, it would be inappropriate here to expand upon Robertson's research.
22 *Evening News, Good Time Girl*, 30 April 1948.
23 PRO TNA MEPO 2/8342, Jan Read to Harold Scott, 6 May 1948.
24 Ibid.
25 MH 102/1138, Minute 1, 22 May 1947.
26 Robertson, *Good Time Girl*, p. 159.

27 See Donald Thomas, *An Underworld At War: Spivs, Deserters, Racketeers and Civilians in the Second World War* (London: John Murray, 2003), pp. 243–7 for a full account of the 'Cleft Chin' murder.
28 PRO TNA MEPO 2/8342, Jan Read to Harold Scott, 6 May 1948.
29 PRO TNA MEPO 2/8342, Read to Scott, 7 July 1948.
30 Receipt of this dossier was acknowledged by Jan Read on 27 July 1948. PRO TNA MEPO 2/8342, Read to Fearnley, 27 July 1948.
31 Ibid.
32 PRO TNA MEPO 2/8342, *The Blue Lamp* Treatment, Jan Read, 21 September 1948, p. 11.
33 PRO TNA MEPO 2/8342, Minute 18, 2 August 1948.
34 PRO TNA MEPO 2/8342, *The Blue Lamp* treatment, 21 September 1948.
35 PRO TNA MEPO 2/8342, Minute 20, 30 September 1948.
36 PRO TNA MEPO 2/8342, Minute 29, 5 November 1948. See also PRO TNA MEPO 2/8342, Jan Read to Harold Scott, 20 October 1948.
37 Charles Barr, *Ealing Studios* (London: Cameron & Tayleur, 1977), p. 81.
38 Ibid., p. 82.
39 PRO TNA MEPO 2/8342, *The Blue Lamp* Treatment, Jan Read, 21 September 1948, p. 3.
40 Harper and Porter, *British Cinema of the 1950s: The Decline of Deference* (Oxford: OUP, 2003), p. 60.
41 PRO TNA MEPO 2/8342, *The Blue Lamp* Treatment, Jan Read, 21 September 1948, p. 7.
42 Ibid., pp. 8–9.
43 Ibid., p. 5.
44 Ibid., p. 6.
45 Ibid., p. 14.
46 PRO TNA MEPO 2/8342, Fearnley to Richard Jackson, Met Secretary, 27 October 1948.
47 Ibid.
48 PRO TNA MEPO 2/8342, Fearnley, Minute 20, 30 September 1948.
49 Ibid.
50 PRO TNA MEPO 2/8342, *The Blue Lamp* Treatment, Jan Read, 21 September 1948, p. 6.
51 PRO TNA MEPO 2/8342, Minute 20, 30 September 1948.

52 PRO TNA MEPO 2/8342, Minute 22, 16 October 1948.
53 Chibnall, 'The Teenage Trilogy', p. 139.
54 PRO TNA MEPO 2/8342, Fearnley to Richard Jackson, 27 October 1948.
55 PRO TNA MEPO 2/8342, Minute 29, 5 November 1948.
56 PRO TNA MEPO 2/7576, Minute 2, 30 October 1946.
57 PRO TNA MEPO 2/6979, Minute 48, R. H. Jackson, 20 August 1946.
58 PRO TNA MEPO 2/6979, Minute 19, Percy Fearnley, footnote.
59 PRO TNA HO 45/24098, KH(?) to Baker, Home Office, 4 November 1948.
60 PRO TNA HO 45/24098, Anon., 'Films On The Police', p. 1. Undated, presumably early November 1948.
61 Ibid.
62 Ibid., p. 2.
63 Ibid., p. 3.
64 PRO TNA MEPO 2/7442, anonymous memo headed 'Summary of applications for facilities to make films depicting Police work, etc.', undated (possibly 1938, or early 1939).
65 PRO TNA HO 45/24098, R. H. Jackson to Baker, 19 November 1948; PRO TNA MEPO 2/8342, Minute 29, 5 November 1948.
66 PRO TNA HO 45/24098, Newsam to Scott, 4 January 1949; PRO TNA HO 45/24098, Jackson to Baker, 19 January 1948.
67 PRO TNA HO 45/24098, Griffiths to Baker, 23 November 1948.
68 Ibid.
69 Ibid.
70 See, for example, PRO TNA MEPO 2/6207, Brigadier-General Sir William Horwood, Commissioner of Police of the Metropolis, to William Jeapes, Topical Film Company, 26 January 1921.
71 PRO TNA HO 45/24098, Private Minute, Frank Newsam, 21 December 1948.
72 'Mr. Griffiths's course (1) should be adopted, namely, that we should get together with Gainsborough and Scotland Yard with a view to seeing what could be done to improve the proposed treatment from the national point of view.' Ibid.
73 PRO TNA HO 45/24098, Frank Newsam to Harold Scott, 4 January 1949.

74 Ibid.
75 PRO TNA MEPO 2/8342, Scott to Newsam, 7 January 1949.
76 Donald Zec, 'The Blue Lamp', *Daily Mirror*, 18 January 1950, n.p.
77 PRO TNA MEPO 2/8342, Scott to Newsam, 7 January 1949.
78 PRO TNA MEPO 2/8342, Newsam to Scott, 20 January 1949.
79 Ibid.
80 PRO TNA MEPO 2/8342, Read to Fearnley, 1 December 1948.
81 PRO TNA MEPO 2/8342, Percy Fearnley to District Commander Quincey, 3 December 1948.
82 PRO TNA MEPO 2/8342, Minute 38, Percy Fearnley, 6 January 1949.
83 Ibid.
84 Geoffrey Macnab, *J. Arthur Rank and the British Film Industry* (London and New York: Routledge, 1993), p. 164.
85 Paul Swann, *The Hollywood Feature Film in Post-war Britain*, p. 90.
86 Ibid.
87 Ian Jarvie, for instance, has argued that the 75 per cent *ad valorem* tax was an

> anomalous measure, ill-thought-out, and inconsistent with both film policy and trade policy. Imposed hastily and *ad hoc*, it did not raise any revenue but had the unintended consequence of encouraging the production of high-quality American films in British studios; the beginning of a trend to American production in Europe – known as 'runaway' production – that eventually opened up the US domestic market to European-made films.

Ian Jarvie, 'British Trade Policy versus Hollywood, 1947–1948: "Food before Flicks"', *Historical Journal of Film, Radio and Television* (vol. 6, no. 1, 1986), p. 19.

88 Gallup, *Gallup International* (September 1947), quoted in Paul Swann, *The Hollywood Feature Film in Post-war Britain*, p. 93.
89 Robert Murphy, 'Rank's Attempt on the American Market', p. 166 (pp. 164–78), James Curran and Vincent Porter (eds), *British Cinema History* (London: Weidenfeld & Nicolson, 1983).
90 Robert Murphy, 'Under the Shadow of Hollywood' in Charles Barr (ed.), *All Our Yesterdays: 90 Years of British Cinema* (London: BFI, 1986), p. 61.

91 Macnab, *J. Arthur Rank*, p. 184.
92 Margaret Dickinson and Simon Hartog, 'Interview: Sir Harold Wilson', *Screen* (vol. 22, no. 3, 1981), pp. 19–20.
93 Anon., 'Revolt Against Quota & Trading Terms Grows', *To-day's Cinema* (vol. 71, no. 5668, 1948), p. 14.
94 Ibid.
95 Harper and Porter, *British Cinema of the 1950s: The Decline of Deference* (Oxford: OUP, 2007), p. 35.
96 Ibid.
97 Ibid., p. 36; see also Justine Ashby, 'Betty Box, "The Lady in Charge"', in Justine Ashby and Andrew Higson (eds), *British Cinema, Past and Present* (London and New York: Routledge, 2000), p. 170.
98 Ibid., p. 57.
99 PRO TNA MEPO 2/8342, Percy Fearnley, Minute 38, 6 January 1949.
100 PRO TNA MEPO 2/8342, Percy Fearnley, Minute 20, 30 September 1948.
101 PRO TNA MEPO 2/8342, Fearnley to Read, 7 January 1949.
102 PRO TNA MEPO 2/8342, Balcon to Fearnley, 12 January 1949.
103 PRO TNA MEPO 2/8342, Minute 45, Fearnley, 27 January 1949.
104 Barr, *Ealing Studios*, p. 85.
105 PRO TNA MEPO 2/8342, First Draft Script, p. 75.
106 Ibid., p. 31.
107 T. E. B. Clarke, *The Blue Lamp* shooting script, 27 May 1949. I am grateful to Professor Tim O'Sullivan and Simon Relph for granting me access to this resource. All references to the final shooting script are sourced from Basil Dearden's personal copy of the shooting script.
108 PRO TNA MEPO 2/8342, Percy Fearnley to Assistant Commissioners 'A', 'C' and 'D', 11 May 1949.
109 Ibid.
110 PRO TNA MEPO 2/8342, Fearnley to R. H. Jackson, Met Secretary, Minute 51, 13 May 1949.
111 T. E. B. Clarke, *The Blue Lamp* shooting script, 27 May 1949, pp. 92–6.
112 PRO TNA MEPO 2/8342, Minute 105, Percy Fearnley, 27 July 1949.
113 See, for example, PRO TNA MEPO 2/8342, Percy Fearnley, Minute 83, 11 July 1949, which records the arrangement of one such screening, observation and discussion.

114 PRO TNA MEPO 2/8342, Elizabeth Bather, Superintendent of Met Women Police, to Percy Fearnley, 11 July 1949.
115 PRO TNA MEPO 2/8342, Percy Fearnley to Michael Relph, 11 July 1949.
116 PRO TNA MEPO 2/8342, Minute 51, Percy Fearnley to R. L. Jackson, 13 May 1949.
117 PRO TNA MEPO 2/8342, Inspector Leonard Pearcey, 21 June 1949.
118 Michael Relph, *The Blue Lamp* shooting schedule, 27 May 1949. I am grateful to Professor Tim O'Sullivan and Simon Relph for granting me access to this resource.
119 PRO TNA MEPO 2/8342, Minute 112, Percy Fearnley, 11 August 1949.
120 PRO TNA MEPO 2/8342, Percy Fearnley to Met Police Receiver, 14 September 1949.
121 PRO TNA MEPO 2/8342, Minute 74, Percy Fearnley, 24 June 1949.
122 PRO TNA MEPO 2/8342, Minute 61, Percy Fearnley, 14 June 1949.
123 PRO TNA MEPO 2/8342, Minute 52, Percy Fearnley to R. L. Jackson, 20 May 1949.
124 PRO TNA MEPO 2/8342, Minute 51, Percy Fearnley to R. L. Jackson, 13 May 1949.
125 Ibid.
126 PRO TNA MEPO 2/8342, 'Note of Meeting at Elliott House on 4 May, 1949', Percy Fearnley.
127 PRO TNA MEPO 2/8342, Minute 125, Percy Fearnley to Met Receiver, 14 September 1949.
128 PRO TNA MEPO 2/8342, Minute 129, Percy to Met Receiver, 1 October 1949.
129 Ibid.
130 PRO TNA MEPO 2/8342, Minute 136, Percy Fearnley, 11 November 1949.
131 PRO TNA MEPO 2/8342, Percy Fearnley to Assistant Commissioner 'D' Branch, Arthur Young, Minute 160, 23 January 1950.
132 PRO TNA MEPO 2/8342, Percy Fearnley, Minute 144, 8 December 1949.
133 PRO TNA HO 45/17415, Clement Attlee to Home Secretary, Samuel Hoare, 17 October 1938.

134 Anon., '"The Blue Lamp" Exhibition: An Intriguing Show', *Kinematograph Weekly*, 2 February 1950, n.p.
135 Ibid.
136 Anon., 'London Crime Film', *Evening Standard*, 17 January 1950, n.p.
137 Fred Redman, 'The Story That Had to Be Told', *Sunday Pictorial*, 15 January 1950, n.p.
138 Donald Zec, 'The Blue Lamp', *Daily Mirror*, 18 January 1950, n.p.
139 Anon., 'New Film Shows Pc 999 at Work', *The Star*, 17 January 1950, p. 5.
140 Anon., 'Latest Crime Film', *Yorkshire Post*, 18 January 1950, n.p.; Anon., 'Film On The Beat', *Liverpool Post*, 18 January 1950, n.p.; Anon., 'The Blue Lamp: Thriller From Ealing Studios', *Scotsman*, 18 January 1950, n.p.; Anon., 'The Policeman's Lot Makes Good Film', *Glasgow Herald*, 18 January 1950, n.p.
141 'It may be captious to complain that you can't lawfully arrest an over-seventeen girl who is missing from home merely because she fails to produce an identity card … Concede also that Jimmy Hanley, who arrests her, lets her walk in front of him to Paddington Green Police Station, so that it doesn't look like an arrest'. Anon., 'The Constable and the Law', *Police Review*, 27 January 1950, n.p.
142 Ibid.
143 Ibid.
144 Ibid.
145 Ibid.
146 P.H., 'The Blue Lamp', *The Daily Herald*, 20 January 1950, n.p.

5

Real life as the Metropolitan Police insisted upon us seeing it: Division of labour and the collaborative production of *Street Corner*, 1950–3

The previous two chapters have located and defined the status of 'the producer' within a series of texts made collaboratively between the Metropolitan Police (hereafter 'Met') Press Bureau and British film studios, focusing predominantly upon the instigation of a more progressive public relations policy by the Met and how this policy was implemented by the Met's PIO, Percy Fearnley. Vincent Porter has traced the variability of what he calls 'the creative contribution of the producer'[1], noting that this variability 'frequently depended on the limits which were imposed on the producer's creative freedom by changes in technology, the availability of production finance and the resultant division of labour'.[2] Porter continues by historicizing the relationships between the producer and these three categories. He acknowledges the complexities inherent in attempting to locate the producer by quoting an interview with David Lean. When asked why Alec (Trevor Howard) and Laura (Celia Johnson) do not consummate their on-screen relationship in *Brief Encounter* (which Lean directed and his long-time collaborator Ronald Neame produced under the auspices of Rank's supposedly untrammelled Independent Producers umbrella), 'Lean replied: "This was real life as J. Arthur Rank insisted upon us seeing it".[3] During the production of *The Blue Lamp*, the Met Press Bureau possessed a level of influence akin to Rank's over

Brief Encounter; the Press Bureau rendered Michael Relph's position irrelevant, despite his control of labour, production finance and technology. Relph is hardly visible in the production files housed in the National Archives. With *The Blue Lamp*'s two successors, *Street Corner* (Muriel Box, London Independent Producers, 1953) and *The Long Arm* (Charles Frend, Ealing Studios, 1956), Fearnley took the principles of mediation and control first applied within a feature film context to *The Blue Lamp* and expanded upon them, further obfuscating the role of the producer in these texts.

At this point, it is prudent to return to the work of Raymond Williams when considering the function of the producer of these collaborative texts; his assertion that the 'progress of culture is dependent upon the material conditions for culture' illuminates Fearnley's position of power over these collaborative projects.[4] In these instances, the traditional control of production finance, division of labour and technology held by the named film producers is not of equal stature to the control of 'the material conditions for culture' wielded by Fearnley.

With *This Modern Age: Scotland Yard* and *The Girl from Scotland Yard*, Percy Fearnley and the Met Press Bureau began experimenting with the control of cultural production by playing off the producers' need for access with the Met's desire for entertainment masked as propaganda, or 'real life as *the Met* insisted upon us seeing it'. With *The Blue Lamp*, Fearnley honed his previous experience and expanded his influence to encompass feature film production, occupying the role of producer by controlling 'the material conditions for culture'.

The Blue Lamp proved a commercial and critical success at the British box office, opening in early 1950 to become the most popular film of the year.[5] It is clear that Percy Fearnley, who was so keen to begin his reign as PIO by 'bring[ing] film Companies into line', approved of the final product.[6] In February 1950, *The Police Review* carried the following summary of *The Blue Lamp*'s release:

Film-goers who see it may not realise how much Ealing Studios owe to the help they received from Scotland Yard. The idea of a full length feature film of the Police was first conceived by Mr. P. H. Fearnley, the Public Information Officer at Scotland Yard, and his department was instrumental in securing the full co-operation between the Police and the film's directors which is the secret of its success. Advice and technical assistance was given throughout the making of the film and many changes were made at the request of the Police.[7]

Despite the internal recognition Fearnley received for his work on *The Blue Lamp* and its experimental supporting-feature predecessors *This Modern Age: Scotland Yard* and *The Girl from Scotland Yard*, Fearnley did not receive a screen credit for his contribution – possibly by design, as the intention of the entertainment-as-propaganda experiment Fearnley undertook relied on the fact that 'film-goers who see it may not realise' the entertainment they have just consumed was (at least) co-produced by the Met itself. As I have argued in previous chapters, Fearnley adopted the position of producer during the collaborative processes involved in these films with a view to establishing a coherent programme of feature filmmaking that masked propaganda as entertainment, thus increasing the legitimacy of the police by using cinema to manipulate the image of the police within Britain's social consciousness. *The Blue Lamp*, as textual analysts have observed, is constructed with the tenets of 'social stability', 'community'[8] and family – both in literal and professional terms – as its central focus.[9] As Eugene McLaughlin has pointed out, the film is at pains to stress that the Met – 'a police force stretched to the limits' – is responsible for maintaining social stability, and with it the 'old London' values of 'duty, obligation and responsibility'.[10] This stress was the product of the Press Bureau's interventions in the collaborative process. These interventions were crucial to the box office success of the film, too, as through the acquiescence of *The Blue Lamp*'s named producers to the Met's wishes, the film depicted a previously unseen aspect of the work of Scotland Yard, and therefore the film existed as a voyeuristic curiosity in a crowded marketplace.

Despite the successful conclusion of the previous collaborative film project, the potential for friction within the process is exemplified by *Street Corner* (Muriel Box, London Independent Producers, 1953) – the only film for which Percy Fearnley received a credit of any sort (he is listed in the opening credit as 'Technical Advisor'). The film – which was the Met Press Bureau's next involvement with a feature-length film after *The Blue Lamp* – harked back in structure and theme both to *The Girl from Scotland Yard* and *The Blue Lamp* but, unlike its predecessors, the production of 1953's *Street Corner* was beset with problems from beginning to end. These problems were characterized by a constant struggle for control between the Met and its director-producer team of Muriel and Sydney Box. The 'interaction between culture [filmmaker] and social organization [the Met]' proved to be the catalyst for a series of disputes.[11] Muriel Box, writing in her 1974 memoir, noted that 'innumerable battles with Scotland Yard bedevilled us', causing the production to reach the filming stage only after 'the seventh or eighth draft of the policewoman screenplay'.[12] This chapter, then, looks in detail at the production processes of *Street Corner*, utilizing the extant Met correspondence housed at the National Archives to evaluate the extent to which the 'innumerable battles' between the Met and the Boxes were centred around which institution held meaning-making power over the film's production.

5.1 Fearnley's influence

The production's instigation was in itself a contested moment; Sydney Box, having recently left his position as overseer of Gainsborough Studio's production schedule, approached Percy Fearnley directly in early November 1951 'with a proposal to make a feature film on the Women Police, a treatment for which he had already bought'.[13] However, Concanen Productions – a relatively new production company set up by Terrence and Derrick de Marney – had beaten Box to it, having already approached the Met Press Bureau with a similar proposal tentatively titled *The Blue Stocking*.[14] Sydney Box's treatment had been purchased from Jan Read and Ted Willis, who had written the well-received treatment for *The Blue Lamp* three years prior, and, despite the earlier approach from Concancen Productions, Fearnley was more receptive to the idea of collaborating again with Sydney Box. He noted in a private minute that

> while it is no part of our business to prejudge the claims of rival companies ... we can go ahead with Sidney [sic] Box with much greater confidence if only because he has the money behind him to produce a good film.[15]

However, Fearnley was unwilling to express this preference publicly. He instead asked the Secretary of the British Film Producers Association – a body for film producers equivalent to the exhibition industry's Cinematograph Exhibitors Association[16] – to mitigate between the two companies in order to prevent duplication of content.[17] The British Film Producers Association (BFPA) had no jurisdiction over either Concanen or London Independent Producers – neither company were members of the Association and, if they were, the BFPA's primary responsibility only involved analyzing production schedules with a view to advising on the suitability of the Board of Trade's exhibition quota for indigenous product on British cinema screens. However, the BFPA's Secretary wrote back to Fearnley in early December with confirmation that Concanen had agreed to withdraw their project, therefore paving the way for Sydney Box to proceed with his collaboration with the Met. Fearnley had already made the Home Office aware of Concanen's request for collaboration, and the Home Office – no doubt buoyed by the success of *The Blue Lamp* in spite of their attempt to veto the project[18] – had permitted the Met to proceed with the collaboration with Concanen. However, Fearnley chose to not inform the Home Office of the change of producer and was backed up by Met Commissioner Harold Scott in this decision.[19] *Good-Time Girl*, for which Sydney Box assumed the role of producer, caused considerable controversy within the Home Office in 1948. The Conservative MP Cuthbert Headlam had written directly to James Chuter Ede, the then Home Secretary, in May of that year following *Picture Post*'s coverage of the production of *Good-Time Girl*:

> I cannot believe that the publication of pictures of this description in an illustrated paper, or of the reproduction in a film of the scenes which they depict, can be in the public interest; nor can I understand how such a film can pass the censorship which presumably it must have done?[20]

Headlam's letter, alongside other petitions received, caused the Home Office to consider a public rebuttal to Sydney Box directly in the form of a Parliamentary Question, to be answered by the Home Secretary.[21] Because of this controversy, stemming from Sydney Box's defence of the film's content (he wrote an article for the *Newcastle Journal* in the wake of criticism of the film in which he claimed that *Good-Time Girl* 'is true of a big social problem'[22]), it is doubtful whether the Home Office would have reacted positively to the news that Sydney Box had been given the responsibility of producing a film collaboratively with the Met, particularly given the fact that the Conservative Party – members of whom had reacted so vociferously to *Good-Time Girl* – had won the election of October 1951. It is therefore expedient of Percy Fearnley to omit the mention of this change of producer to the Home Office.

Fearnley wrote to Sydney Box outlining the terms of the collaboration on 6 December 1951. These six conditions included 'submitt[ing] for the Commissioner's approval a treatment and subsequently a script' prior to the final granting of shooting facilities.[23] Box replied six days later, stating that 'these conditions are completely acceptable to us'.[24] No mention, however, was made of the level of control the Met would hold over the publicity materials to be used for the film's exploitation or the method of the film's release, the latter of which proved to be a considerable object of disagreement. Fearnley's next step was to send to Sydney Box a three-page document outlining cases in which the Women Police had played a crucial role,[25] in much the same manner as Robert Fabian's dossier on the Antiquis murder was sent to Jan Read to aid the production of *The Blue Lamp*.[26] The six cases detailed in the document involve a jeweller receiving stolen goods, a fifteen-year-old runaway who appeared to have been working as a prostitute, a Women Police Constable being struck by two assailants in the course of an arrest, two homeless young lovers who were apprehended and sent to a shelter by a Woman Police Constable, the breaking of a large prostitution ring and the apprehension of a military deserter. Of these six cases, four made their way into *Street Corner*; the inclusion of the military deserter Edna (Eleanor Summerfield) and her husband, Dave (Ronald Howard), can be traced to Fearnley's memo, and so too can the finale of the film in which a Woman Police Constable is attacked by two men. The jeweller, Muller (Charles Victor), who fences stolen goods for the two central criminal characters of the film, is also an inclusion based on the content of Fearnley's memo. As with *The Blue Lamp*, Fearnley had again exerted significant influence over the content of the final film by releasing 'insider' information to the filmmakers.

Jan Read began a series of research visits following the receipt of the above document. These research visits – which, by now, the Met were familiar with – included trips to Peto House (the Women Police training school), and a meeting with Elizabeth Bather, the Superintendent of the Women Police Branch and the UK's highest-ranking female police officer, at Peel House. The scheduled research visits were not as thorough as on previous collaborative film projects, possibly due to Fearnley's unwillingness to schedule a comprehensive series of visits, and the fact that Jan Read had previously undertaken a similar series of visits in preparing *The Blue Lamp*. Fearnley minuted the following:

> I have had a number of discussions with Sidney Box about the preliminary research work ... and have indicated to him that the Force would be saved a considerable amount of time (and probably irritation as well) if the research work could be cut to a minimum. I pointed out that the trouble with all writers who are strange to the Police is that it takes them a considerable time, and many visits, to secure the atmosphere, and suggested that in view of the fact that Jan Read, with whom he had worked, was writing a series of scripts for the B.B.C. Television Service, he might like to use him on the preliminaries.
>
> Mr. Box subsequently informed me that he had discussed my suggestion with Mr. Read and that the latter had agreed to prepare a rough treatment, partly based on knowledge he gained while writing the original 'Blue Lamp' script.[27]

This minute is a significant demonstration of the influence held by Fearnley over the project; not only did he have a final refusal on the script progressing into production, but he had also suggested to Sydney Box that, from the Met's perspective, the employment of Jan Read to write the treatment was preferred. Jan Read, as I have mentioned in the previous chapter, was a friend of Harold Scott's daughter,[28] and was trusted by the Press Bureau for this reason and for his previous involvement with *The Blue Lamp*.

On 10 March 1952, Jan Read provided Percy Fearnley with a treatment for the film, prospectively titled *West End Central*.[29] This treatment, which bears little resemblance to the final film, was received cautiously by Fearnley, who minuted the following:

There is a considerable amount of revision to do and I would prefer that [the Assistant Commissioners and Elizabeth Bather] are not troubled until we have found a reasonably good working script.

...

It should be borne in mind that there are a considerable number of omissions and that many sequences of Women Police activities and incidents based on true occurrences have yet to be included.

The present treatment may not yet be as good as that for 'The Blue Lamp' but the atmosphere is already there ... I think we have a good foundation for a film which can excel 'The Blue Lamp' and do far more than it did for police recruitment, provided of course that we can curb the known enthusiasm of Sidney Box, if we find that necessary.[30]

The final comment is unclear, but it is presumably a reference to Box's involvement in *Good-Time Girl*, and his ebullient defence of the film in the press.

A copy of the *West End Central* treatment has been preserved in the Met archive, along with handwritten comments from Percy Fearnley. It bears more resemblance to *The Girl from Scotland Yard* than *The Blue Lamp*. The treatment begins with the training of a young, university-educated, middle-class new recruit to the Women Police, and intersperses her induction with a crime story involving the hijacking of a jeweller's van by 'a couple of spivs'.[31] The female group dynamic for which Muriel Box has been credited is present in Jan Read's treatment; however, the new recruit, Joyce, befriends Lucy, 'a decided flirt [who is] much in demand at section house dances',[32] and the motherly Sargeant Ramsey takes Joyce under her wing at West End Central Police Station. The episodic structure of *Street Corner* also has its roots in Jan Read's treatment; interspersed with the central Women Police narrative are sub-plots involving lost children, apprehending drunks and the aforementioned jewel robbery. Very few of these sub-plots and training sequences made their way into the finished film. Jan Read did, however, first introduce the Soho environ of the Down-Beat Club and its proprietors, Ray and Chick, the two central criminal characters who use the club as a front, played by Terence Morgan and Michael Medwin, respectively in *Street Corner*:

> A couple of young men, Ray Daniels and Chick Farrar, both in their early twenties, both of flash appearance, in fact typical C. R. O. [Criminal Record Office] boys, are sitting at a table in the rear. Ray is grumbling about a transaction with one, Sam Friedman, obviously a fence, and Chick replies that Sam may be stingy but that he is dependable.[33]

The character of Sam Friedman, 'a Polish Jew who has come to England during the Hitler terror' who operates a jewellery shop,[34] is re-christened as Muller in the completed film. In both Jan Read's treatment and the final product, he is blackmailed by Ray and Chick; Friedman has only dealt with Ray, so Chick and an accomplice are able to visit his shop posing as CID inspectors who identify stolen jewellery in his possession, blackmailing him for £500 in order for no charges to be brought against him. This sequence's roots are firmly found within Jan Read's treatment.[35]

Although Fearnley chose not to provide the Assistant Commissioners with copies of Jan Read's treatment, he noted that 'the Commissioner, however, is interested in this film and would no doubt like to see the treatment at this stage'.[36] Harold Scott had presided over the reinvigoration of the Press Bureau; during his Commissionership, the Bureau had embraced film production in an unprecedented manner, and Scott's continued interest does seem to indicate that collaboration with British film producers was key to his public relations strategy. He expressed enthusiasm for Jan Read's treatment, acknowledging after reading *West End Central* that 'this has the makings of a good film'.[37] Following the Commissioner's minute, Fearnley returned a mediated copy of the treatment to Sydney Box and

Jan Read the following day in person. His mediations were principally made in the interests of accuracy; he felt no need to suggest major amendments as he had already supplied Read with source materials for adaptation. He summarized the meeting as follows:

> I suggested a number of changes and deletions ... and also suggested they might like to bring in a dog sequence with a chase and arrest towards the end.[38]

This again provides evidence of Fearnley's control of the project; not only did he provide the core cases from which Jan Read's treatment was produced, but he also suggested the dog sequence, which forms the principal chase of the final act.

5.2 The script

Sydney Box wrote to Fearnley on 2 May 1952 to update him on the progress made on the first draft of the script:

> This note is only to confirm that the typist has today delivered copies of a first draft of 157 pages(!) which Jan [Read] and I propose to reduce to around 100 before presenting it for your approval.[39]

Thus began a torturous period in the production of *Street Corner*; before the script reached the shooting stage, a further seven significant rewrites were called.[40] Unfortunately, no drafts of the script survive in the Public Record Office; however, the correspondence detailing the interventions made by Fearnley and Superintendent Elizabeth Bather – both by now veterans of this process – is extant.

The script itself was produced collaboratively between Sydney and Muriel Box and Jan Read. Box sent six copies of their shortened effort to the Met Press Bureau thirteen days later, but it was dismissed by Fearnley as a 'typical Hollywood effort', and as bearing 'little if any resemblance to the original treatment'.[41] Based on this draft of the script, Fearnley minuted that the 'Commissioner would not be prepared to grant facilities for this story',[42] and sought to prevent the script reaching production by writing to ATL Watkins, the Secretary of the British Board of Film Censors (BBFC). The letter is reproduced in full below:

> You will remember that some time ago we had telephone conversations about Mr. Derrick de Marney and Mr. Sydney Box who had both made approaches to us about the possibility of making a film on the Women Police, and that in the end we submitted the matter to the British Film Producers' Association who gave Mr. Box the 'all clear' to go ahead.
>
> Subsequently we granted facilities to Mr. Jan Read, on behalf of Mr. Box, to prepare the rough treatment. This was submitted to us and accepted by us as a basis for the film. We have now received from Mr. Box the enclosed copy of the so far untitled script which bears little if any resemblance to the original treatment. It is not the kind of script for which the Commissioner would be prepared to grant any shooting facilities other than normal facilities afforded film companies for shooting in the streets of London. I propose to see Mr. Box later this week and inform him accordingly.

In the meantime I thought you might like to see the script.[43] Watkins responded two days later (23 May 1952), returning the script as Sydney Box had already sent a copy to the BBFC as 'part of the normal censorship process'.[44] Significantly, Watkins added that

> when we have read it and formed our own views I will get in touch with you and get some further idea of your reactions.[45]

While the BBFC were (and still are) theoretically an independent, trade-led film classification body, this demonstrates the potential for the Met and, by extension, other state control agencies and departments to influence their processes. The purpose of Fearnley's letter seems to have been to make the BBFC aware that the Met were not willing to support the production of the film based on the current draft of the script. His letter therefore reads as a subtle petition for censorship. It would appear from the correspondence that Percy Fearnley was known to the BBFC, and on friendly terms with their examiners; the letter, for instance, begins with the informal 'Dear Watkins'.[46]

Fearnley wrote to the BBFC six days after receiving the script and, after the receipt of Watkins' response, Fearnley arranged a meeting with Sydney Box. In the meeting, Fearnley 'asked Mr Box to re-write the script entirely + offered various suggestions for inclusion'.[47] Contradicting his earlier statement, Fearnley also allowed research visits for the filmmakers, scheduling a meeting at short notice for Sydney and Muriel Box with Elizabeth Bather.[48] Muriel Box also requested a visit to West End Central Station, and was assigned a Woman Police officer to shadow for an afternoon in late June 1952.[49] The visit seemed to have an impact upon Muriel Box, who wrote of the time spent at West End Central in her autobiography:

> While examining the cell where Emmeline Pankhurst was imprisoned, I could not help wondering what that eminent suffragette would have said if she could have glimpsed the future and seen me, a woman-director, in the company of a female in the higher ranks of the police force, nattering away on the spot where she was forcibly fed.[50]

Muriel Box's autobiography details the gender discrimination she experienced over the course of her career and how her feminist politics have influenced her work. On the surface, her feminism appears to have made her an ideal candidate for the direction of a female group film such as *Street Corner*. However, notions of authorship regarding *Street Corner* must remain contested; while Muriel Box was responsible for co-writing the script and directing the film, the Met's interventions in the project were extensive, influential and numerous.

Muriel and Sydney Box appear to have been continuing to revise the script while undertaking the series of research visits, handing in a revised script for mediation by the Press Bureau on 15 June 1952.[51] After reading this draft of the script, Percy Fearnley sent five pages of procedural queries ('Do Women P.C.'s have cups of tea in their offices or in the canteen?', 'Do civilian clerks in the Court's service take payment of fines?') to the Met's division of Women Police for clarification.[52] Woman Police Sargeant Lambourne (who, three years earlier, had first alerted Scotland Yard to the suspicious nature of the man later identified as the 'Acid Bath' killer, John George Haigh) responded with a series of clarifications on 24 June,[53] and these were collated into an eleven-page memo sent to Sydney Box by Percy Fearnley a week later.[54] The amendments suggested therein were largely made for the purposes of accuracy; issues such as the number of desks at West End Central and the number of stripes on a Woman Police Constable's uniform were raised, for instance.[55] However, certain amendments were suggested for the purposes of image management; Fearnley was concerned that the 'Women Police dialogue should be more persuasive and less "smart alec"',[56] and he suggested that the Women Police officers 'might well be more conversational' in their tone on one occasion,[57] and that 'Pauline's dialogue in this scene [should be] rather brighter'.[58] At several points in this memo, Fearnley provides rewritten sections of dialogue for Sydney Box to incorporate into the script. These sections are spoken, verbatim, in the final cut of the film.[59]

Fearnley also objected to a scene involving the Met breaking down a door:

> Also, in this and other scenes, [Mr Fearnley] was in favour of eliminating the chopper and the breaking down of the door and substituting the finding of the key to the door under the mat.[60]

The image management amendments suggested by Fearnley were designed to construct a holistic image of the women police; by suggesting the omission of 'smart alec' dialogue and its replacement with more conversational elements along with the gentler method of intrusion into the suspect's house, the Press Bureau were stressing approachability in place of action. In a meeting between Sydney Box, William MacQuitty, Superintendent Elizabeth Bather and Percy Fearnley, Box agreed to all of their suggestions and 'agreed to try to improve the dialogue in the next script, which he hopes will be the final effort'.[61]

His optimism was unfounded, however, as the script went through a fourth, fifth, sixth and seventh draft before being signed off by the Met. The fourth to sixth drafts were completed in twenty days between 7 July and 27 July and the penultimate draft was enthusiastically received by Percy Fearnley:

> After six efforts we now have a script which has the makings of a good film. In some respects I think it is better written than 'The Blue Lamp'. If the film is produced and directed as well as the script is written it should at least equal 'The Blue Lamp'! … There will be another script to incorporate our suggestions, but I do not think there will be need to waste people's time reading it.[62]

However, the intensive and seemingly interminable series of rewrites requested by the Met took their toll on Sydney and Muriel Box. Muriel's diary entry for 26 July – presumably the day that the sixth rewrite was completed – attests to this:

> We start shooting exteriors on September 28th and interiors on October 13th at the Gate studio. Our troubles with Scotland Yard never ending.
>
> Every time we attempt to make a film we think it can't be worse than the last one, but in a different way it always is and just now

we are both being driven frantic – so much so, that Sydney has vanished in the car for the week-end, unable to bear it any longer.[63]

The issues regarding the script seem to originate not from the Press Bureau, but from the Women Police – and their Superintendent in particular. An undated two-page memo from Elizabeth Bather, presumably presented to Percy Fearnley in mid-July 1952, outlined her opinion of the script and the many issues she had with the Boxes work.[64] This memo seems to indicate Press Bureau mismanagement of the project; one may speculate that, had Bather been involved in preliminary discussions between the Boxes and the Press Bureau in late 1951, the problems with the project might have been remedied at an early stage. The Women Police's first involvement with the Boxes came in May 1952, two drafts into the scriptwriting stage, and their input up until Elizabeth Bather's memo had been limited to one brief meeting with the producers in that month followed by a series of invited responses to Percy Fearnley's questions on police procedure. Bather's memo indicates the level of dissatisfaction within the Women Police regarding the script:

> I am still very disappointed and perturbed about the script … The stories are, for the most part, so completely improbable and in no way give a true picture of our work … The main crime story is, I suppose, all right, but it couldn't, surely, be more ordinary. The only thing I really object to is the last sequence. If a P.C. is available, I cannot see why the W.P.C. has to be knocked about like that, and I think it is most undesirable.
>
> I still think the dialogue is 'smart alec' and I don't think any of the policewomen have the manner and approach of real women. My view in this is endorsed by others who have read it, and it is a thing we feel very strongly about.[65]

All of Bather's suggestions received a response from Percy Fearnley in the form of pencilled notes in the margin. In these notes, he acceded to her requests with the exception of her thoughts on the final sequence. While Bather was reluctant to include the violence against Lucy (Barbara Murray) at the hands of Ray and Chick in the final sequence of the film, Fearnley was more receptive, proposing the following rewrite:

> It is proposed that these scenes should be recast so that Lucy does not rush wildly into danger but goes up to the men and makes some sort of routine enquiry about their Road Fund licence or driving licence. The object is to delay them sufficiently to allow time for the return of Angus. The men are naturally anxious to get away and the violence in this scene can begin as a result of their attempt to get away from Lucy's questioning.[66]

Fearnley scheduled two meetings with Sydney Box on 11 and 13 August to 'put forward a number of suggestions including the majority' in Elizabeth Bather's memo.[67] Bather was present at the second meeting, and she compiled comprehensive notes on this 'most satisfactory' meeting, professing to feeling 'happier about the whole thing' at the meeting's conclusion.[68] Prior to Bather's assertive intervention in the mediation process, neither Richard Jackson, Percy Fearnley, nor Harold Scott saw fit to involve her more fully in the film's production.

Elizabeth Bather's notes indicate how she made three crucial suggestions that helped to shape the final film. She contributed to Fearnley's rewrite of the film's ending, again muddying the tracing of the authorial voice within *Street Corner*:

> The final shots will be altered. The W.P.C. will 'phone "999" ' herself and Angus will not appear. She will then go back to the Mews and when she sees Ray, etc. getting into the car she will go up and try to delay the car by snatching for the ignition key, etc. She will be outside the car, the others inside and she will be hit away from the side of the car and will fall on the cobbles. This will avoid the

shooting and judo. Angus will either come in the wireless car or as the officer on the beat.[69]

Bather's amendments downplay the danger for women in police employment; while the female officer is assaulted in the final scene, the original script drafts call for her to be shot in the line of duty following a judo fight with her assailants (itself probably requested originally by Percy Fearnley following the PR success achieved through the inclusion of Dixon's shooting in *The Blue Lamp*). Bather also requested the addition of two sequences – one involving 'a W.P.C. on the beat ... talking to a member of the public and explaining why she joined the Force', and another 'showing either Joyce or Pauline discussing the question of marriage with a man recently returned from abroad and explaining to him why she would want to stay on in the Force after marriage'.[70] These two sequences were not included in the final cut of the film; however, the exploitation folder issued by the film's distributor describes the following segment in the synopsis:

> At the Chelsea Police Station Pauline deals with a constant succession of human problems. She is in love with her work, glad to have the opportunities it gives her to extend a helping hand to people. Although it nearly breaks her heart, she refuses marriage when it is offered on condition that she leaves the force. Her fiancé has second thoughts, however, and she is able to look forward to life with the man she loves with the added satisfaction of continuing her worthwhile job as a policewoman.[71]

All three of her mediations were made for the purposes of image management: the first to downplay the threat to life involved in police work; the second to enable the film to act as an 'animated recruitment poster' in much the same way as *The Blue Lamp* and the third to counter the popular perception that Women Police officers were unable to marry (the marriage bar in the Women Police Force was lifted in 1945).

The day after these amendments were given to Sydney Box, Fearnley wrote to the producer conveying the Commissioner's final consent to the film, 'subject to your submission in due course of alternative pages for the script incorporating the various additions and suggestions which were made to you at our two meetings'.[72] Fearnley seemed to be aware of the difficult nature of this project's script development for Sydney Box, and thanked the producer 'for the way you have tried to understand our problems, and your obvious sincere desire to meet us on so many points'.[73] The mediation process may have been prolonged compared to that of *The Blue Lamp* and its documentary predecessors, but nevertheless the changes suggested by the Press Bureau and Women Police were incorporated into the final shooting script – the Met still retained control of the project. This fact was cemented on 21 August, less than three weeks before the shooting of *Street Corner* (which, at this point, was still untitled) commenced. On this date, Sydney Box sent a three-page memo to all members of the production unit informing them that pages, including script amendments made by the Met, would be circulated in the coming week.[74]

5.3 Shooting *Street Corner*

Filming commenced on 8 September, as detailed in a copy of the shooting schedule sent to Fearnley on 11 August. The level of control Fearnley felt he retained over the project is demonstrated by his scribbled note on top of his filed shooting schedule; as the schedule was sent prior to the two meetings with Sydney Box to discuss Elizabeth Bather's suggested amendments, Fearnley had pencilled:

This shooting schedule must *not* be taken as firm. PERCY FEARNLEY.[75]

The Commissioner had yet to give his final consent to the film progressing to the shooting stage, so Fearnley did indeed hold considerable influence over the shooting schedule at that moment in time. Nevertheless, following Box's decision to acquiesce to the demands issued by Elizabeth Bather, the shooting commenced according to schedule, with assistance from the Press Bureau, which arranged to provide uniforms, cars and locations upon request from the producers.[76] As with *The Blue Lamp*, a fee was levied for all materials provided by the Met. These materials included police cars and locations, but also props for the studio-set sequences of the film, including desks, chairs and other police-issue furnishings.[77] This fee also included the wages and pension contributions of Woman Police Sargeant Lambourne, who was attached to the production unit at the request of the Press Bureau (and not at the request of Sydney or Muriel Box) 'to give advice to the Producer and Director on police procedure, deportment, etc.'[78] While it was at the request of the Press Bureau that she be attached to the production, she appears to have been well received by the filmmakers; images of Lambourne adjusting the uniforms of supporting cast members attest to her usefulness on set.[79] Unfortunately for the researcher, she was not requested to file day-to-day reports of her activities during the filming process.

Further amendments to the script were issued by Sydney Box on 12 September, four days into the filming.[80] These amendments were not called for by the Press Bureau, and consist of very minor amendments to the police procedural language used; the most likely explanation for these notes may lie with WPS Lambourne, who was four days into her secondment to the production unit. Regardless of the origins of these notes, they do provide further evidence of Sydney Box's struggle to grasp the Met's need for accuracy in the filmic depiction of police procedure.

After this final set of rewrites, no more disputes between the Met and the film producers were raised regarding issues on set, and the filming process was allowed to continue without any further interventions. However, during the shoot, the Met clashed with senior figures within the Rank empire regarding the film's premiere and publicity. Fearnley wrote to Sydney Box on 26 September 1952, outlining the Met's policy regarding publicity for film collaborations. The contents of the letter are revealing, and point to the Met's desired reception of the film:

> Any information to the Press about that co-operation, and the reasons for it, is usually issued by us; and our normal practice is to refrain from telling the Press much, if anything at all, about police participation in a film until the Unit has finished location work.[81]

For the producer, the fact that the Met were collaborating with London Independent Producers in the making of a film would have been in itself an eminently marketable element of the film in an age where the appetites of cinemagoers were sated by stories grounded within the mechanisms of the everyday. However, by not drawing attention to their involvement, the Met Press Bureau may have been hoping that, by not marketing their input in the production, the film would be received not as a collaborative work involving a state control agency, but as an independently made crime film. The Press Bureau may have felt that *Street Corner*'s reception as entertainment, and not as propaganda, would be a more beneficial piece of image management.

On a more simplistic level, Fearnley admitted to Box that 'the purpose behind these steps is to avoid Press criticism of police participation in the Policewoman film'.[82] In September 1952, a press furore was developing around 'cosh boys' – a recently realized phenomenon of juvenile delinquency predicated around increasing incident figures of robbery with violence amongst under 21s since the end of the Second World War. *The Times* of 18 July 1952 reported three robberies on cashiers transporting cash in the streets of London on the previous afternoon,[83] and three months later the same paper reported on the sentencing of four under 21s for a particularly brutal crime that had taken place earlier in the summer, in which coshes and an air pistol were used to rob a 79-year-old woman in her home:

> Mr. Justice Oliver said that he wished persons who were opposed to flogging and whipping could hear [prosecution] counsel's statement. Passing sentence, he said that the Criminal Justice Act, 1948, impressed upon the Courts that they should not send people under 21 to prison unless there was nothing else to do. In another section the power to order defendants 'a jolly good hiding' in cases of that kind was taken away.[84]

The Criminal Justice Act, 1948, had removed corporal punishment as a sentencing option for court cases; this despite its frequent use as a sentencing option in cases involving under 21s. However, by mid-1952, a campaign led by the Lord Chief Justice, Rayner Goddard, to reintroduce corporal punishment as a measure to combat the perceived crime wave was gaining momentum in response to sensationalistic newspaper headlines peppering the tabloids.

Goddard presented the case for repealing the legislation outlawing corporal punishment in a *Picture Post* article of 22 November 1952, entitled 'Should we flog the thugs?':

> With this great increase in violent crime, the superior courts should be given power, in their discretion, to inflict corporal punishment for all forms of felonious violence ... I do not believe it would do away with crime, but I think it might very substantially reduce it.[85]

It is within the context of a widening panic surrounding the effectiveness of the instruments of law and order in halting the increase in violent crime figures that *Street Corner* was being produced. In order to construct a popular perception of the police as responding directly to this panic, and to prevent criticism from the media being aimed at the Met's collaboration on the production of *Street Corner* in the midst of a crime wave, Percy Fearnley withdrew an invitation to the reporters of the *Evening News* to observe the filming of a scene on location, and he instructed his staff 'to say nothing about our association with the film, unless absolutely pressed, until the Unit gets into the Studio'.[86] At this point, it was of the utmost importance to Fearnley that the Met's allocation of police resources to a film production was not leaked to the press. The Press Bureau, from the outset, had sought to limit the encroachment upon police time inherent in the collaborative production process with the potential for criticism of misallocation in mind. This – given the Met's unenthusiastic response to the first few drafts of the script – had backfired, and he was now directly responsible for having committed considerable police resources to the film's production at a time when this commitment might garner the most criticism.

Despite the possible outcry from the press, even more resources were committed to the project, increasing the risk of the press reporting the production of the film. The Met Commissioner, Harold Scott, visited the studio set in October to observe the filming and was approached by Sydney Box about the possibility of providing a police dog and uniformed officer for use in the film's finale.[87] The Commissioner agreed to this request on the condition that

> no publicity is sought or given about the use of the dog until such time as the Commissioner has had an opportunity of seeing the film.[88]

Clearly, two months after the 'cosh boy' panic broke and despite the fact that the filmmakers had completed all shooting on police locations, the Met were still wary of possible press criticism regarding the misallocation of police resources in the midst of what was popularly perceived to be a crime wave. Despite the additional commitment to the film and the stringent monitoring and mediation processes, the Commissioner still chose to withhold the Met's blessing of the film:

The Commissioner does not wish to say whether he is agreeable to credit being given to the Metropolitan Police for their help until he has seen the film.[89]

As the tacit acknowledgement of the Met's involvement in *The Blue Lamp* seemed to add to that film's publicity machine, Sydney Box may have been anxious to secure a similar arrangement for *Street Corner*. However, mindful of the press reaction to the film in light of the upsurge in contemporary crime figures, this credit was withheld until the last possible moment, until the Press Bureau was confident that the content of the film would not bring the Force into disrepute.

Despite repeated calls from the Met that their cooperation in the film's production not be publicized, Alan Arnold – publicist for the Rank Organisation who was responsible for distributing the film – provided the Met Press Bureau with five publicity stills taken during the filming.[90] With the consent of the Met, these stills would then be issued to cinemas and the press prior to the film's release. Two of these stills depict WPS Lambourne adjusting the uniforms of the film's stars, and a third is an image of the police dog and his handler in the witness box, taken in a courtroom set in Gate Studios. In his letter, Arnold acknowledges his speculative approach to publicising the film:

> These stills are not absolutely vital to our publicity series, but a selection of perhaps three out of the five would be an interesting addition to have as informal evidence of your co-operation.
>
> However, you may have good grounds for not wishing them to remain in the series, and it is this consideration which causes me to send them to you for a decision.[91]

The importance of the Met's cooperation in the publicity process to both the producer and the publicist is demonstrated here, but, despite this, all of the stills were rejected by Percy Fearnley on behalf of the Commissioner.[92]

Shooting ceased in November 1952, and the editing process and further post-production processes began in early 1953. The Met were still to give their final consent to be officially recognized for their contribution to the film, as a letter sent to Percy Fearnley by Sydney Box in January 1953 makes apparent:

> We are about to record the music for the POLICEWOMAN film and in order to do this it is necessary for us to know the exact length of the titles. This we cannot calculate until we know the length which should be allowed for the Scotland Yard credit, if in fact this is to be included. I have not forgotten that its inclusion is subject to the decision of the Commissioner when he sees the film with you at a date to be agreed, but it would help us considerably if you could indicate now the wording which you suggest should be used.[93]

Fearnley replied with the wording for the credit that did finally appear on the completed film – 'We acknowledge with gratitude the help given by the Commissioner of Police of the Metropolis and men and women of the Metropolitan Police to whom we dedicate this film.'[94] Fearnley's use of the exclusive 'we' here is telling, and indicative of where Fearnley perceived his position within the filmmaking process to be.

The film was privately screened for Commissioner Harold Scott, the Assistant Commissioner of 'A' Branch, Elizabeth Bather and Percy Fearnley only on 23 February 1953.[95] While no direct response was filed, it would appear that no further mediations were requested; the Commissioner granted permission for the Boxes to use the Met credit, which appears in the final film. As the film has its premiere scheduled for early March, expediency may have played its part in the lack of extant written material regarding the Met's response to the private screening.

No record of a negative response to the final title, *Street Corner*, exists. This is surprising given the controversies surrounding the previous collaboration between the Met Women Police and a filmmaker; during the production of *The Girl from Scotland Yard*, Elizabeth Bather reacted angrily to the use of the word 'girl' in the title on several occasions.[96] Jan Read's original treatment carried the title *West End Central*,[97] Sydney Box referred to the film as *Policewoman* on numerous occasions,[98] and subsequent internal correspondence within the Met referred to the project as *Policewoman* too.[99] The first mention of the title appears in a letter from Rank's Managing Director, John Davis, sent to Percy Fearnley on 4 February 1953, in which he announced that 'the Policewoman film ... has now been entitled "Street Corner"'.[100] Again, expediency may have played a part in the lack of controversy from the Met surrounding the title.

This letter was sent to address the issue of the film's premiere – an issue first raised by Percy Fearnley in August of the previous year in a letter sent to Sydney Box. While the Met retained a significant element of control over the production of the film, the issues raised by the film's premiere highlight the fact that, regardless of this control, the exploitation of the film remained an uncontrollable element:

> As you know, the Metropolitan Police are frequently called upon for duty at film and theatre First Nights in the West End, and no doubt they will be called upon for similar duty on the first night of the Policewoman film. I think it would be a nice gesture if arrangements could be made for the first night to be devoted to Metropolitan Police charities, or in other words for the film to have a Gala Premiere to send it on its way. Such a Premiere would I think help the film along probably just as much as it would help the Metropolitan Police.[101]

Such a letter is evocative of the Met Press Bureau's first incursion into the collaborative filmmaking process with *Scotland Yard 1921: For the King, the Law, the People* (Edmund Distin-Maddick, The Topical Film Company, 1921). For that film, which was directly commissioned by the then-Commissioner, William Horwood, proceeds from the film were channelled directly into the Met's benevolent funds.[102] However, unlike *Scotland Yard 1921* – which was a project completely controlled by the Met – the Press Bureau failed to achieve the outcome they desired with *Street Corner*. The film was distributed by General Film Distributors which, like the Boxes' London Independent Producers, was an organization within the Rank empire. While Rank's senior management had given the Boxes free reign on the production side, they were more heavily involved with *Street Corner*'s distribution and exhibition – hence the last-minute decision by Rank's Managing Director, John Davis, to name the film *Street Corner* without prior consultation. The Met's request that the film be allocated a Gala Premiere was also denied by John Davis in a letter addressed to Percy Fearnley:

> [*Street Corner*] is being presented in the West End of London on March 12th [1953], and we have decided not to present it with a Charity Premiere opening.
>
> I, therefore, regret that I am unable to accede to the request which was the subject matter of our previous correspondence.[103]

This denial remained the only negative response from film interests to a request from the Met Press Bureau throughout the production of *Street Corner*. However, it did not seem to douse the Met's enthusiasm for the project; Fearnley arranged for the Press Bureau to distribute 450 tickets to the film's premiere to those involved with the production, and requested that the Met Central Band appear prior to the film, along with fifty-uniformed Met officers (both male and female) – including the police dog, Rap, featured in the film.[104] However, this allocation was cut as John Davis decided to deny the Met any seats for the premiere – he instead decided to invite them to the press screening, which took place a day earlier at 10:40 am.[105] The only guests of the Met to attend the premiere were the Fleet Street crime reporters – and Rap's handler, P. C. Grimshaw-Brown.[106]

During the production of *The Blue Lamp*, Percy Fearnley occupied the position of producer of the text by wresting control of story, script, locations and other material conditions away from the traditional (and named) producer of the film. The box office success of that film strengthened Percy Fearnley's hand for *Street Corner*; Sydney Box was willing to acquiesce to all suggestions made by Fearnley because the previous and sole full-length fiction film collaboration with the Met Press Bureau resulted in a slew of awards and impressive financial returns. Fearnley seemed to be aware of his newly established position as a reliable mediator/controller of the production. If he was not, he nevertheless issued suggestions with far wider implications than on his previous film collaborations; his interjections resulted in the appointments of both the named producer, Sydney Box, and the trusted Met collaborator Jan Read as writer. Once these individuals were in position, he still retained wide and far-reaching control of the project, using his position to demand over half a dozen script rewrites and retaining a veto on the location shooting schedule. With Fearnley fully established and now a veteran of the collaborative film production process, it may have been anticipated that further collaborations would progress apace in which the image of the British police force would be continually reconstructed and re-legitimized. However, the rise of television and its subsequent effect upon the British film industry, alongside changing patterns of consumption and the political climate of the mid-1950s prevented further collaborations of this ilk past the focus of the next chapter – *The Long Arm* (Charles Frend, Ealing Studios, 1957).

Notes

1 Vincent Porter, 'Making and Meaning: The Role of the Producer in British Films', *Journal of British Cinema and Television* (vol. 9, no. 1, 2012), pp. 7–25 (p. 8).

2 Ibid.
3 Derek Malcolm, *A Century of Films* (London: I. B. Tauris, 2000), p. 36, quoted in Porter, 'Making and Meaning', p. 15.
4 Raymond Williams, *Culture and Society 1780–1950* (London: Penguin, 1976), p. 263.
5 Sue Harper and Vincent Porter, *British Cinema of the 1950s: The Decline of Deference* (Oxford: OUP, 2003), p. 247.
6 Public Record Office, The National Archives (hereafter 'PRO TNA'), MEPO 2/7849, Percy Fearnley to Metropolitan Police Secretary, Hamilton Howgrave-Graham, 10 September 1946.
7 PRO TNA MEPO 2/8342, Anon., 'Success of "The Blue Lamp", *Police Review*, 3 February 1950.
8 Eugene McLaughlin, 'From Reel to Ideal: *The Blue Lamp* and the Popular Cultural Construction of the English "Bobby"', *Crime, Media Culture* (vol. 1, no. 1, 2005), p. 19.
9 Charles Barr, *Ealing Studios* (London: Cameron & Tayleur, 1977), p. 84.
10 McLaughlin, *From Reel to Ideal*, p. 19.
11 Raymond Williams, *Culture and Society 1780–1950* (London: Penguin, 1976), p. 263. My insertions.
12 Muriel Box, *Odd Woman Out* (London: Leslie Frewin, 1977), p. 218.
13 PRO TNA MEPO 2/9040, Minute 1, Percy Fearnley, 13 November 1951.
14 PRO TNA MEPO 2/9040, E. W. Wingrove to Percy Fearnley, 3 December 1951.
15 PRO TNA MEPO 2/9040, Minute 4, 5 December 1951; Harold Scott scribbled 'I agree' after Fearnley's comment, also.
16 Harper and Porter, *British Cinema of the 1950s*, p. 6.
17 PRO TNA MEPO 2/9040, Minute 1, Percy Fearnley, 13 November 1951.
18 HO 45/24098, Griffiths to Baker, 23 November 1948.
19 PRO TNA MEPO 2/9040, Percy Fearnley, Minute 4, 5 December 1951.
20 MH 102/1138, Cuthbert Headlam to Home Secretary, 22 May 1948.
21 MH 102/1140, George Griffith to Mr. Ross, 7 July 1948.
22 Sydney Box, 'My film is true of a big social problem', *Newcastle Journal*, 23 June 1948.
23 PRO TNA MEPO 2/9040, Percy Fearnley to Sydney Box, 6 December 1951.

24 PRO TNA MEPO 2/9040, Sydney Box to Percy Fearnley, 13 December 1951.
25 PRO TNA MEPO 2/9040, untitled, undated, anonymous document following P. A. Rhodes' letter to Percy Fearnley acknowledging receipt of said document, dated 4 February 1952.
26 Receipt of this dossier was acknowledged by Jan Read on 27 July 1948. PRO TNA MEPO 2/8342, Jan Read to Percy Fearnley, 27 July 1948.
27 PRO TNA MEPO 2/9040, Minute 13, Percy Fearnley, 19 February 1952.
28 PRO TNA MEPO 2/8342, Jan Read to Harold Scott, 6 May 1948.
29 PRO TNA MEPO 2/9040, *West End Central*, Jan Read (undated).
30 PRO TNA MEPO 2/9040, Minute 13, Percy Fearnley, 19 February 1952.
31 PRO TNA MEPO 2/9040, *West End Central*, Jan Read (undated), p. 2.
32 Ibid., p. 3.
33 Ibid., p. 7.
34 Ibid., p. 11.
35 Ibid., p. 12.
36 PRO TNA MEPO 2/9040, Minute 13, Percy Fearnley, 19 February 1952.
37 PRO TNA MEPO 2/9040, Minute 16, Harold Scott, 12 March 1952.
38 PRO TNA MEPO 2/9040, Percy Fearnley, 14 April 1952.
39 PRO TNA MEPO 2/9040, Sydney Box to Percy Fearnley, 2 May 1952.
40 This note demonstrates that Jan Read played a further part in the film beyond the authorship of the treatment. Read is not credited as the scriptwriter for *Street Corner*, however.
41 PRO TNA MEPO 2/9040, Percy Fearnley, Minute 21, 21 May 1952.
42 Ibid.
43 PRO TNA MEPO 2/9040, Percy Fearnley to ATL Watkins, British Board of Film Censorship, 21 May 1952.
44 PRO TNA MEPO 2/9040, ATL Watkins to Percy Fearnley, 23 May 1952.
45 Ibid.
46 Ibid.
47 PRO TNA MEPO 2/9040, Minute 22, Percy Fearnley, 27 May 1952.
48 PRO TNA MEPO 2/9040, Minute 25, author's inscription unclear, 28 February 1952.
49 PRO TNA MEPO 2/9040, Minute 26, Percy Fearnley, 23 June 1952.
50 Muriel Box, *Odd Woman Out*, p. 215.

51 The Press Bureau appear to have not acknowledged receipt of the script in the *Street Corner* file. However, the recommended additions to the script sent to Sydney Box are prefaced with 'Following are the amendments requested by Mr. P. H. Fearnley in the draft treatment of June 15'. See PRO TNA MEPO 2/9040, Minutes 28 (Elizabeth Bather, 24 June 1952) and 33A (Anon., 7 July 1952).
52 PRO TNA MEPO 2/9040, '"Policewomen": Notes on Revised Script', Percy Fearnley, undated (mid-June 1952).
53 PRO TNA MEPO 2/9040, 'Answers to Queries Raised on "Policewomen" Script', Woman Police Sargeant Alexandra Lambourne, 24 June 1952.
54 PRO TNA MEPO 2/9040, 'Policewoman', Percy Fearnley, 1 July 1952.
55 Ibid., pp. 2–3.
56 PRO TNA MEPO 2/9040, Minute 34, Percy Fearnley, 7 July 1952.
57 PRO TNA MEPO 2/9040, 'Policewoman', Percy Fearnley, 1 July 1952, p. 3.
58 Ibid., p. 4.
59 See pp. 2–3, 5, 7 and 10, ibid.
60 Ibid., p. 6.
61 PRO TNA MEPO 2/9040, Minute 34, Percy Fearnley, 7 July 1952.
62 PRO TNA MEPO 2/9040, Minute 39, Percy Fearnley, 28 July 1952.
63 Muriel Box, *Odd Woman Out*, p. 218.
64 PRO TNA MEPO 2/9040, 'The Policewomen Film', Elizabeth Bather, undated.
65 Ibid.
66 PRO TNA MEPO 2/9040, 'Policewoman', Percy Fearnley, 1 July 1952, p. 11.
67 PRO TNA MEPO 2/9040, Minute 41, Percy Fearnley, 12 August 1952.
68 PRO TNA MEPO 2/9040, Elizabeth Bather, 'Notes on meeting re film', 13 August 1952.
69 Ibid.
70 Ibid.
71 *Street Corner* exploitation folder dated 18 January 1954, courtesy of the Steve Chibnall Archive.
72 PRO TNA MEPO 2/9040, Percy Fearnley to Sydney Box, 14 August 1952.

73 Ibid.
74 PRO TNA MEPO 2/9040, Box to London Independent Producers Production Unit, 21 August 1952.
75 PRO TNA MEPO 2/9040, London Independent Producers Ltd, '"Policewoman" Provisional Shooting Schedule, 11 August 1952, p. 1.
76 See PRO TNA MEPO 2/9040, Percy Fearnley to Receivers Office, 4 September 1952.
77 PRO TNA MEPO 2/9040, Percy Fearnley to Receivers Office, 6 October 1952.
78 PRO TNA MEPO 2/9040, Minute 52, Percy Fearnley, 22 August 1952.
79 These images are preserved in PRO TNA MEPO 2/9040.
80 PRO TNA MEPO 2/9040, Sydney Box, 'Further Notes on Script', 12 September 1952.
81 PRO TNA MEPO 2/9040, Percy Fearnley to Sydney Box, 26 September 1952.
82 Ibid.
83 Anon., 'Three Robberies in London Streets', *The Times*, 18 July 1952, p. 3.
84 Anon., 'Old Woman Robbed With Violence', *The Times*, 15 October 1952, p. 2.
85 Rayner Goddard, Lord Chief Justice, 'Should we flog the thugs?', *Picture Post*, 22 November 1952, p. 34.
86 PRO TNA MEPO 2/9040, Percy Fearnley to Sydney Box, 26 September 1952
87 PRO TNA MEPO 2/9040, Percy Fearnley to Chief Inspector Peck, 27 October 1952.
88 PRO TNA MEPO 2/9040, Percy Fearnley to Sydney Box, 28 October 1952.
89 Ibid.
90 PRO TNA MEPO 2/9040, Alan Arnold to Percy Fearnley, 2 October 1952.
91 Ibid.
92 PRO TNA MEPO 2/9040, Percy Fearnley to Alan Arnold, 6 October 1952.
93 PRO TNA MEPO 2/9040, Sydney Box to Fearnley, 15 January 1953.
94 PRO TNA MEPO 2/9040, Fearnley to Sydney Box, 22 January 1953.

95 PRO TNA MEPO 2/9040, Minute 89, Percy Fearnley, 4 February 1953.
96 See PRO TNA MEPO 2/7850, Elizabeth Bather to Percy Fearnley, 19 February 1947; PRO TNA MEPO 2/7850, Percy Fearnley to Hamilton Howgrave-Graham, Minute 16, 20 March 1947, and agreement from Bather's supervisor at PRO TNA MEPO 2/7850, Minute 19, Assistant Commissioner 'A', Alexander Robertson, to Hamilton Howgrave-Graham, 26 March 1947.
97 PRO TNA MEPO 2/9040, *West End Central*, Jan Read, 7 March 1952.
98 See, for example, PRO TNA MEPO 2/9040, Sydney Box to Percy Fearnley, 2 May 1952.
99 PRO TNA MEPO 2/9040, Elizabeth Bather to Percy Fearnley, 5 August 1952.
100 PRO TNA MEPO 2/9040, John Davis to Percy Fearnley, 4 February 53.
101 PRO TNA MEPO 2/9040, Percy Fearnley to Sydney Box, 13 August 1952.
102 PRO TNA MEPO 2/6207, Brigadier-General Sir William Horwood, Commissioner of Police of the Metropolis, circular to the Press, 9 March 1921.
103 PRO TNA MEPO 2/9040, John Davis, Managing Director, J. Arthur Rank Organisation, to Percy Fearnley, 4 February 1953.
104 PRO TNA MEPO 2/9040, Percy Fearnley to David Pursall, J. Arthur Rank Organisation, 27 February 1953. See also PRO TNA MEPO 2/9040, Minute 99, 10 March 1953, in which it is stated that 'arrangements made … for P.C. Grimshaw-Brown (in uniform) and Rap to be present in the foyer from 8:15 p.m. and for the dog to be taken care of while the P.C. is seeing the film.'
105 PRO TNA MEPO 2/9040, Percy Fearnley to all Met departments, 5 March 1953.
106 PRO TNA MEPO 2/9040, Percy Fearnley, Minute 96A, undated. See also, PRO TNA MEPO 2/9040, Minute 99, 10 March 1953.

6

'The machine at work': Forensic filmmaking and *The Long Arm*, 1951–6

The production of *The Long Arm* (Charles Frend, Ealing Studios, 1956), the next feature-length collaboration between the Metropolitan Police (hereafter abbreviated to 'Met') and a British film studio, was typified by upheaval and change brought about by changing patterns of cinema attendance and film production alongside a structural reorganization of the Met. This period of change – both within the British film industry and within society as a whole – dragged across the prolonged six-year production of *The Long Arm* and also incorporated the production and release of *Street Corner*, affecting the former more severely than the latter.

Charles Barr has summarized this era as follows:

> 1951 was a watershed year for British films as a whole, and the period 1952–58 was an extraordinarily dead one. 1951 was Festival of Britain year, and Michael Frayn sees the Festival as the end of an era, the end of the ten-year dominance of the 'herbivores, or gentle ruminants' and their philosophy; it was the year in which the Conservative party regained office.[1]

The return to power of the Conservatives and the Labour-organized Festival of Britain, ushered in a new era of consumerism as rationing was phased out and new technologies – with television foremost of these – became more readily available to households. The advent of television and the death of the age of the 'herbivore', as Frayn characterized those key players in the late 1940s political consensus, brought with them changing patterns of consumption which had a direct impact upon the British film industry; John Ellis has noted, for example, that cinema 'attendances had dropped from the 1946 peak of 1,635 million to 1,182 million in 1955'.[2]

6.1 1955

The year 1955 is a crucial date for Ealing Studios and the Met Press Bureau. While Charles Barr – and, in a wider context, a variety of social historians – mark 1951 as a watershed year for both the British film industry and the country, 1955 proved to be the year in which a variety of events caused the irretrievable loss of both the machinery and cultural climate capitalized upon by Percy Fearnley's series of film collaborations between the British film industry and the Met Press Bureau. Ealing Studios relocated in 1957 after the British Broadcasting Corporation purchased their longstanding premises in 1955. *The Long Arm* was the final film produced by Ealing Studios in Ealing, and the film represents the end of several eras. Not only was it the last film produced at Ealing, but it was also the last collaborative film production between the British film industry and the Met Press Bureau during Percy Fearnley's custodianship. While continuing production at MGM's Elstree Studios for a time, Michael Balcon's Ealing Studios ceased production in 1959, and with it the era of cinema as the primary means of disseminating propaganda as entertainment ended. The aesthetic modes utilized in *The Blue Lamp*, *Street Corner*, *The Long Arm* and their second-feature forebears were deemed outdated; their lack of truly independent critical edge set them apart and prematurely aged them in the age of the British New Wave, *Z Cars* and the Angry Young Men. Barr's eulogy to Ealing in the 1950s reflects this:

Ealing never loses its allegiance to the ideal community defined in *Passport to Pimlico* and *The Blue Lamp*; stable, gentle, innocent, already consciously backward-looking, and based on the elaborate set of loyalties and renunciations that will now be familiar. This community recedes inexorably into the past. Partly, the specific processes of post-war history leave it behind: partly, its own internal frailty, its lack of dynamism, renders it vulnerable to the passage of time as such, like a preserved mummy crumbling when exposed to the air.[3]

Ealing not so much crumbled 'when exposed to the air' of 1950s consumerism and a reticence to embrace new technologies, but rather its ethos was assimilated into a new medium – helped largely by the success of one of its own. Ted Willis – the writer of *The Blue Lamp*'s treatment and, as I have documented, the originator of many of the film's key tropes – resurrected his most famous character, P. C. George Dixon, for a successful six-episode TV series in the same year as its broadcaster, the BBC, purchased Ealing. Willis writes that

> Dixon happened with astonishing speed. In March 1955 the idea of a home-grown police series for BBC television was first discussed at a chance meeting between myself and Ronnie Waldman, Head of Light Entertainment. By summer of the same year, the first series of six programmes went to air. They were so successful that Ronnie asked for more. And more. And more.[4]

The contribution of television *and* also of *Dixon of Dock Green* to the demise of Ealing and the Met Press Bureau's film collaboration programme provides the final irony, as the tone adopted by the films of both Balcon and Fearnley did not end with *The Long Arm*, as Susan Sydney-Smith has remarked:

> During the post-war period, television not only took over the Ealing Studios in 1955, but also began to erode its regular audience ... [D]espite the onslaught, the values of the studio, along with

personnel nonetheless 'infiltrated the conqueror' ... [Ealing's] ideology became absorbed and deeply embedded in television, as indicated by the pastoral connotations of soaps like *The Grove Family* and the police series, *Dixon of Dock Green*.[5]

While *Dixon of Dock Green* was proving a huge success when screened in the living rooms of the British public, the Press Bureau collaborations produced in the wake of its progenitor failed to recapture the success of *The Blue Lamp*. The closure of Ealing Studios occurring alongside the rise of the televised police series (including *Fabian of the Yard*, first aired in 1954), reorganization at the Met (Harold Scott was replaced as Commissioner by John Nott-Bower in August 1953) and changing patterns of consumption in the mid-1950s signified the end of the 'herbivorous', paternalistic approach to entertainment-propaganda.

1955, then, for the collaborative process of film production between the Met and the British film industry, is a far more pertinent watershed year than 1951 for the reasons detailed above. Perhaps the most damaging event of that year to the public image of police benevolence disseminated by Fearnley's film collaborations, though, occurred in November 1955. In that month, a detailed report was delivered to Commissioner John Nott-Bower regarding corruption in the Met – but, more damagingly, the report was also leaked to the *Daily Mail*:

> The report revealed 'a vast amount of bribery and corruption among certain uniformed police officers attached to West End Central police station' after an investigation involving 'club proprietors, prostitutes, gaming-house owners, brothel-keepers and men living on immoral earnings' ... The following day the article was further attacked by Sir Laurence Dunne, the Chief Magistrate and by the Joint Under-Secretary at the Home Office who described the piece variously as: 'misleading', 'mischievous', 'unwarranted', and 'unsubstantiated', and condemned its probable effect on public

confidence in the Force. In fact, there is every reason to believe that, with the exception of one or two sentences, the article was substantially accurate, but the reaction to stories of this type is not necessarily dependent on their accuracy.[6]

At the same time as the *Daily Mail* article, a West End Central detective sergeant stood trial for 'conspiring to defeat the course of justice by fabricating evidence at the trial of Joseph Grech, a notorious "vice baron"', further deepening the public perception of an endemic state of police corruption, particularly in the West End of London.[7] It is again an ironic coincidence that the station in the eye of the storm, West End Central, was the setting for *Street Corner*. What these events – along with the rise of *Dixon of Dock Green* (which, while written by Ted Willis and benefitting from his research during *The Blue Lamp*, was produced independently of the Met Press Bureau), the fall of Ealing, and the beginning of the British New Wave – signified was that the British public were approaching controlled images of the machinery of law and order with a more critical eye. No longer, in the words so memorably contained in the *Daily Herald*'s review of *The Blue Lamp*, were British audiences willing to let 'the quickness of the hand deceive the eye'.[8]

6.2 'Pull it to pieces': The first stage of production

The Long Arm's tumultuous journey from conception to release took six years, during which time four different directors and three different writers were attached to the project. Within the context of Ealing's post-1955 productions, *The Long Arm* is not an exception; Charles Barr has noted that *Barnacle Bill* (Charles Frend, 1957) and *Davy* (Michael Relph, 1958), both released in the years after *The Long Arm* and after Ealing had moved to MGM's Borehamwood studio, 'had unusually long gestation periods' of two years or more.[9] Neither came close to the six-year period between the first mooting of the idea by Michael Balcon and the film's eventual release. The production was also affected by political instability; over the course of the production, three general elections were held, and Harold Scott retired from his position as Met Commissioner, being replaced by John Nott-Bower in 1953. *The Blue Lamp* remained a constant point of reference during the long gestation of *The Long Arm*, as it did during the *Street Corner* collaboration; with the success of *The Blue Lamp* fresh in the minds of both Ealing Studios and the Met Press Bureau, at which Percy Fearnley still held the post of PIO, Michael Balcon wrote in November 1950 to solidify a proposal previously discussed with Fearnley:

> I wish to confirm that we would like to make a film at these studios [Ealing] based on the work of Scotland Yard.
>
> We would not in any case be able to fit it into our programme until 1952, and I understand that this would also be the earliest time at which you could give us the necessary facilities. We would, however, like to proceed with the lengthy task of scriptwriting at the earliest possible opportunity and if, as you suggest, you could sort out some promising material for us in the next two months, we could then put one of our best writers on to the subject and I feel confident that we could achieve something as successful from both our points of view as THE BLUE LAMP.[10]

Fearnley had clearly advised Balcon that a film on the Women Police was a priority on the Met's schedule, and also that preliminary research on that film was about to commence – therefore putting additional strain upon the Met Press Bureau's resources.

The fact that Fearnley had informed Balcon that he was unable to fulfil a collaborative project until 1952 and the end of *Street Corner*'s production is indicative of three key points. Fearnley was aware that Ealing wanted 'to concentrate more on Scotland Yard and the CID than the Uniform Branch – in other words, the film should be "The Blue Lamp" in reverse'.[11] By informing Balcon that he was to go ahead with a project on the Women Police, Fearnley seemed to indicate that, from a public relations viewpoint, the plain-clothes aspects of the Met were not of an immediate priority for the Press Bureau in terms of image management work. Secondly, it would also seem to underline Fearnley's preference for working with Sydney Box over Michael Balcon; Sydney Box, while at Gainsborough Studios, was responsible for the initial stages of *The Blue Lamp*'s production before the project was reallocated to Michael Balcon's Ealing Studios following Gainsborough's closure in early 1949. Box had employed Jan Read as the scenario writer for *The Blue Lamp* and, as the extant correspondence demonstrated in the early days of *The Blue Lamp*'s production, he was both acquiescent to the Press Bureau's mediations and also a family friend of the Met Commissioner, Harold Scott.[12] Therefore, Box was deemed controllable, whereas – as I have discussed at an earlier point – Michael Balcon had suggested various alterations to the project his studio inherited, such as a change of setting from 'the East End to the Paddington district'.[13] Despite Fearnley's protestations, Balcon's location change was carried through.

It may have been with Balcon's resilience in mind when compared to Box's pliability that the proposed Ealing film was held until 1952 in favour of the latter's Women Police project. Finally, the decision to hold over the production is also evidence of the limited capacity of the Press Bureau; in order to effectively produce the filmic text by offering mediations on content in exchange for filmmaking facilities, there was a requirement – albeit unspoken – that the PIO occupy a central position in the production. As there was only one PIO, the Press Bureau could only collaboratively produce one filmic text at a time.

The summoning of the successes of *The Blue Lamp* piqued the interest of Met Secretary, Richard Jackson, who wrote in a private minute to Harold Scott that 'if it should prove anything like as good as *The Blue Lamp* I think it is worth doing. Do you agree?'[14]

Scott replied to the affirmative, and Jackson took it upon himself to draft a letter to Frank Newsam, the Permanent Under-Secretary of State to the Home Office, who had demanded to be informed 'at an early stage in any future venture of this kind involving official co-operation on your part and the provision of police facilities, so that it can be decided whether any particular project would best be dealt with on a national rather than on a purely Metropolitan basis'.[15] In Jackson's letter, ghost-written for Harold Scott, he provided a brief overview of Balcon's proposal and refers to *The Blue Lamp* twice, noting that the film 'would be complementary to 'The Blue Lamp'.[16]

Richard Jackson's enthusiasm for *The Blue Lamp*'s follow-up with Ealing Studios was not quite matched by Percy Fearnley, who appeared to take a step back at this early stage; indeed, Jackson's commandeering of the project during November and December 1950 is evocative of the approach of his predecessor, Hamilton Howgrave-Graham. Howgrave-Graham occupied the position of Met Secretary between 1927 and 1946, and, prior to Percy Fearnley's appointment, he was responsible for managing film collaborations.[17] Jackson's intervention in this case, however, is a reminder that the Met Secretary (a position equal in rank to Assistant Commissioner) was organizationally superior within the Met. Fearnley began to take an active role in the production process of this film following a prompt by Hal Mason, Ealing's long-serving General Manager, who wrote to Fearnley on 5 January 1951:

> T. E. B. Clarke's present assignment will be completed by the end of this week. As you know, Sir Michael is most anxious for him to work on our proposed Scotland Yard subject and we have purposely avoided getting him involved on any new subject for this reason. Therefore, would it be possible for him to come and see you within the next week or ten days for a preliminary discussion so that work generally on this subject can be started.[18]

T. E. B. Clarke was of course known to the Press Bureau as a previous collaborator on the Ealing draft of *The Blue Lamp*'s script and, while there are no comments on Clarke's appointment on file from the Met, it can safely be assumed that, given the success of their previous collaboration and Fearnley's preference to work with previous collaborators, Clarke's appointment would have been welcomed. Clarke's stock was, however, at its highest in the early 1950s; one presumes that the 'present assignment' Hal Mason mentioned that Clarke was finalizing would have been *The Titfield Thunderbolt* (Charles Crichton, Ealing Studios, 1953) and *The Lavender Hill Mob* (Charles Crichton, Ealing Studios, 1951) – for which Clarke would win his one and only Oscar in 1953 for Best Writing, Story and Screenplay – was close to being released. Perhaps because of this, Clarke was removed from the project less than a month after he was appointed – Hal Mason informed Fearnley that Clarke 'was now not available to write the script' in a meeting between the two at Ealing Studios on 9 February 1951, and also that 'they were proposing to engage an outside writer, Mr. Frank Harvey, who wrote the script for "Seven Days to Noon" and "I Spy Strangers".'[19] Harvey also wrote the original stage script for *Brighton Rock* – the film version of which provided a significant contribution to the British crime cinema moral panic of 1947. Charles Barr has noted that during Michael Balcon's custodianship, Ealing Studios was typified by the values of 'teamwork, loyalty, puritanism, a valuing of craftsmanship and reliability over flair; a certain insularity',[20] and he traces how these values surfaced in the output of the studio.[21] Therefore, the appointment of the 'outside writer' to a project that, apparently, was intended as a continuation of one of the studio's biggest box-office successes, is surprisingly out of character for Ealing Studios.

Harvey's appointment, and Michael Relph's desire for Harvey to undertake a series of research visits, was met cautiously by Fearnley:

Mr. Michael Relph, Associate Producer of the film, suggested that Mr. Harvey be given facilities to meet and talk to C.I.D. Officers, sit with them in their offices and go out with them on duty. I informed him that I did not think this was necessary and I doubted very much whether the Commissioner would agree to such facilities being granted.

I suggested in the first place Mr. Harvey should be asked to write a rough treatment and send it to us so that we could, if need be, pull it to pieces and prepare another treatment on which a script could subsequently be based.[22]

Fearnley, by now, was confident in his preferred approach to the collaborative production process; having orchestrated the productions of two supporting features and, in *The Blue Lamp*, one feature film, he preferred to keep distance between the scriptwriters and working police officers in order to both minimize the burden of resources upon the Met and also to ensure that the Press Bureau retained as much central control of the project as possible. Fearnley's preference to continue to work with the contacts he had previously established in the film industry – Sydney Box and Jan Read in particular – may have stemmed from the fact that they were willing to adhere to Fearnley's preferred working practices. However, Michael Relph's involvement with the Met during the production of *The Blue Lamp* was limited; Relph had taken control of the project after Gainsborough's closure, and his first meeting with Fearnley was in January 1949.[23] By this point, the majority of preparatory work had been completed, as the film had been in early pre-production for seven months prior to any involvement from Ealing Studios. As such, both Relph and Harvey were largely unknown collaborators to the Press Bureau and, particularly with the above request in mind, seemed unfamiliar with the Met's preferred working practices.

Regardless of his lack of collaborative experience with either Frank Harvey or Michael Relph, Fearnley's confidence in his ability to manipulate the creative processes of production is clear in the private minute above – his position, and that of his Press Bureau colleagues, is to take the independent depiction of the Met and to 'pull it to pieces and prepare another treatment' – a process within which is sited the key ideological intervention. Fearnley had already expressed this course of action with regards to this project on several occasions – three months prior to his meeting at Ealing with Harvey and Relph, he had already told the Met Secretary that Ealing Studios 'will leave the building up of the story to us ... the script would be written around various clues – which we would provide – as was done for "The Blue Lamp".[24] The 'clues' were indeed provided in much the same manner as had been established during the production of *The Blue Lamp*, when the provision of Robert Fabian's dossier on the Antiquis murder had proved so influential upon the final film.[25] Instead of providing the filmmakers with a dossier on one incident which the Press Bureau felt would be of benefit to them when adapted, Fearnley instead provided nine, pre-empting the multiple cases sent to Sydney Box during *Street Corner*'s production.[26] Unfortunately, the content of these case summaries has not survived; however, an extant minute lists the cases as 'Antiquis murder, Forgery Case £5 and £10 Bank of England Notes, Forgery of British National Health Insurance Stamps, Forgery of Clothing Coupons, Mayfair Play-Boys Case, Detective as Decoy, Deserter Chased Across River, Attack on Rent Collector, Cases of Special Interest'[27]. These case summaries had been sent to Balcon directly who 'propose[d] to study the subjects very carefully indeed and in due course will hand them to Mr. T. E. B. Clarke.'[28] Twelve days later, Balcon passed the case summaries on to Basil Dearden and Michael Relph and, in doing so, he reunited *The Blue Lamp's* director/producer/writer team of, respectively, Dearden, Relph and Clarke in readiness for their second film on the activities of the Met.[29] As Clarke was unable to complete the project, and the film went through (at least) three more writers, one more producer and two more directors before reaching the script stage, it may have been anticipated that the influence of these cases would not make their way into the final production.

The pre-production period of *The Long Arm*, in which all research and scriptwriting duties were undertaken – was continually held up by a series of unspecified delays. The longest delay – of an astonishing two years and five months between July 1951 and December 1953 – can be attributed to the production of *Street Corner*, an account of which comprises Chapter 4 of this work. By July 1951, however, the project had already been worked on intermittently for seven months. During the equivalent seven months of even a project as troubled as *Street Corner*, all research had been undertaken and the final draft of the script had been delivered in preparation for the shooting stage two months later (see Table 6.1).

One presumes that the delays may have arisen due to uncertainty from Ealing Studios and the continual re-evaluation of the studio's position within the J. Arthur Rank Organisation; these uncertainties appear to have manifested themselves in the first seven months of *The Long Arm*'s production through the reallocation of writing duties for the film. First T. E. B. Clarke, and then Frank Harvey, were appointed as scriptwriters for the film, and the project received its third writer in July 1951 in the form of W. P. Lipscomb. Lipscomb – a 64-year-old veteran of the late silent era – was an experienced scriptwriter, and had just completed the script for *Where No Vultures Fly* (Harry Watt, Ealing Studios, 1951) when he was 'asked by Sir Michael Balcon to prepare the first rough treatment' for the as yet untitled Scotland Yard project.[30] Lipscomb met with Fearnley to discuss the scripting preliminaries, but appears not to have brought any ideas of his own to the meeting. Fearnley's summary of the meeting is as follows:

> Ealing Studios still have no idea how to deal with the film or what story to portray. I suggested to Mr. Lipscoombe [*sic*] that the story

Table 6.1 *The Long Arm* and *Street Corner* production timelines

	The Blue Lamp	Street Corner	The Long Arm
January-50	Release of film		
...			
November-50			Letter from Michael Balcon received at Press Bureau proposing new collaboration
December-50			
January-51			Permission given by Home Office; Clarke, Dearden and Relph appointed to project
February-51			Frank Harvey appointed writer
...			
July-51			W. P. Lipscomb appointed scenario writer
...			
November-51		Box approaches Met	
December-51		Concanen Productions withdraw their project	
January-52			
February-52		Box received supplementary material from Fearnley	
March-52		Jan Read's treatment delivered to Fearnley	
April-52			
May-52		Script delivered	
June-52		Rewrites	
July-52		Rewrites	
August-52		Rewrites	
September-52		Film begins shooting	
...			
January-53		Music recorded	

216 *The Metropolitan Police and the British Film Industry, 1919–1956*

	The Blue Lamp	*Street Corner*	*The Long Arm*
February-53			
March-53		Film released	
...			
December-53			Project restarted; Pat Jackson appointed
...			
November-54			Project again restarted; Charles Frend appointed
December-54			Treatment (from Robert Barr's outline) given to Met
January-55			Permission from Home Office re-obtained
July/October-55			Pat Jackson shoots *The Feminine Touch* and Basil Dearden shoots *Who Done It?* at Ealing
August-55			Script copies received by Fearnley from Frend
September-55			
October-55			Film begins shooting
November-55			
December-55			
January-56			Ealing Studios closes following end of shoot
February-56			Rough cut screened to Fearnley
...			
January-57			16mm print received by Met

should, if possible, include the majority of departments at C.O., police and civil, so as to show the machine at work and that it might be useful to bring Police and Press co-operation into it.[31]

The lack of direction on Ealing's part would have suited Fearnley, in that more flexibility for shaping the story would be afforded to the Press Bureau instead of – as was the case with previous projects – chipping away at an externally-moulded script. His hope that the film should demonstrate 'the machine at work' is telling, and is emblematic of his desire to conduct public relations on behalf of the Met through cinema; his comment is an evolution of John Baird's speech given at the press screening of *Scotland Yard 1921: For the King, the Law, the People* (Edmund Distin-Maddick, Topical Film Company, 1921):

> It is a Film of propaganda to show you citizens of the Metropolis and other places where the Film may be shown exactly what the Police do for you, to create a liaison between the Public and the Force, and to increase... that kindness of feeling and thankfulness to our 'Men in Blue'.[32]

Fearnley – as I have demonstrated in the preceding chapters – developed the approach first attempted by the fledgling Press Bureau in 1921 across all of his collaborative filmmaking projects, primarily by omitting all references to propaganda and instead obliquely masking propaganda as entertainment. However, his desired outcome 'to show the machine at work' is no different to that of his interwar predecessors – through purporting to transparently demonstrate the inner workings of the Met, it was hoped that these cinematic collaborations would 'create a liaison between the Public and the Force'. While the desired outcome remained unchanged over the period between the Press Bureau's formation in 1919 and Fearnley's minute written in July 1951, his methods – and Harold Scott's risky appointment of a seasoned journalist to an internal public relations position – proved far more successful than any approach adopted in relation to the British film industry during the interwar years.

As a result of the meeting between Lipscomb and Fearnley, the production appeared to gather pace, and a series of research visits were scheduled for W. P. Lipscomb to view 'the machine at work' before writing his treatment. These visits were as comprehensive, if not more so, than those scheduled for Jan Read in June 1948 in preparation for *The Blue Lamp*'s treatment; they included observation of the Information and Map Rooms alongside time spent with Fearnley during a press briefing and further visits to the Criminal Record Office and the Fingerprint Department.[33] Interestingly, a visit was also arranged to the Met's Control Room based in London's South Bank for the Festival of Britain. While the Festival did incorporate many touring elements aimed at engaging the whole country, its focal point was situated in the South Bank area, and Lipscomb's visit took place just under three months after King George VI opened the Festival in May 1951. Fearnley's desire for the proposed film to incorporate elements of the Festival is indicative of his wish for the Met to ride the bandwagon of optimism surrounding the Festival of Britain. David Kynaston – one of many historians who have provided accounts of the Festival's significance[34] – succinctly describes the contemporaneous importance of the Festival:

> Whatever individual visitors felt about it, no one could deny that the Festival of Britain was a major national event, the most important yet since the war. For some, looking backwards, it marked the reward for six attritional years of gradually edging towards some sort of peacetime normality; for others, looking forward, it was the welcome harbinger not only of Britain's long-awaited revival as a major force after her early post-war difficulties but of a whole way of more contemporary living.[35]

While *The Blue Lamp* sought to change public perception of the Met's effectiveness in the midst of those 'attritional years', Fearnley's direction that Lipscomb visit the Festival Control Room seems to indicate that the Press Bureau wanted *The Blue Lamp*'s follow-up to piggyback on the national mood of optimism fostered by the Festival of Britain. This was not to be the case, due to the amount of time that had passed between the research visits and *The Long Arm*'s release – however, the climactic scenes of the film are set in that great monolith to the Festival, the Royal Festival Hall. Despite Fearnley's due care and attention to the research process, Lipscomb's treatment was not forthcoming, and Lipscomb played no further part in the film's production – even though all research visits had been completed. The source material does not provide an explanation for his sudden disappearance from the project.

Indeed, no correspondence was exchanged between the Met and Ealing Studios for the next two months. During that time, Concanen Productions had approached the Press Bureau with a proposal to make a film based on the work of the Women Police – a project that, despite initially being accepted by the Press Bureau as a collaborative endeavour, was shelved due to Sydney Box's application to make what would become *Street Corner*. As Fearnley was eager for a depiction of the Women Police on screen, he wrote to Michael Balcon following up the progress of the Scotland Yard film while simultaneously making clear his preference to schedule Concanen's proposal over the Ealing film:

> Are you making any progress with the proposal to make another Scotland Yard film next year? I am asking this question now because we are in the middle of discussions with another company about a full length feature film on the work of the Women Police. We have indicated to them that we are interested in the proposal and will probably be willing to help them, but we cannot give them a provisional date until we have something firm from you about when you wish to produce your second film on Scotland Yard.[36]

Michael Balcon spoke to Fearnley, informing him that 'Ealing Studios are not yet decided on the treatment for this proposed C.I.D. film' and he was willing for the Women Police film to proceed in its place. The project, in line with the Press Bureau's policy of collaborating on one film at a time, was held over until late December 1953, during which time *Street Corner* was started and completed, and Harold Scott had retired as Met Commissioner, with John Nott-Bower taking his place.

In December 1953, presumably before Ealing Studios began negotiations regarding the sale of their premises to the BBC, Michael Balcon wrote to Percy Fearnley in order to inform him that Ealing 'are now in a position to commence research at an early date, and, therefore, we would be grateful if you would accept this as our formal applications for these facilities [to produce a film about the Metropolitan Police and/or Scotland Yard]'.[37] Pat Jackson, 'who as you know is a film director of high repute', was appointed to the project at this time, becoming the second director after Basil Dearden to be recruited to make the film.[38] As with the appointment of the film's second writer, Frank Harvey, Pat Jackson as the director of the prospective film marks a break with the Ealing tradition – but not as significant a break, and one which the Met might not have been troubled by. Jackson was, like many an Ealing director, an alumnus of the British Documentary Movement, having directed such key shorts as *The First Days* (GPO Film Unit, 1939) alongside Humphrey Jennings, *Builders* (GPO Film Unit, 1942) and the feature-length *Western Approaches* (Crown Film Unit, 1944). After the war, Jackson became involved in feature-length fiction filmmaking and, most pertinently, co-wrote (with Jan Read, no less) and directed *White Corridors* (Vic Films, 1951), a medical drama set in a National Health Service hospital. As his oeuvre suggests an aptitude for exhibiting the machinery of state and includes a series of collaborations with individuals involved with previous Met Press Bureau aided films, it is unsurprising that no objections were raised by the Press Bureau regarding Jackson's involvement. Pat Jackson's enthusiasm had led him to pre-empt Balcon's letter, as he had already visited Percy Fearnley:

Mr. Pat Jackson has already been to see me and I am arranging for him to visit a number of departments here ... If we can equal 'The Blue Lamp' our mutual efforts will be worth while [sic].[39]

Whether these preliminary visits took place is unclear, as again the project was postponed – one presumes by the uncertainty surrounding the future of Ealing Studios. Pat Jackson was reassigned by Michael Balcon, drawing upon expertize gained during the production of *White Corridors* to direct *The Feminine Touch* (Ealing Studios, 1956) – his only Ealing film and one which again revolved around the National Health Service. The only constant, by this time, in the production was the use of *The Blue Lamp* as a continual point of reference and comparison – again, the desire to 'equal' *The Blue Lamp* is expressed by Fearnley. This iteration, though, is of added importance given that *Street Corner* was released nine months prior to Fearnley's letter to Balcon, indicating that *Street Corner* had failed to live up to the Press Bureau's expectations.

6.3 The production gathers pace

The project was restarted following a phone call between Hal Mason and Percy Fearnley in October 1954, and the Ealing veteran Charles Frend became the third director appointed to the project.[40] Frend was, like Basil Dearden, an experienced Ealing staple, responsible for two of the studio's most successful wartime films, *The Foreman went to France* (1942) and *San Demetrio London* (1943) alongside some of their most successful postwar films, including *Scott of the Antarctic* (1948) and *The Cruel Sea* (1953). In discussing Ealing's coterie of directors, Charles Barr groups Frend alongside Dearden and Charles Crichton, noting that

> these three stay at least 15 years and between them direct 43 films, close to half of the entire Ealing total from 1938. They are

continuously active on a wide range of projects without establishing any immediately identifiable consistency of theme or style.[41]

Charles Frend's appointment to *The Long Arm* marks a return to Ealing solidity following the four years of instability surrounding the collaboration, and provides further evidence for Barr's assertion that Ealing's 'own internal frailty, its lack of dynamism, renders it vulnerable to the passage of time'.[42] Frend was dependable, but was not going to provide a film that broke from Ealing's past and gave the studio the dynamism and flair it required to adapt to the vastly different societal climate that *The Long Arm* would encounter during its release.

Regardless of this, Charles Frend was a far more involved director in his project than Dearden was with *The Blue Lamp*, or Muriel Box with *Street Corner*. Visits were arranged for Charles Frend – not, as in previous collaborations, the film's treatment writer – to see the Information Room, Map Room and the Criminal Record Office in action in November 1954.[43] Inviting the director to participate in the preliminary research visits had a significant impact upon the final film, of which large portions are set in one of those three rooms. Frend expressed his gratitude in a sincere letter to Percy Fearnley sent the day after his visit:

> This is just to thank you for arranging such a splendid day for me yesterday and for the excellent lunch which you so kindly gave me. I can truthfully say that every minute of the day was interesting to me and will, I hope, prove the first step towards making an authentic film. Everyone I met was most kind and helpful and I am most grateful to them for the trouble they took and the time they spent in showing me their departments and making me feel not a nuisance, but thoroughly at home.[44]

Unlike the previous collaborations between the British film industry and the Met Press Bureau, the director was far more involved in liaising with the Press Bureau than the writer in the case of *The Long Arm*. The film, as a result, is visually more forensic in its examination of the processes of detection and the machinery of Scotland Yard when compared to its predecessors.

On the same day as Charles Frend was visiting various aspects of Scotland Yard, the writer Robert Barr mailed a rough treatment simultaneously to both Michael Balcon and Percy Fearnley. Fearnley's copy included a covering letter, in which he wrote to Fearnley that

> As you so shrewdly said: this might lead to discussion, and discussion will lead to something better. So – tear away.⁴⁵

The fact that Ealing was willing to have the research visits overlap with the writing of the treatment, rather than the former complementing the latter, is indicative of a hurried pre-production process; indeed, Robert Barr acknowledged this, stating that 'it is a rather fast job as [Ealing] wanted it in a few days, and it didn't leave time for much research'.⁴⁶

While the recruitment of Charles Frend displayed lack of dynamism on the part of Ealing Studios, Robert Barr's employment on the project is an example of the exact opposite. Barr was an early pioneer of the television magazine format and was heavily involved in pushing the boundaries of television producing and writing in the late 1940s. His letter to Fearnley begins with 'My dear Percy' – a familiarity that may derive professionally from Barr's frequenting of the Press Bureau during the writing of *I Made News* (1951), a weekly television documentary 'featuring the dramatized true story of a protagonist who had made the news that week', or which may derive from a shared trade, as both Barr and Fearnley were previously Fleet Street reporters.⁴⁷ Barr's primary employment was as a proponent of the fledgling British television production industry, and his use by Ealing is surprising; during one episode of *I Made News*, Barr 'introduced the Fabian character, leading to the subsequent film series *Fabian of the Yard'* which starred the recently-retired Inspector Robert Fabian himself.[48] *Fabian of the Yard* was broadcast on television, and its success softened the audience for *Dixon of Dock Green*.

Barr's expertise in developing the celebrity real-life Scotland Yard detective is readily apparent in his treatment; after two pages of summarizing the roles of the various Met departments, including that of the Commissioner, Barr settles on a primary focus on 'C' Department – 'the department which [gives] Scotland Yard its fame as a "detective agency".[49] He then offers a pen picture of the Department's head, Assistant Commissioner Ronald Howe:

> He is a barrister who came to the Yard from the office of Director of Public Prosecutions. He dresses with exceptional neatness and doesn't 'write much on paper'. It is said that when studying files and reports there are only two types of 'minutes' he writes – a short one and a long one. The short one is 'No', and the long one 'Yes'.[50]

Barr's outline complemented Charles Frend's forensic approach to *The Long Arm* and is unusual when compared to previous collaborative film projects involving the Met. The outline has more in common with a behind-closed-doors glimpse of Scotland Yard found in a Sunday newspaper; of its twenty pages, the first ten contain detailed summaries of the key departments operating from the Yard, including the Criminal Record Office, Map Room, Information Room and so forth. Barr mused on page ten that

> the problem remains then to find a plot that will show the headquarters machine in action, a plot that will draw strength from 'character', 'method' and 'atmosphere', and which in return will illuminate and explain the peculiarly British complex of administration and action which is housed at New Scotland Yard.[51]

Fearnley's stated desire, expressed in a private minute in 1951, that the film depict 'the machine at work' is echoed here by Robert Barr, and it indicates the level of influence Fearnley had over the production.[52] On several occasions in the outline, Robert Barr noted that its contents are all 'subject to correction by Mr. Fearnley' and this alongside the echo of Fearnley's sentiments that the film should show 'the machine at work' leaves no doubt that Fearnley occupied the most influential position of power over the production, in much the same way as *The Blue Lamp* and *Street Corner*.[53]

The final film bears no resemblance whatsoever to Barr's treatment, which focuses upon three Superintendents and is episodic, including cases involving an illicit pornography-printing organization and the discovery of a dismembered corpse. No response from the Met regarding the treatment has been recorded, but Fearnley met with Charles Frend, Robert Barr and the Associate Producer, Tom Morahan, in January 1955 to discuss the treatment.[54] Fearnley minuted that 'afterwards Mr. Frend said he would submit another treatment which would include many of the points raised during the discussion'.[55] It may be safe to assume that Fearnley objected to the cases upon which Barr suggested that the film be based (the dismembered corpse narrative would have stirred contemporary memories of the murder of Stanley Setty, for instance), but I have no evidence for this; unusually, the treatment is not marked with Fearnley's characteristic pencilled annotations and crossings-out in red.

Given the period of time that had elapsed since Fearnley received the consent of the Home Office to undertake the collaboration, he wrote again to the Home Office to inform them of the progress of the project. His remarks seem to indicate his frustration at the time elapsed; he states that, since 1951, 'Ealing Studios have made various unsuccessful attempts to get a treatment for our approval', and confirmed that the production was postponed from 1953 'at our request'.[56] While soliciting the Home Office's consent to continue with the production, he again evoked *The Blue Lamp*, making use of the familiar refrain that 'if it is anywhere near as good ... it will be worth doing'.[57] Whether consent was granted due to this evocation or trust in Fearnley's leadership of the Press Bureau is unclear, but the Home Office did agree for the project to continue, and further research trips were scheduled for Charles Frend in preparation for the writing of a script.[58]

A further six months elapsed between the Home Office reiterating their consent for the film to progress with Press Bureau involvement and the delivery of a completed script. During this period, no significant contact was recorded between the Met and Ealing Studios, and unfortunately, no script drafts have been preserved in the Public Record Office collection of papers relating to the film. However, from the mediations proposed by the Met, it is clear that a version of this script was carried forward to the shooting stage. During the production of the script, Charles Frend and Tom Morahan visited several blocks of police accommodation and were invited on two trips in an Area Wireless Car – for Frend, these trips were his second and third, and are an indicator of his hands-on approach to the project when compared to Basil Dearden and Muriel Box on the previous feature-length collaborations.[59]

One minute recorded in this period notes the delivery of a rough draft of the script, which appears to have been written solely by Charles Frend. This, however, was not positively received, and Fearnley visited Ealing to offer his thoughts:

> I saw Mr. C. Frend and Mr. Morahan at Ealing Studios and pointed out to them that the script was in such a rough state and so full of inaccuracies that I did not think it would be right to circulate it ... I detailed the many errors in the script and they agreed to re-write it in the light of what I had said. They admitted that it was still far short of what they wanted it to be.[60]

Percy Fearnley, during the production of *The Blue Lamp* and to a greater extent during *Street Corner*, fulfilled the traditional position of producer of the text by controlling the material conditions required for the film and by also holding the final veto on the project. In this instance, it is evident that Fearnley holds the position of power in the production and, in judging the content of the script and prescribing rewrites, is occupying a role of equal, if not superior, power to that of the film's named producer, Tom Morahan.

After Fearnley ordered that the script be rewritten, Michael Balcon prioritized the production of the film, presumably aware of the fact that this film would be the last to be shot *by* Ealing *at* Ealing, by scheduling the sound-stage filming for October 1955 – giving three months for the script to be finalized, for consent to be granted by the Met and for a shooting script to be produced.[61] This put a series of constraints upon Fearnley's Press Bureau – he noted that the 'second rough script ... will have to be the one on which approval is given or refused' and, when compared to the seven rewrites demanded by the Met of the *Street Corner* script, this gave little room for Fearnley to influence the script's content.[62] However, at no point during the correspondence in this period was the sale of Ealing's studio buildings to the BBC explicitly referenced, although the impending sale is tangible in the correspondence and one assumes, given the lack of enquiry from Fearnley regarding why the project was subject to such tight deadlines, that the Press Bureau was aware of the sale.

Charles Frend mailed six copies of the second draft of the script to Fearnley on 16 August 1955, along with detailed maps proposing locations for street filming close to Trafalgar Square and off Piccadilly, both in central London. At this point, only Percy Fearnley saw the scripts and, on 24 August, Fearnley recommended to the Met Secretary that the Commissioner offer his consent for the film to proceed.[63] He noted that 'the script is very workmanlike and I am reasonably satisfied that it will be a very good one by the time shooting begins'.[64] He offered several mediations for the purpose of accuracy in a letter sent on the same day, in which he stated that 'all of the suggested changes have been made only to ensure the accuracy of Metropolitan Police procedure or practice'.[65] However, two points were deemed contentious – the opening sequence in which the Stones factory safe is robbed by a dummy nightwatchman, who the Scotland Yard detectives fail to apprehend when investigating an alarm call at the factory, and the proposed title, 'Phantom Fingers':

> I think we should tell Ealing Studios that we do not like the title 'Phantom Fingers'. I think it is a shocking title + could drive cinemagoers to other films.[66]

Fearnley, here, is expressing an opinion more akin to that of a film producer than a public relations officer for the Met, and it is a pertinent example of his progress within the field of film production since the early years of his appointment as PIO, during which period his sole purpose was to ensure that the Met appeared in a positive light in any film collaborations.

The issue of the title is an interesting one, and through it one can explore the complex series of relationships that existed between Ealing, the Met and the Rank Organisation. Ealing and the Met appeared to agree on the unsuitability of 'Phantom Fingers'; Fearnley wrote in a minute that 'I don't like the title. Neither do Ealing' and sent Charles Frend a similar expression in which Fearnley acknowledged that his objection went above his stated role as a Met advisor on the script's accuracy:[67]

> I hesitate to breach a subject that is not really our concern, but I think I should mention that 'Phantom Fingers' does not, somehow, appear to us to be a suitable title for the film. Would it be possible, do you think, to review the title with a view to finding an alternative?[68]

This letter's timidity is disingenuous, as Fearnley *already knew* that Ealing Studios did not like the title. Ealing had requested that Fearnley object to the title; in a letter sent by Fearnley to Assistant Commissioner Richard Jackson in August 1955, Fearnley stated the following:

Incidentally Ealing Studios would like us to say that we don't like the title 'Phantom Fingers', which has been thrust upon them by the publicity people of Rank Organisation, who are distributing the film. I have already told them that I think it is a title which immediately makes me think of a second rate film.[69]

The relationship between Rank and Ealing is not the focus of my research; this has been covered elsewhere.[70] This episode does convey the genial working relationship between the Met and Ealing, and the way in which Ealing felt confident in taking the Met 'on side' in order to influence the distribution of the film, the control of which lay with the Rank Organisation. Given the imposition of the title *Street Corner* by Rank upon the previous collaboration, the Met was probably equally concerned at the top-down approach to film marketing and distribution displayed by Rank.

The opening scenes involving the dummy nightwatchman provide an example of the Met Press Bureau objecting to film content for the purposes of image management. Although he acknowledged that the 'scenes … were cleverly written to meet possible police criticism', they 'seem to me to need more "dressing up"'.[71] What this 'dressing up' entailed is unclear but, as the scene depicts a false nightwatchman outwitting the combined minds of a wireless car full of detectives, Fearnley's objection is an obvious one. As a result, Fearnley and Charles Frend met to rewrite the opening of the film in late August. He handwrote the following as a postscript on a letter sent the next day to the Assistant Commissioner of 'C' Branch, Robert Jackson:

> We did 22 pages of new opening y'day + these are now at the front [of the attached script], with the pages they replaced at the back. There will be some minor changes throughout the script arising from the new opening.[72]

This is again further evidence of Fearnley's powerful position within the film's production, and the familiarity he was acquiring with the process of filmmaking; during this meeting, he was involved directly in rewriting a fifth of the film's script. In the same letter, he also expressed an awareness of the need for flexibility regarding his mediations for accuracy in order to benefit the box-office potential of the film:

> Jack Hawkins has been signed up to play the part of Halliday, which has been specially written for him. He may be given a little more work to do that would ordinarily be done by a C.I.D. Superintendent. I think, however, that we must allow a little film licence here because Ealing want the "star" to feature in the film as much as possible; the portrayal, so far as the script is concerned, is excellent. We can well leave Hawkins to make this part come to life.[73]

Despite the above demonstrating Fearnley's new-found comfort with the production process, his rewriting of the script's opening with Charles Frend lacked the understanding of 'film licence' he was willing to concede to allow Hawkins to feature prominently in the film. It would appear that Fearnley's rewrites omitted the nightwatchman call to action sequence entirely, which therefore would have significant repercussions upon the rest of the script, as the narrative almost entirely revolves around this opening sequence and its depiction of the guile of the criminal. A memo was drafted by Ealing, with no individual signatory but – as Charles Frend participated in Fearnley's rewriting session – presumably from Tom Morahan and Michael Balcon principally:

> We believe that when the NIGHT WATCHMAN was knocked out of the story, this script suffered serious damage. These are the main points we would like to make:-
>
> 1. The night-watchman-trick made a considerable impact. It proved that the man had nerve and cunning. It *established a personality* for 'Chummie' which was immensely valuable to the story.

2. Once this personality was established, and the police were on the scene, the story took shape.
3. With the abolition of the NIGHT WATCHMAN, many – very many – of the scenes in the first half of the script lose their point, their edge … The small changes which have been made in them cannot disguise the fact that they are no longer hitting their mark.
4. Even scenes towards the end of the script – any scene in which 'Chummie' is mentioned, or in which any memory of him is conjured up for the audience – lose their edge and their interest.
5. Countless small incidents and lines throughout the script are now thrown off-centre.[74]

Fearnley, here, was faced with a choice between producing a film according to the doctrines of 'control' – of enforcing the omission of the nightwatchman and therefore requesting the complete rewriting of the script – or of making concessions towards the entertainment value of the film, and of incorporating 'film licence' to bolster the film's chances at the box office. He chose the latter – a decision possibly borne of necessity due to time constraints, but it regardless was a decision that he probably would not have made in the early years of his appointment. To choose the safer option of omitting the nightwatchman entirely would have been to date the final film even more than it already, inevitably (given the proliferation of television narrative forms and the decline of Ealing), would appear in its original form.

Filming began in mid-October 1955, with many scenes shot on location with the assistance of Caernarvon Police and the Met. Commissioner Nott-Bower had allocated a Chief Inspector as a technical advisor to the filming but, unlike previous collaborations, he did not file reports for the attention of the Commissioner and the Press Bureau. During November, the Commissioner's Office itself became a film set during the evening – an obligation which at times meant that 70 Ealing Studios personnel were 'on set' during the filming.⁷⁵ The Press Bureau also arranged for temporary structural changes to the Commissioner's Office:

> In order to film certain scenes in authentic surroundings, the film unit will work in the Commissioner's Office during the nights of 18th and 25th November.
>
> During the evenings preceding the filming, prefabricated false arches will be erected in the ground floor corridor alongside A.C.C.'s room [Assistant Commissioner, 'C' Branch] and in the mezzanine floor corridor alongside the Deputy Commissioner's room.⁷⁶

Not only were the Met involved in the pre-production stages of the film, alongside the sourcing of locations, but they were also willing to commit a significant element of personnel and premises to the project at the price of impeding the day-to-day functionality of the Met.

Filming was completed by early January 1956, by which point Ealing had – with the help of Percy Fearnley – strong-armed Rank into replacing their proposed title with *The Long Arm*. The press picked up on the fact that the film would be the final cinema feature filmed at the studios in Ealing, and the *Daily Mail* sent a reporter to cover the final day of the shoot:

> When Charles Frend, director of the Jack Hawkins Scotland Yard thriller, 'The Long Arm', called his final 'Cut' he was saying goodbye to Ealing, but not to Ealing Pictures.
>
> The B.B.C. will keep Ealing busy with TV films. But so far as the cinema public is concerned 'The Long Arm' completed last night except for a few 'tidying up' shots, will be the last film to go out from Ealing.
>
> In other words yesterday's scene in a replica of Scotland Yard's Information Room spelt the end of the studios where Alec Guinness found international fame.⁷⁷

The fact that the final scene shot at Ealing by Balcon's enterprise depicted Scotland Yard's Information Room provides a neat, symbolic closure; not only was this moment a goodbye to the Ealing tradition, but it was also the end of Percy Fearnley's programme of collaborative film production.

However, this was not the end of the film's mediation process. Percy Fearnley's influence over the project spread not just to the pre-production stage, but also to the film's post-production. Six weeks after the final scene was shot, 'two rough cuts' were screened for Fearnley and, as a result, he noted that 'various deletions' were agreed 'which have resulted in its length being reduced from two hours, 10 minutes, to one hour, 49 minutes'.[78] The objections raised by Fearnley to this material were not recorded. What this incident highlights, though, is the level of trust placed in Fearnley by the Commissioner, John Nott-Bower. In fact, Nott-Bower is completely absent from the entire production process of *The Long Arm*; while Fearnley was continuing the work instigated by his predecessor, Harold Scott, in using public relations policy to influence the image of the Met in filmic depictions of the force, it would seem that Scott's successor had very little interest in using cinema in this way. Nott-Bower's lack of interest in Fearnley's work, alongside the advancements made during the 1950s discussed earlier in this chapter, may help to explain why Fearnley never again embarked on a collaborative filmmaking project despite his decade of experience in this area.

On 4 July 1951, Fearnley suggested to W. P. Lipscomb that 'it might be useful to bring Police and Press co-operation into' the film they were exploring at that point.[79] Five years had elapsed since the suggestion was made, but Fearnley's desire to incorporate police-press collaboration in the plot came to fruition; a key plot point of the film involves the co-opting of Fleet Street into the hunt for 'Chummie'. This was picked up on with great pride by the *Daily Mail*:

The only clue was a crumpled copy of the *Daily Mail* with an address scribbled on it. But it was enough for 'The Long Arm' – of the law ... the *Daily Mail* circulation department is able to put the police on the track of a safebreaker. By explaining certain markings the copy of the newspaper is tracked back to its Manchester printing office and from there back to the wholesalers. They in turn find the village shopkeeper who delivered it to a North Wales garage.[80]

This inclusion is demonstrative of Fearnley's public relations approach; he also, somewhat tongue-in-cheek, mentioned to the Assistant Commissioner of 'C' Branch that this sequence

> shows one more aspect of how the Press can help the police. These scenes should be an insurance against bad press write-ups of the film![81]

While this indeed is a clever ploy, it ultimately failed. The film was released in June 1956 to largely indifferent reviews, typified by *The Times*' response to the film. Their reviewer notes 'that a neat if not particularly distinguished plot ... has been lifted to something like a documentary level of realism', but that 'minor implausibilities that might pass unnoticed in a routine film studio thriller suddenly face not only the camera lens but the magnifying glass of reality' – indicating that Fearnley's experiment in foregrounding film licence at the expense of accuracy may have proven detrimental to the final film.[82] It is also indicative of how Fearnley's wish to produce a film to equal *The Blue Lamp*, reiterated on several occasions during the production of *The Long Arm*, was an unachievable goal in the post-1955 culture of Britain; without the direct encouragement of Harold Scott's replacement as Commissioner and in the light of competing media platforms and a wilting Ealing institution, the film did not receive – as was custom in previous collaborations – a private screening for the higher echelons of the Met, nor did it receive a premiere fanfare in the West End. *The Long Arm* file closes with a note thanking Hal Mason for the receipt of a 16mm copy of the film for preservation in the Met Film Library, and with the closure of the file came the end of Fearnley's reign as the head of a programme of entertainment as propaganda.[83]

Notes

1 Charles Barr, *Ealing Studios* (London: Cameron and Tayleur, 1977), p. 146.
2 John Ellis, 'Made in Ealing,' *Screen* (vol. 16, no. 1, 1975), p. 85 (pp. 78–127).
3 Ibid., p. 177.
4 Ted Willis, *Evening All: 50 Years Over a Hot Typewriter* (London: Macmillan, 1991), p. 124.
5 Susan Sydney-Smith, *Beyond Dixon of Dock Green: Early British Police Series* (London: I. B. Tauris, 2002), p. 36.
6 Steve Chibnall, *Law-and-Order News* (London: Tavistock, 1977), pp. 162–3.
7 Ibid., p. 162.
8 P.H., 'The Blue Lamp', *The Daily Herald*, 20 January 1950.
9 Charles Barr, 'Against the Grain: Kenneth Tynan at Ealing,' in Mark Duguid, Lee Freeman, Keith Johnston, Melanie Williams (eds.), *Ealing Revisited* (London: BFI Palgrave, 2012), p. 209 (pp. 206–16).
10 Public Record Office, The National Archives (hereafter abbreviated to 'PRO TNA'), PRO TNA MEPO 2/8736, Michael Balcon, Managing Director, Ealing Studios, to Percy Fearnley, Public Information Officer, Met, 2 November 1950.
11 PRO TNA MEPO 2/8736, Minute 5, Percy Fearnley, 13 November 1951.
12 When a series of alterations suggested by the Met to *The Blue Lamp*'s treatment were put to Jan Read, Sydney Box and Ted Willis, they, with equanimity, 'agreed to do so'. PRO TNA PRO TNA MEPO 2/8342, Minute 38, Percy Fearnley, 6 January 1949. See also PRO TNA PRO TNA MEPO 2/8342, Jan Read to Harold Scott, 6 May 1948, for evidence of Jan Read's closeness to Harold Scott.
13 PRO TNA MEPO 2/8342, Minute 38, Percy Fearnley, 6 January 1949.

14 PRO TNA MEPO 2/8736, Minute 3, Richard Jackson, Met Secretary, to Harold Scott, Commissioner of Police of the Metropolis, 9 November 1950.
15 PRO TNA MEPO 2/8342, Sir Frank Newsam, Permanent Under-Secretary of State to the Home Office, to Harold Scott, 20 January 1949.
16 PRO TNA MEPO 2/8736, Harold Scott to Frank Newsam, 5 December 1950.
17 See PRO TNA HO 144/22544 for full details of Hamilton Howgrave-Graham's appointment and see Chapter 1 for a full breakdown of Howgrave-Graham's reticent approach to collaborating with the British film industry.
18 PRO TNA MEPO 2/8736, Hal Mason, General Manager, Ealing Studios, to Percy Fearnley, 5 January 1951.
19 PRO TNA MEPO 2/8736, Minute 15, Percy Fearnley, 10 February 1951.
20 Charles Barr, *Ealing Studios* (London: Cameron & Tayleur, 1977), p. 49.
21 Ibid., pp. 44–9.
22 PRO TNA MEPO 2/8736, Minute 15, Percy Fearnley, 10 February 1951.
23 PRO TNA MEPO 2/8342, Balcon to Fearnley, 12 January 1949.
24 PRO TNA MEPO 2/8736, Minute 5, Percy Fearnley, 13 November 1951.
25 Receipt of this dossier was acknowledged by Jan Read on 27 July 1948. PRO TNA PRO TNA MEPO 2/8342, Read to Fearnley, 27 July 1948.
26 PRO TNA MEPO 2/9040, untitled, undated, anonymous document following P. A. Rhodes' letter to Percy Fearnley acknowledging receipt of said document, dated 4 February 1952.
27 PRO TNA MEPO 2/8736, Minute 12A, Percy Fearnley, undated (referring to letter of 15 January 1951).
28 PRO TNA MEPO 2/8736, Balcon to Fearnley, 17 January 1951.
29 PRO TNA MEPO 2/8736, Hal Mason, General Manager, Ealing Studios, to Fearnley, 29 January 1951.
30 PRO TNA MEPO 2/8736, Minute 16, Percy Fearnley, 4 July 1951.
31 Ibid.
32 Ibid.
33 PRO TNA MEPO 2/8736, Minute 18, Percy Fearnley, 5 July 1951; Minute 19, Percy Fearnley, 24 July 1951; Minute 20, Percy Fearnley, 27 July 1951.
34 See Mary Banham and Bevis Hillier (eds.), *A Tonic to the Nation: Festival of Britain*, 1951 (London: Thames & Hudson, 1976); Becky E.

Conekin, *The Autobiography of a Nation: The 1951 Festival of Britain* (Manchester: MUP, 2003); Sarah Street, 'Cinema, Colour and the Festival of Britain, 1951', *Visual Culture in Britain* (vol. 13, no. 1, 2012), pp. 83–99.
35 David Kynaston, *Family Britain 1951–57* (London and New York: Bloomsbury, 2009), p. 7.
36 PRO TNA MEPO 2/8736, 'Postscript to private letter written by P.I.O. on 24.9.51', Percy Fearnley to Michael Balcon.
37 PRO TNA MEPO 2/8736, Balcon to Fearnley, 30 December 1953.
38 Ibid.
39 PRO TNA MEPO 2/8736, Fearnley to Balcon, 5 January 1954.
40 PRO TNA MEPO 2/8736, Minute 24, Percy Fearnley, 27 October 1954.
41 Barr, *Ealing Studios*, p. 46.
42 Ibid., p. 177.
43 PRO TNA MEPO 2/8736, Minute 25, S. Broad, 8 November 1954.
44 PRO TNA MEPO 2/8736, Charles Frend to Percy Fearnley, 10 November 1954.
45 PRO TNA MEPO 2/8736, Robert Barr to Percy Fearnley, 9 November 1954.
46 Ibid.
47 Sydney-Smith, *Beyond Dixon of Dock Green*, p. 66.
48 Ibid.
49 PRO TNA MEPO 2/8736, Robert Barr, 'SCOTLAND YARD STORY', undated, p. 2.
50 Ibid., p. 3.
51 Ibid., p. 10.
52 PRO TNA MEPO 2/8736, Minute 16, Percy Fearnley, 4 July 1951.
53 PRO TNA MEPO 2/8736, Robert Barr, 'SCOTLAND YARD STORY', undated, p. 10.
54 PRO TNA MEPO 2/8736, Minute 32, Percy Fearnley, 17 January 1955.
55 Ibid.
56 PRO TNA MEPO 2/8736, Percy Fearnley to Philip Allen, Home Office, 10 January 1955.
57 Ibid.
58 PRO TNA MEPO 2/8736, Charles Frend to Percy Fearnley, 17 January 1955.

59 PRO TNA MEPO 2/8736, Minute 44, 2 April 1955 and Minute 45, 4 April 1955 – both authors illegible.
60 PRO TNA MEPO 2/8736, Minute 46, Percy Fearnley, 17 June 1955.
61 PRO TNA MEPO 2/8736, Minute 47, Percy Fearnley, 11 July 1955.
62 Ibid.
63 PRO TNA MEPO 2/8736, Minute 55, Percy Fearnley, 24 August 1955.
64 Ibid.
65 PRO TNA MEPO 2/8736, Fearnley to Frend, 24 August 1955.
66 PRO TNA MEPO 2/8736, Minute 55, Percy Fearnley, 24 August 1955.
67 PRO TNA MEPO 2/8736, Minute 60, Percy Fearnley, 13 September 1955.
68 PRO TNA MEPO 2/8736, Fearnley to Frend, 13 September 1955.
69 PRO TNA MEPO 2/8736, Fearnley to Assistant Commissioner 'C' Branch, Robert Jackson, 23 August 1955.
70 Ellis, Made in Ealing, pp. 82–118; see also Geoffrey Macnab, *J. Arthur Rank and the British Film Industry* (Abingdon: Routledge, 1993), pp. 51–120.
71 PRO TNA MEPO 2/8736, Fearnley to Jackson, 23 August 1955.
72 Ibid., postscript.
73 Ibid.
74 PRO TNA MEPO 2/8736, Ealing Studios to the Met Press Bureau, 29 August 1955.
75 PRO TNA MEPO 2/8736, Memorandum, Percy Fearnley, 16 November 1955.
76 Ibid.
77 Cecil Wilson, "'Cut' – And the Ealing Story Ends', *Daily Mail*, 5 January 1955.
78 PRO TNA MEPO 2/8736, Minute 93, Percy Fearnley, 24 February 1956.
79 PRO TNA MEPO 2/8736, Minute 16, Percy Fearnley, 4 July 1951.
80 Cecil Wilson, 'Just One Clue For 'The Long Arm', *Daily Mail*, 5 January 1955.
81 PRO TNA MEPO 2/8736, Fearnley to Jackson, 23 August 1955.
82 Anon., 'The Arts', *The Times*, 25 June 1956, p. 12.
83 See PRO TNA MEPO 2/7963 for papers relating to the 'rental' of films contained within the Met Film Library.

7

Conclusion: Further areas of research

This research has revolved around the extent to which the Metropolitan Police exercised control over a series of feature films collaboratively produced between 1948 and 1956. Using primary source materials held at the Public Record Office in the Metropolitan Police (hereafter 'Met') collection, I have been able to identify – from such sensitive materials as private notes between senior Met officers and scripts annotated with mediations from the Met – the level of influence held by the Met's PIO, Percy Fearnley, over three feature films and two supporting features, and the progression of his confidence in approaching collaborative film projects made between British film studios and the Met. These three features – *The Blue Lamp* (Basil Dearden, Ealing Studios, 1950), *Street Corner* (Muriel Box, London Independent Producers, 1953) and *The Long Arm* (Charles Frend, Ealing Studios, 1956) – have been the subject of much secondary research, the majority of which has focused upon 'fixing the meaning of a film'.[1] The production of these films as discrete entities (independent of the machinations of Ealing, Rank, Gainsborough, Michael Balcon and Sydney Box) has been neglected; the focus of my research – the Met's production files and the analysis of the power relationships documented within – has conformed to John Ellis' 1978 treatise regarding the empirical neglect of the study of production:

> Writing about film production has generally been a ghetto of cinema criticism. As most film criticism has seen its main function

as fixing the meaning of a film, then ideas of production have been called in only as another witness to the interpretation.[2]

Only recently has the study of the role of the producer been researched, principally through the work of Andrew Spicer.[3] Spicer has addressed the reasons behind the dearth of research on the role of the producer, and his thoughts echo those of Ellis':

> This lack of attention to producers is largely the result of the long shadow of the *auteur* theory, which, in its conventional form, has elevated the director as the key creative influence within filmmaking, expressing a personal vision with a distinctive aesthetic 'signature'. As a consequence, the producer has been relegated to the role of organiser and financier, concerned only with a saleable product and often actively hostile to creativity, or, at best, a trimmer, fearful of the radical or the experimental, seeking an acceptable compromise.[4]

Spicer continues by discussing the reflections offered by Michael Balcon and Sydney Box on the role of the producer, before providing a definition of the producer-role as 'mediator and facilitator'.[5] Spicer's definition is reminiscent of Sarah Street's discussion of Filippo Del Giudice:

> Responsible for initiating projects, arranging finance, labour and negotiating with distributors, at first glance the producer would appear to be a facilitator or... an 'administrator' of the creative film production process.[6]

Both Spicer and Street utilize an empirical approach to the study of the producer, as do I; Spicer, for instance, justifies his focal point of the 'film-making process itself' rather than on 'the textual analysis of specific films' as a methodological necessity 'in order to be clear about the nature of the choices that were open' to the producer.[7] However, my research focus problematizes the fledgling study of the producer; extant secondary research on the role of the film producer has focused upon such figures as Balcon, Box, Robert Clark and – further afield – the work of Hollywood powerbrokers such as David O. Selznick, but have not yet taken into account the influence of external bodies such as the Met upon entertainment film collaborations.[8] On more than one occasion, the significance of Percy Fearnley's mediation and facilitation outstripped the contributions of the named producer; the only element that traditionally falls within a producer's remit that Fearnley did not directly influence was the sourcing and allocation of production finance. Was *Fearnley*, then, the producer of these texts?

Spicer's definition of the role of the producer as mediator and facilitator also recalls Raymond William's discussion of the production of culture:

> The progress of culture is dependent upon the material conditions for culture; and, in particular, the social organization of any period of history limits the cultural possibilities of that period. Yet all through history there is a constant interaction between culture and social organization ... There is a continuity both between various forms of social organization and various forms of culture, but the cultural continuity is the more marked because, for one thing, it is easier to envisage possibilities than to put them into practice, and also because change and progress in society have always been resisted for as long as possible by those interested persons who, being for the moment at the top, stand to lose by any readjustment within the whole.[9]

Williams' account provides, for the purpose of my research, a more relevant definition of the producer; Fearnley was a member of the 'social organization' responsible for limiting the 'cultural possibilities' of the film productions by ensuring that they existed as public relations exercises and, in order to achieve this goal, he was given control of 'the material conditions for [the production of] culture'. For the films that form my corpus, finance was not the primary material condition for the production of culture; in an age where documentary realism proved the dominant aesthetic, sating a hunger for behind-the-scenes glimpses of the machinery of state and control-required permission and access to be granted by those – such as Fearnley – who wielded the authority to grant that permission and access. The control of finance, therefore, is of less importance than the control of access. This point is readily demonstrated by a comparison of the financial returns and social impact of, for instance, an expensive melodrama such as *Saraband for Dead Lovers* (Basil Dearden, Ealing Studios, 1948) and a modestly budgeted realist film such as *The Blue Lamp* (Basil Dearden, Ealing Studios, 1950).[10]

While the research objective may seem superficially straightforward, charting the influence of the Met's PIO upon these films has necessitated a study of the history of public relations initiatives within the Met and the wider civil service. Fearnley took public relations practice – which found its way into the Met in 1919 with the establishment of the Press Bureau – and adapted it to fit a more holistic model of image management, whereby the films in question sought not just to change the public's opinion of the Met's handling of a certain case, but to create a public image of paternalistic benevolence for *all ranks and all activity* within Scotland Yard. This was achieved not by deflecting the attention of the media (both written and visual) away from the Met, as had been the case during the interwar years, but by actively encouraging this attention and mediating projects – by effectively shaping the films in partnership with the film studios and newspapers. While this project proved fruitful in the decade immediately following the Second World War, 1955 proved a turning point in which television, police corruption scandals, the decline of Ealing Studios, the disinterest of the Met's Commissioner, the rise of consumerism and the beginning of the British New Wave brought about a new, more modern context for cinema. Fearnley's film collaborations appeared aged beyond their years and were received with disinterest. However, the hunger for glimpses of the machinery of Scotland Yard was still present; Susan Sydney-Smith has pointed out that, by the sixth episode of *Dixon of Dock Green*'s first series, broadcast in 1955, 'the audience ... increased to 49 per cent of the potential viewing public'.[11] An individual response recorded by the BBC's Audience Research Report is also of interest:

> A methods engineer ... remarked of the series that 'more could and should be done on these lines for bringing the public services to our notice'.[12]

This was not to be achieved on the cinema screen, however, as the success of *Dixon of Dock Green* testifies to a changing pattern of consumption; Fearnley's creations are suitable for viewing in the home, but lacked the draw required to persuade those audiences to see these images in the cinema. However, these changing consumptive modes did not signal the end of the collaborative police procedural, which instead responded to the rise of television by moving away from a purely London focus. Manchester Police – whose archive is not as immediately accessible as the Met papers – cooperated with Hammer Films on the production of *Hell is a City* (Val Guest, 1960), for instance, and the collaborative development of the Northern policier may be a suitable object of further study.

Susan Sydney-Smith has traced the development of early television police series throughout this period and onwards; it is worth noting that both *Fabian of the Yard* (broadcast from 1954 until 1957) and *Dixon of Dock Green* (broadcast from 1955 until 1976) ran alongside the production period of *The Long Arm*, and that *Fabian*'s writer, Robert Barr, was involved in a writing capacity on *The Long Arm*.[13] Even earlier than this, Robert Barr was involved in two productions in which the Met were utilized on an advisory capacity – *War on Crime* (1950) and *Pilgrim Street* (1953).[14] Jan Read – who had collaborated with the Met on *The Blue Lamp* and *Street Corner* – was also working on *Dixon of Dock Green* alongside his fellow collaborator on *The*

Blue Lamp, Ted Willis. Television's takeover of the mode of delivery pioneered by Percy Fearnley and expressed in cinematic form was fully established by the mid-1950s, with personnel moving between the two media, Ealing's studio complex passing into BBC ownership and audiences expressing their preference for television as the ideal medium 'for bringing the public services to our notice'. However, as Susan Sydney-Smith correctly emphasizes, this exchange is not conducted solely from film to television, as *The Long Arm*'s production makes evident:

> Charles Barr's suggestion, that we should perceive one of the last Ealing productions, *The Long Arm* (1956), as a television police series pilot-feature is slightly misleading in that it once again sees television as dependent upon film. Given its early date, it is more the case that television series like *War on Crime* (1951) actually influenced these productions. This is especially so as both series and film were written and produced by Robert Barr.[15]

Despite the fact that Barr's input in the writing of *The Long Arm*, as I have discussed, was minimal and largely ignored, with Charles Frend writing the final screenplay, Sydney-Smith demonstrates that the Met's film collaborations in the 1950s are heavily reliant upon expertize gained through early television. Nevertheless, the mode of address – which can be summarized as propaganda as entertainment – was pioneered through the Met Press Bureau's film collaborations.

Steve Chibnall has discussed this mode of address with regards to relationships between newsmen and police image management during the 1960s. His conclusions are just as applicable to the consumption of the moving image of the police:

> Things began to change in the sixties as the increasing media accent on newness, vitality, and irreverence symbolized by youth began to undermine the acceptability of the established police image. The friendly bobby and the painstaking sleuth began to appear rather

slow and old-fashioned. They represented the old order and the old values of safety and dependability which were altogether unsuited to the irresponsible, exciting, aggressive, glamorous mood of the times which the newspapers found themselves articulating.[16]

The police image of the 'friendly bobby' had, in film, already been eroded by the 1960s as I have discussed in relation to *The Long Arm*. Having reached its most impactful at the release of *The Blue Lamp*, *The Long Arm* represents the death of this cinematic representation and television's appropriation of the cultural construction of the 'friendly bobby and the painstaking sleuth', until the 1960s and the rise of 'what may be regarded as the British Northern policier'.[17]

7.1 What next for the Press Bureau?

My research, then, acts as a prelude to three key source texts; Sydney-Smith's work in television addresses what happened next with the police procedural, while Steve Chibnall's *Law-and-Order News* documents the relationships between the Met and the media in the 1960s and 1970s. The third text, Lord Justice Leveson's *An Inquiry into the Culture, Practices and Ethics of the Press*, was instigated in 2011 following a phone hacking scandal that brought the relationship between the police and the press into the spotlight. Both Chibnall and Leveson address levels of transparency and control inherent in the troubled symbiosis between the police and the press – a symbiosis first established in 1919 with the formation of the Met Press Bureau, and a process that I have historicized with an emphasis on the Press Bureau's dealings with the British film industry. Notwithstanding these texts, and my own, there still remains a gap in existing knowledge regarding the Met Press Bureau's involvement with the written press; a gap which, in order to fully understand the terms of Leveson, must be addressed. The Leveson Inquiry's terms of reference included the following:

> To inquire into the culture, practices and ethics of the press, including:
>
> (a) contacts and relationships between national newspapers and politicians, and the conduct of each;
> (b) contacts and the relationship between the press and the police, and the conduct of each.[18]

If Chibnall provides the history of these 'cultures, practices and ethics' during the 1960s and 1970s, the prehistory – that period between 1919 and the mid-1960s – remains an unknown quantity.

Policing in Britain and Northern Ireland has been mired by a century of crises – from the 'Third Degree' controversy of the 1920s to endemic corruption in the 1970s, most recently culminating in the phone-hacking scandal, which acted as the catalyst for Leveson. In each of these cases – as traced by Mawby in his seminal post-Leveson article – there is an attempt to address the ensuing chaos of perception through image management.[19] Perception, here, is key – regardless of reality. I would argue that this has, since the first attempt to suppress the unauthorized *Secrets of Scotland Yard* serial in 1919, always been the case. Mawby explores the terms of Leveson's investigation; while, in assessing the reality of the evidence, 'in general the police escaped excoriation', the Met was significantly damaged by the perception of wrongdoing:[20]

> At face value, the extent of links between the [Met] and NI (News International) are shocking, fuelling suspicions of inappropriately close relations. However, the Leveson Report dispelled the notion that the relationships were corrupt or had influenced decision-making ... The perception referred to is that the [Met] had become too close to [News International].[21]

Whether perception marries with reality is – and always has been – an irrelevance, but the fact that the perception of impropriety was allowed to manifest through poor decision-making caused damage to the legitimacy to the notion of policing by consent. This process – of the management of perception – has been traced in this book at a number of key points, but the most significant of these instances is the transformational perception management work undertaken in 1950 with the release of *The Blue Lamp*. Over a decade on from Leveson, and with a new wealth of evidence in the public realm, the manifestation of this perception management work post-Leveson remains a valuable object of further study.

The Met were not the only state control agency making use of public relations policy to harness the influence of the British film industry; while extensive research has been conducted, primarily courtesy of James Chapman, Scott Anthony and Luke McKernan, on the relationships between newsreel filmmakers, documentarists and the Ministry of Information during the First and Second World Wars, the Home Office were also conducting their own film collaborations through their public relations office.[22] Inspired by the success of *The Blue Lamp*, Ealing Studios and the Home Office collaborated on the production of *I Believe in You* (Basil Dearden, 1952). The Home Office sought to apply the same entertainment-as-propaganda approach to the Probation Service as Fearnley was applying to the Met, but their attempts to control the project bear similarity to the approach taken by the Met to the film industry during the interwar years. The production file for this project is housed in the Public Record Office, and provides an important companion to the texts discussed in my research.[23] The production processes of the British prison film cycle of the mid-1950s, including *Yield to the Night* (J. Lee Thompson, Associated-British, 1956) and *Turn the Key Softly* (Jack Lee, Chiltern, 1953), are also worthy of further study in this respect;

the Home Office refused to collaborate on these projects despite being approached by both production houses.

Chibnall has discussed the next step for the Met Press Bureau in great detail, and, in evidence provided to the Leveson Inquiry, Rob Mawby acknowledged that his research 'remains the seminal study of English crime reporting'.[24] The key development for the Press Bureau from the late 1950s onwards involved growth – not just within the Met, but in the adoption of similar methods in regional police forces:

> It was not until the late 1960s that other forces followed the Met's example and established press offices. In the intervening period these departments have developed to the extent that 'press office' is now a misnomer ... [They] have developed into departments responsible for internal communications, operational support, media liaison and public relations.[25]

The growth continues; from one man in a dingy Scotland Yard basement in 1919, public relations within the British police extended to 408 professionals according to figures gathered in 2007. In 2001, there were only 215 police press officers; it is a fair assumption to make that this exponential increase has continued.[26]

A larger Information Room was opened at Scotland Yard in 1957, and in 1967, G. D. Gregory was appointed head of public relations.[27] It is unclear at what point Fearnley left the Press Bureau; he was born in 1907, and would have been sixty in 1967; therefore it would appear that Fearnley's retirement instigated Gregory's appointment. Gregory possessed a similar background to Fearnley's, and was – like his predecessor – keen to involve the press regardless of the opinions of Scotland Yard's police contingent:

> The appointee, G. D. Gregory, was recruited from industry and brought considerable experience in the publicity field. He immediately set about a task of image-reconstruction, gathering a number of men with newspaper experience into his staff and

making sure that the Public Relations Department was never considered a quiet field into which ineffectual policemen could be put out to graze, as it is in some provincial forces. It is significant that one of Gregory's first moves was to sponsor the investigation of a young freelance journalist, Peter Laurie. It was a move which Laurie maintains was met with hostility by many senior officers at the Yard and amazement from many more junior.[28]

Gregory's policy of co-opting the press into the work of Scotland Yard and investing them within the image-management project, masking control with the gauze of transparency, was a policy first instigated within the Met by Percy Fearnley. Fearnley's approach to public relations work within the Met during the 1940s and onwards effectively shaped the future of public relations within the Met. His pioneering approach to the film industry is continued today, on a much larger scale, through the Met (here an element of the Met, and not the whole of the Met):

> The Film Unit is the sole Metropolitan Police Department responsible for managing the industry filming moving activity [sic] (tracking, low loader, 'A' frame or specialist vehicle shots) on the roads covered by the 32 London Boroughs (City of London is not included). Our advice must be sought in the first instance and we will assess the nature of the scene with you.[29]

The Met's approach today to film collaborations is split in two, mirroring the approach taken since the formation of the Press Bureau in 1919. Filming in the Met district is assisted by the Film Unit, but film collaborations for the purposes of image management are dealt with separately by the Directorate of Media and Communications (DMCs), where the ghost of Fearnley still lingers. He requested the following in 1946:

> I think we should 'vet' all film scripts submitted to us and also invite other film Companies to get into the habit of submitting

their scripts before commencing shooting. By so doing, we can ensure to some degree, that the Police are not held up to ridicule on the cinema screen, as they so often have been ... My view is that one of our biggest tasks here is not to bring the Press into line (because it is coming into line slowly but surely), but to bring film Companies into line; and if we can do this, we shall have done a tremendous job which will redound to the credit of the Police in this country around the world.[30]

Today, this policy still exists:

From time to time, DMC will consider and undertake non-chargeable documentary and educational filming of the Metropolitan Police, officers, staff, services and/or publicity related filming of police campaigns and concerns.

This is most likely where the filming will provide relevant publicity or promotion of the Metropolitan Police and where it will be beneficial to the community they serve.[31]

'Bringing film companies into line' is still a primary objective for the Met, and Percy Fearnley's first twelve years at the Met instigated this process. To understand the processes of managing today's public image of the police, one must refer back to the period immediately following the Second World War and the mediative practices harnessed in those early film collaborations.

Notes

1 John Ellis, 'Made in Ealing', *Screen* (vol. 16, no. 1, 1975), p. 78.
2 Ibid.
3 Andrew Spicer, 'The Production Line: Reflections on the Role of the Producer in British Cinema', *Journal of British Cinema and Television* (vol. 1, no. 1, November 2004), pp. 33–50; Andrew Spicer, *Sydney Box* (Manchester: MUP, 2006); Andrew Spicer, A. T. McKenna and

Christopher Meir (eds), *Beyond the Bottom Line: The Producer in Film and Television Studies* (London: Continuum, 2014).
4   Spicer, *Sydney Box*, p. 1.
5   Ibid., p. 3.
6   Sarah Street, *British Cinema in Documents* (London: Routledge, 2000), p. 39.
7   Ibid.
8   Vincent Porter, 'The Robert Clark Account: Films Released in Britain by Associated British Pictures, British Lion, MGM, and Warner Bros, 1946–1957', *Historical Journal of Film, Radio and Television* (vol. 20, no. 4, 2000), pp. 469–511; Alan David Vertrees, *Selznick's Vision: Gone With The Wind and Hollywood Filmmaking* (Texas: University of Texas Press, 1997); Charles Barr, *Ealing Studios* (London: Cameron & Tayleur, 1977).
9   Raymond Williams, *Culture and Society 1780–1950* (London: Penguin, 1976), p. 263.
10 Burton and O'Sullivan have noted, regarding *Saraband for Dead Lovers*, that 'this expensive experiment in seventeenth-century costume drama became Ealing's costliest failure at the box office'. Alan Burton and Tim O'Sullivan, *The Cinema of Basil Dearden and Michael Relph* (Edinburgh: EUP, 2009), p. 92.
11 Susan Sydney-Smith, *Beyond Dixon of Dock Green: Early British Police Series* (London: I. B. Tauris, 2002), pp. 106–7.
12 Ibid., p. 107.
13 See Sydney-Smith, *Beyond Dixon of Dock Green*, pp. 239–60, for a full chronology of the broadcast of early British police series.
14 Ibid., pp. 67–84.
15 Ibid., p. 116.
16 Steve Chibnall, *Law-and-Order News* (London: Tavistock, 1977), p. 69.
17 Sydney-Smith, *Beyond Dixon of Dock Green*, p. 120.
18 Lord Justice Leveson, *An Inquiry into the Culture, Practices and Ethics of the Press* (London: HMSO, 2012).
19 Rob Mawby, 'The Presentation of Police in Everyday Life: Police–press Relations, Impression Management and the Leveson Inquiry', *Crime, Media, Culture* (vol. 10, no. 3, 2014): pp. 239–57.
20 Ibid., p. 244.
21 Ibid., p. 249.

22 James Chapman, *The British at War: Cinema, State and Propaganda, 1939–45* (London: I. B. Tauris, 2000); Luke McKernan, *Topical Budget: The Great British News Film* (London: BFI, 1992).
23 Public Record Office, The National Archives (hereafter PRO TNA), HO 330/11.
24 Rob Mawby, 'Witness Statement for the Leveson Inquiry', https://www.discoverleveson.com/evidence/Witness_Statement_of_Dr_Rob_Mawby/8054/media (accessed 10 August 2022), p. 5.
25 Ibid., p. 10.
26 Ibid., p. 11.
27 Chibnall, *Law-and-Order News*, p. 72.
28 Ibid.
29 Metropolitan Police Film Unit, 'Our Remit', http://content.met.police.uk/Article/Our-Remit/1400008588920/mpsfilmunit (accessed 28 May 2014).
30 PRO TNA MEPO 2/7849, Minute 1, Percy Fearnley, 10 September 1946.
31 Metropolitan Police Film Unit, 'Publicity and Press', http://content.met.police.uk/Article/Our-Remit/1400008588920/mpsfilmunit (accessed 28 May 2014).

Bibliography

Public record office files

All of the files below are housed at The National Archives, Kew.

BT 13/83
HO 144/22544
HO 330/11
HO 45/10960/340327
HO 45/17415
HO 45/24098
HO 45/24442
MEPO 2/2259
MEPO 2/6207
MEPO 2/6964
MEPO 2/6978
MEPO 2/6979
MEPO 2/7392
MEPO 2/7442
MEPO 2/7576
MEPO 2/7849
MEPO 2/7850
MEPO 2/7950
MEPO 2/7963
MEPO 2/8342
MEPO 2/8393
MEPO 2/8736
MEPO 2/9040
MEPO 2/9352
MH 102/1137
MH 102/1138
MH 102/1140

MH 102/1141
MH 102/1142

Newspaper articles

Anon., 'The Arts', *The Times*, 25 June 1956.
Anon., '"The Blue Lamp" Exhibition: An Intriguing Show', *Kinematograph Weekly*, 2 February 1950.
Anon., 'Black Market', *The Birmingham Mail*, 13 September 1945.
Anon., 'Film on the Beat', *Liverpool Post*, 18 January 1950.
Anon., 'Go to It!', *Documentary News Letter*, July 1940.
Anon., 'Good Time Girl', *Evening News*, 30 April 1948.
Anon., 'Latest Crime Film', *Yorkshire Post*, 18 January 1950.
Anon., 'London Crime Film', *Evening Standard*, 17 January 1950.
Anon., 'New Film Shows Pc 999 at Work', *The Star*, 17 January 1950.
Anon., 'Police Pictures: Tribute to the Work of the Force', *The Times*, 12 March 1921.
Anon., 'Revolt Against Quota & Trading Terms Grows', *To-day's Cinema* (vol. 71, no. 5668), 2 July 1948.
Anon., 'Scotland Yard Film', *The Times*, 28 September 1946.
Anon., 'The Blue Lamp: Thriller from Ealing Studios', *Scotsman*, 18 January 1950.
Anon., 'The Constable and the Law', *Police Review*, 27 January 1950.
Anon., 'The Policeman's Lot Makes Good Film, *Glasgow Herald*, 18 January 1950.
Anon., 'Three Fine Films – Two British & One U.S.', *The Birmingham Mail*, 20 March 1945.
Anon., 'Three Robberies in London Streets', *The Times*, 18 July 1952.
Anon., untitled review of new serials, *Daily Telegraph*, 5 May 1921.
Box, Sydney, 'My Film Is True of a Big Social Problem', *Newcastle Journal*, 23 June 1948.
Davies, Jack, *Brighton Rock* film review, *The Sunday Express*, 11 January 1948.
Fletcher, Helen, 'Why Pick on the Spivs?', *Sunday Graphic*, 29 June 1947.

Goddard, Rayner, Lord Chief Justice, 'Should We Flog the Thugs?', *Picture Post*, 22 November 1952.
Grant, Elspeth, 'Teems with Rain – and Real Life', *Daily Graphic*, 25 November 1947.
Lejeune, C. A., 'Black Country', *The Observer*, 29 June 1947.
Lester, Joan, 'Bold Analysis of Spivery', *Reynolds News*, 4 January 1948.
Majdalany, Fred, 'Now Let's Drop the Spiv', *Daily Mail*, 27 June 1947.
P.H., 'The Blue Lamp', *The Daily Herald*, 20 January 1950.
Ponting, Herbert, 'Education and the Film: Its Place in the Schools', *Manchester Guardian*, 11 September 1917.
Powell, Dilys, 'Films of the Week', *Sunday Times*, 28 November 1947.
Redman, Fred, 'The Story That Had to Be Told', *Sunday Pictorial*, 15 January 1950.
Wilson, Cecil, '"Cut" – And the Ealing Story Ends', *Daily Mail*, 5 January 1955.
Wilson, Cecil, 'Just One Clue for "The Long Arm"', *Daily Mail*, 5 January 1955.
Zec, Donald, 'The Blue Lamp', *Daily Mirror*, 18 January 1950.

Further primary source material

Clarke, T. E. B., *The Blue Lamp* shooting script, 27 May 1949.
Metropolitan Police Film Unit, 'Our Remit', http://content.met.police.uk/Article/Our-Remit/1400008588920/mpsfilmunit (accessed 28 May 2014).
Metropolitan Police Film Unit, 'Publicity and Press', http://content.met.police.uk/Article/Our-Remit/1400008588920/mpsfilmunit (accessed 28 May 2014).
Relph, Michael, *The Blue Lamp* shooting script, 27 May 1949.
Spinks' Auction House, Lot 232, http://www.auction-net.co.uk/viewAuction.php?id=1211&offset=200&PHPSESSID=413f2c0fc4f9dce4b1636a05f7ece50c (accessed 9 January 2012).
Street Corner exploitation folder, dated 18 January 1954, courtesy of the Steve Chibnall Archive.

'The Public Records System', http://www.nationalarchives.gov.uk/informat
ion-management/legislation/public-records-system.htm (accessed 2
June 2014).

Secondary sources

Anthony, Scott, *Public Relations and the Making of Modern Britain: Stephen Tallents and the Birth of a Progressive Media Profession* (Manchester: MUP, 2012).
Ashby, Justine, and Andrew Higson (ed.), *British Cinema, Past and Present* (London: Routledge, 2000).
Ashby, Justine, 'Betty Box, "The Lady in Charge"', in Justine Ashby and Andrew Higson (eds), *British Cinema, Past and Present* (London: Routledge, 2000), pp. 168–78.
Banham, Mary, and Bevis Hillier (eds), *A Tonic to the Nation: Festival of Britain* (London: Thames, 1951).
Barr, Charles (ed.), *All Our Yesterdays: 90 Years of British Cinema* (London: BFI, 1986).
Barr, Charles, 'Against the Grain: Kenneth Tynan at Ealing', in Mark Duguid, Lee Freeman, et al. (eds), *Ealing Revisited* (London: BFI Palgrave, 2012), pp. 206–16.
Barr, Charles, *Ealing Studios* (London: Cameron & Tayleur, 1977).
Box, Muriel, *Odd Woman Out* (London: Leslie Frewin, 1976).
Burton, Alan, and Tim O'Sullivan, *The Cinema of Basil Dearden and Michael Relph* (Edinburgh: EUP, 2009).
Burton, Alan, Tim O'Sullivan and Paul Wells (eds), *Liberal Directions: Basil Dearden and Post-war British Film Culture* (Wiltshire: Flicks Books, 1997).
Chapman, James, *The British at War: Cinema, State and Propaganda, 1939–45* (London: I. B. Tauris, 2000).
Chapman, James, '"Sordidness, Corruption and Violence almost Unrelieved": Critics, Censors and the Post-war British Crime Film', *Contemporary British History* (vol. 22, no. 2, June 2008), pp. 181–201.

Chermak, Steven, and Alexander Weiss, 'Maintaining Legitimacy Using External Communication Strategies: An Analysis of Police-Media Relations', *Journal of Criminal Justice* (no. 33, 2005), pp. 501–12.
Cherrill, Fred, *Cherrill of the Yard* (London: Harper and Collins, 1954).
Chibnall, Steve, and Brian McFarlane, *The British 'B' Film* (London: Palgrave, 2009).
Chibnall, Steve, and Robert Murphy (eds), *British Crime Cinema* (London: Routledge, 1999).
Chibnall, Steve, *Brighton Rock* (London: I. B. Tauris, 2005).
Chibnall, Steve, *Law-and-Order News* (London: Tavistock, 1977).
Chibnall, Steve, 'From *the Snake Pit* to the *Garden of Eden*: A Time of Temptation', in Edward Lamberti (ed.), *Behind the Scenes at the BBFC: Film Classification from the Silver Screen to the Digital Age* (London: Palgrave, 2012), pp. 29–52.
Chibnall, Steve, 'The Teenage Trilogy: *The Blue Lamp, I Believe in You* and *Violent Playground*', in Alan Burton et al. (eds), *Liberal Directions: Basil Dearden and Post-war British Film Culture* (Wiltshire: Flicks Books, 1997), pp. 137–53.
Conekin, Becky E., *The Autobiography of a Nation: The 1951 Festival of Britain* (Manchester: MUP, 2003).
Cox, Barry, John Shirley, and Martin Short, *The Fall of Scotland Yard* (London: Penguin, 1977).
Curran, James, and Vincent Porter (eds), *British Cinema History* (London: Weidenfed & Nicolson, 1983).
Dickinson, Margaret, and Sarah Street, *Cinema and State: The Film Industry and the Government 1927–84* (London: BFI, 2005).
Duguid, Mark, Lee Freeman, Keith Johnson and Melaine Williams (eds), *Ealing Revisited* (London: BFI Palgrave, 2012).
Eagleton, Terry, *Marxism and Literary Criticism* (London: Methuen, 1976).
Ellis, John, 'Made in Ealing', *Screen* (vol. 16, no. 1, 1975), pp. 78–127.
Enticknap, Leo, '*This Modern Age* and the British Non-Fiction Film', in Justine Ashby and Jurgen Habermas (eds), *The Structural Transformation of the Public Sphere: An Inquiry into a Category of Bourgeois Society* (Cambridge: Polity Press, 1989).

Harper, Sue and Vincent Porter, *British Cinema of the 1950s: The Decline of Deference* (Oxford: OUP, 2003).

Higson, Andrew (ed.), *British Cinema, Past and Present* (London: Routledge, 2000).

Hopkins, Harry, *The New Look: A Social History of the Forties and Fifties in Britain* (London: Martin Secker & Walburg, 1963).

Hughes, David, 'The Spivs', in Michael Sissons and Philip French (eds), *Age of Austerity: 1945–1951* (London: Hodder and Stoughton, 1963), pp. 83–95.

Jarvie, Ian, 'British Trade Policy versus Hollywood, 1947–1948: "Food before Flicks"', *Historical Journal of Film, Radio and Television* (vol. 6, no. 1, 1986), pp. 19–41.

Jarvis, Mark, *Conservative Governments, Morality and Social Change in Affluent Britain, 1957–64* (Manchester: MUP, 2005).

Kynaston, David, *Austerity Britain 1945–51* (London: Bloomsbury, 2007).

Kynaston, David, *Family Britain 1951–57* (London: Bloomsbury, 2009).

Lamberti, Edward (ed.), *Behind the Scenes at the BBFC: Film Classification from the Silver Screen to the Digital Age* (London: Palgrave, 2012).

Leishman, Frank, and Paul Mason, *Policing and the Media: Facts, Fictions and Factions* (Devon: Willan, 2003).

Leishman, Frank, From *Dock Green* to *Life on Mars*: Continuity and Change in TV Copland (Gloucester: Cyder Press, 2008).

L'Etang, Jacquie, *Public Relations in Britain: A History of Professional Practice in the 20th Century* (London: Lawrence Erlbaum, 2004).

Leveson, Lord Justice, *An Inquiry into the Culture, Practices and Ethics of the Press* (London: HMSO, 2012).

Macnab, Geoffrey, *J. Arthur Rank and the British Film Industry* (Abingdon: Routledge, 1993).

Macready, General Sir Nevil, *Annals of an Active Life Volume II* (London: Hutchinson, 1924).

Malcolm, Derek, *A Century of Films* (London: I. B. Tauris, 2000).

Mawby, Rob C., 'Chibnall Revisited: Crime Reporters, the Police and Law-and-Order News', *British Journal of Criminology* (no. 50, 2010), pp. 1060–76.

Mawby, Rob C., 'The Presentation of Police in Everyday Life: Police–press Relations, Impression Management and the Leveson Inquiry', *Crime, Media, Culture* (vol. 3, no. 10, 2014), pp. 239–57.

Mawby, Rob C., 'Witness Statement for the Leveson Inquiry', http:/www.levesoninquiry.org.uk/wp-content/uploads/2012/04/Witness-Statement-of-Dr-Rob-Mawby.pdf (accessed 28 May 2014).

McKernan, Luke, *Topical Budget: The Great British News Film* (London: BFI, 1992).

McLaughlin, Eugene, 'From reel to ideal: *The Blue Lamp* and the popular cultural construction of the English "bobby"', *Crime, Media Culture* (vol. 1, no. 1, 2005), pp. 11–30.

Moseley, Rachel and Helen Wheatley, 'Is Archiving a Feminist Issue? Historical Research and the Past, Present and Future of Television Studies', *Cinema Journal* (vol. 47, no. 3, Spring 2008), pp. 152–8.

Murphy, Robert, 'Rank's Attempt on the American Market', in James Curran and Vincent Porter (eds), *British Cinema History* (London: Weidenfeld & Nicolson, 1983), pp. 164–78.

Murphy, Robert, 'Riff-Raff: British Cinema and the Underworld', in Charles Barr (ed.), *All Our Yesterdays: 90 Years of British Cinema* (London: BFI, 1986), pp. 286–305.

Murphy, Robert, 'Under the Shadow of Hollywood', in Charles Barr (ed.), *All Our Yesterdays: 90 Years of British Cinema* (London: BFI, 1986), pp. 47–69.

Murphy, Robert, *Realism and Tinsel* (London: Routledge, 1992).

Porter, Vincent, 'The Robert Clark Account: Films Released in Britain by Associated British Pictures, British Lion, MGM, and Warner Bros., 1946–1957', *Historical Journal of Film, Radio and Television* (vol. 20, no. 4, 2000), pp. 469–512.

Porter, Vincent, 'Making and Meaning: The Role of the Producer in British Films', *Journal of British Cinema and Television* (vol. 9, no. 1, 2012), pp. 7–25.

Procter, Maurice, *The Devil Was Handsome* (London: Hutchinson, 1962), p. 109.

Pronay, Nicholas, ' "The Land of Promise" ': The Projection of Peace Aims in Britain', in K. R. M. Shortt (ed.), *Film and Radio Propaganda in World War II* (Tennessee: University of Tennessee Press, 1983), pp. 51–77.

Pulleine, Tim, 'Spin a Dark Web', in Steve Chibnall, and Robert Murphy (eds), *British Crime Cinema* (London: Routledge, 1999), pp. 27–36.

Reiner, Robert, *The Politics of the Police*, 3rd edn (Oxford: OUP, 2000).

Robertson, James C., '*Good Time Girl*, the BBFC and the Home Office: a Mystery Resolved', *Journal of British Cinema and Television* (vol. 3, no. 1, 2006), pp. 159–61.

Rock, Alex, 'Super Cinemas in the Suburbs: Clifton Cinemas and the Difficulties of Independent Exhibition, 1934–1966', *Post Script* (vol. 30, no. 3, 2011) pp. 38–51.

Sayers, R. S., *The Bank of England, 1891–1944* (Cambridge: CUP, 1976).

Scott, Harold, *Scotland Yard* (London: Mayflower, 1970).

Shortt, K. R. M. (ed.), *Film and Radio Propaganda in World War II* (Tennessee: University of Tennessee Press, 1983).

Sissons, Michael, and Philip French (eds), *Age of Austerity: 1945–1951* (London: Hodder and Stoughton, 1963).

Smithies, Edward, *The Black Economy in England Since 1914* (Dublin: Gill and Macmillan, 1984).

Spicer, Andrew, A. T. McKenna and Christopher Meir (eds), *Beyond the Bottom Line: The Producer in Film and Television Studies* (London: Continuum, 2014).

Spicer, Andrew, *Sydney Box* (Manchester: MUP, 2006).

Spicer, Andrew, 'The Production Line: Reflections on the Role of the Producer in British Cinema', *Journal of British Cinema and Television* (vol. 1, no. 1, November 2004), pp. 33–50.

Street, Sarah, *British Cinema in Documents* (London: Routledge, 2000).

Street, Sarah, 'Cinema, Colour and the Festival of Britain, 1951', *Visual Culture in Britain* (vol. 13, no. 1, 2012), pp. 83–99.

Swann, Paul, *The Hollywood Feature Film in Postwar* Britain (London: Croom Helm, 1987).

Sydney-Smith, Susan, *Beyond Dixon of Dock Green: Early British Police Series* (London: I. B. Tauris, 2002).

Thomas, Donald, *An Underworld at War: Spivs, Deserters, Racketeers and Civilians in the Second World War* (London: John Murray, 2003).
Trewin, J. C. (ed.), *The Journal of William Charles Macready 1832–1851* (London: Longmans, 1967).
Tunstall, Jeremy, *The Media in Britain* (London: Constable, 1983).
Vertrees, Alan David, *Selznick's Vision:* Gone with the Wind *and Hollywood Filmmaking* (Texas: University of Texas Press, 1997).
Williams, Raymond, *Culture and Society 1780–1950* (London: Penguin, 1976).
Williams, Raymond, *Keywords* (London: Flamingo, 1988).
Willis, Ted, *Evening All: 50 Years Over a Hot Typewriter* (London: Macmillan, 1991).
Wollen, Peter, 'Riff-Raff Realism', *Sight & Sound* (vol. 8, no. 4, April 1998), pp. 18–22.
Wood, John Carter, '"The Third Degree": Press Reporting, Crime Fiction and Police Powers in 1920s Britain', *Twentieth Century British History* (no. 21, 2010), pp. 464–85.

Annotated Filmography

Title	Details	Notes
Scotland Yard 1921: For the King, the Law, the People	Dir. Edmund Distin-Maddick Prod. Topical Film Company Rel. 1921.	Film commissioned and fully controlled by Scotland Yard; the first foray into cinema by the Metropolitan Police Press Bureau. **LOST.**
Scotland Yard	Dir. James Youngdeer Prod. The Frederick White Co. Rel. 1921.	Six-part serial written by an ex-Chief Inspector. Early example of the Met suppressing uncontrollable independent visual depictions of the machinery of Scotland Yard. **LOST.**
War and Order	Dir. Charles Hasse Prod. General Post Office Film Unit Rel. 1940	Short; within the British Documentary Movement pantheon. Commissioned by the Ministry of Information.
This Modern Age: Scotland Yard	Dir. John Monck Prod. Rank Film Co. Rel. 1946.	Documentary made collaboratively between Met Press Bureau and Rank via Production Facilities (Film) Ltd. **UNOBTAINABLE.**
Children on Trial	Dir. Jack Lee Prod. Crown Film Unit Rel. 1946.	Drama-doc providing an example of how the Crown Film Unit, controlled by the Central Office of Information, produced propaganda films depicting crime to benefit state institutions (in this case, Approved Schools).
The Girl from Scotland Yard	Dir. Paul Barralet Prod. Paul Barralet Productions Rel. 1947.	'B' feature made collaboratively between the Met Press Bureau and Paul Barralet Productions.

Title	Details	Notes
Good Time Girl	Dir. David Macdonald Prod. Gainsborough Pictures Rel. 1948.	State assisted in the depiction of Juvenile Court and Approved Schools, but failed to retain control of content. Was compared in the Press with *Children on Trial*.
The Blue Lamp	Dir. Basil Dearden Prod. Ealing Studios Rel. 1950.	Collaboration between Ealing and the Met Press Bureau, with more of a leaning towards the latter than the former.
I Believe in You	Dir. Basil Dearden Prod. Ealing Studios Rel. 1952.	Fractious collaboration between Ealing and the Probation Service via the Home Office. Provides an example of the reticence of most government departments in dealing with the media. Based on a tell-all book by a former Probation Officer.
Street Corner	Dir. Muriel Box Prod. London Independent Producers Ltd Rel. 1953.	Collaboration between Sydney Box and the Met Press Bureau. Provides an example of how another film company, not Ealing, dealt with state processes of control.
The Long Arm	Dir. Charles Frend Prod. Ealing Studios Rel. 1956.	Collaboration between Ealing and the Met Press Bureau. Final Ealing film to be released. The collaborative process, by this point, is polished and slick.

Index

Ad valorem tax 140–5
archival processes 16–18
Attlee, Clement 100, 156
auteur theory 15

Baim, Harold 76
Baird, Sir John 33–4
Balcon, Sir Michael 140, 144–6, 151, 204, 208, 219, 227
Ball, Sir Joseph 57–8
Barralet, Paul 87–92, 101–8
Barr, Charles 128, 204–5, 211, 221
Barr, Robert 223–5, 243
Bather, Elizabeth 91–2, 94–7, 102–4, 151, 175, 177, 181, 183–7, 194
Beddington, Jack 59
Black market 80–1, 85, 96, 98–101, 119
Blue Lamp, The 1–3, 62, 86, 115–39, 145, 150–9, 170–1, 187, 209
 release and reception 156
 script redrafting by T. E. B. Clarke 146–9
Bogarde, Dirk 126
Box, Muriel 172, 181–4
Box, Sydney 144, 172, 174–7, 179–80, 182–4, 187, 191
Brighton Rock 118, 120, 148, 211
Britain Can Take It 64
British Board of Film Censors 121–2, 180–1
British Broadcasting Corporation 204–6, 227, 232, 243–4
British Council 61
British crime cinema 9, 115, 118–23
British Film Producers Association 173
Byng, Viscount 40, 55

Cavalcanti, Alberto 62, 88
Central Office of Information 82–3, 132–3, 135, 247
Chamberlain, Neville 57
Chapman, James 67, 118–19, 122, 247
Cherrill, Fred 82–3
Chibnall, Steve 5, 7
 Law-and-Order News 6, 11, 14, 244–5
Cinematograph Films Act (1927) 40–2
Clark, Kenneth 58–60
Clarke, T. E. B. 128–30, 146–50, 210–11
'Cleft Chin' case 124
Conservative Party 174
crime in society 12, 13
crime reporters 5, 28, 72–4, 80, 248
Criminal Justice Act 1948 189–91
Cripps, Stafford 156

Dancing With Crime 118
Davis, John 144, 194–5
De Antiquis, Alec 125–6, 147
Dearden, Basil 128, 150
Dickinson, Margaret 6, 7
Distin-Maddick, Edmund 29–31
Dixon of Dock Green 205–6, 224, 243
Documentary News Letter 57

Eagleton, Terry 7–8
Ealing Studios 140, 142, 144, 153–4, 159–60, 207–22, 225
Ellis, John 15, 204, 239–40
Enticknap, Leo 77, 86

Fabian, Robert 125–6, 175, 213
Fabian of the Yard 206, 224
Fearnley, Percy Horne 69–88, 91–3, 96–7, 101–5, 124–5, 127, 130–5, 137, 145, 150–4, 159,

170–83, 187, 195, 208–13, 225, 248–9
  appointment 70–1
  background 14, 21–2, 118
  Festival of Britain 218–19
  Film producers (role of) 15, 67–9, 89–91, 95, 116, 159, 169–72, 185–9, 193–6, 213–17, 226–33, 239–42
49th Parallel 64
Frederick White Company 36–9
Frend, Charles 221, 223–7

Gainsborough Studios 123–4, 128, 136, 140, 142, 144, 159
Game, Sir Philip 45–9, 55, 60, 62, 65, 66–7, 102, 156
Games, Abram 82, 132
Girl From Scotland Yard, The 75, 87–108, 116, 117, 118, 170, 177
'Golden Age' of crime reporting 13
Good-Time Girl 118, 122–5, 136, 174, 177
GPO Film Unit 58–62, 66, 68, 79, 220

Habermas, Jurgen 4–5, 7
Haigh, Ernest (ex-Chief Inspector, Scotland Yard) 28, 36–9
Hanley, Jimmy 131
Harper, Sue 129, 144
Home Guard *see* Local Defence Volunteers
Home Office 82, 85–6, 122, 132–3, 138–9, 174, 210, 225–6, 247
Homes For All 86
Horwood, Sir William 28, 36, 40–1
Howe, Ronald 72, 78–82, 84–5, 224
Howgrave-Graham, Hamilton 34–5, 42, 48, 55, 60, 62, 63, 68, 78, 94, 134, 210
Hughes, David 100–1
Hulton, Edward 26

It Always Rains On Sunday 118

Jackson, Pat 220
Jackson, R. L. 85, 151, 209
Jarvis, Mark 12
Jeapes, William 25, 29, 31
Juvenile delinquency 132

Kinematograph Weekly 35–8
Kynaston, David 100, 218

Labour Party 100, 141
Lee, Bernard 131
Lee, Sir Kenneth 58
Lee, Norman 41–2
L'Etang, Jacqui 7
Leveson Inquiry 7, 245–7
Local Defence Volunteers 63, 66–7
location filming 41–5, 74
Long Arm, The 62, 170, 207–14, 217–35

Mackendrick, Alexander 153
Macnab, Geoffrey 141–2
Macready, Sir Nevil 23, 26
Marxist cultural theory 5, 7
Mawby, Rob 13, 246
McKernan, Luke 25, 247
Metropolitan Police Benevolent Fund 32, 195–6
Ministry of Information 56, 59
  Films Division 56–60, 62, 132
Morrison, Herbert 69
Moseley, Rachel 17
Murphy, Robert 116, 119

National Archives, The 15–16
National Union of Police and Prison Officers 24, 27
News International *see* Leveson Inquiry
Newsam, Sir Frank 135, 137–9, 145, 210
newspapers 74–5, 233–4, 245–6

Night Beat 118, 121–3
Nolbandov, Sergei 79, 88
No Orchids For Miss Blandish 121–3
Noose 101, 118, 121–3
Nott-Bower, Sir John 206, 220, 231, 233

Peto, Dorothy 89–91
police corruption 3, 206–8, 246
Police Strikes of 1918 24
Porter, Vincent 129, 144, 169
Procter, Maurice 6
Pronay, Nicholas 57
Public Information Officer 117, 209
   extent of role and influence in 21st century 248
   international versions of the role 22
   origins in UK 27–8, 50, 70–3
public relations machinery 242–3
   Bank of England 24, 26
   during Second World War 56–61, 63, 98
   Educational possibilities 25, 32–3, 133
   Empire Marketing Board 40
   Home Office 133–4
   in influencing the popular film industry 76, 117, 155, 188–91, 212, 226–7
   Metropolitan Police Press Bureau 22–3, 115–19, 155–8, 179, 188–92, 208–9, 217, 233
   formation 26
   Use of for police recruitment 33, 82, 88, 96, 105, 130–1, 158
   The use of to elicit a response from neutral United States 64

Rank, J. Arthur 77, 78–9, 169
   Ad valorem tax and subsequent production drive 141–4
   General Film Distributors 195

Production Facilities (Film) Ltd 76, 84, 89
Rank Organisation 78, 142, 192, 214, 228–9, 232
Read, Jan 123–9, 139–40, 145, 147, 149, 173, 175, 177–80, 220, 243
Reiner, Robert 5–6, 9–11, 116
Relph, Michael 151–2, 170, 211–12
Rivers-Bodilly, George 27
Robertson, James C. 124
rule of law
   consent 10, 13, 22, 23, 117

Scotland Yard 1921 For the King, the Law, the People 26, 28, 29–35, 56, 66, 137, 195–6, 217
Scott, Sir Harold 13–14, 69–71, 85, 91, 102–3, 106, 117, 123–5, 127, 130, 135–6, 138–9, 145, 177, 191, 217
Secrets of Scotland Yard 28, 35–9, 137, 246
Shell Film Unit 59
Shpayer-Makov, Haia 5
Smith, G. Ivan 76, 78–9, 84
Spicer, Andrew 15, 240
Street, Sarah 6, 7, 14, 16, 240
Street Corner 62, 170
Swann, Paul 141
Sydney-Smith, Susan 6, 205–6, 243–4

television 223–4, 243–4
They Made Me A Fugitive 118, 122
Thomas, Donald 13
This Modern Age: Scotland Yard 56, 75–9, 85, 88, 89, 91, 115, 132, 170
Topical Budget 25, 26
Trenchard, Lord 43–5, 55

War and Order 56, 58–69, 79, 102
Warner, Jack 126
Waterloo Road 101

Watt, Harry 62–3, 65–7, 79
Wheatley, Helen 17
Wide Boy 101
Williams, Raymond 7, 8, 170, 241
Willis, Ted 128–9, 139–40, 145, 147, 149, 173, 205

Wilson, Harold 142
Women Police 81, 87–95, 174–5, 182, 184, 188–9, 209
   recruitment campaign 106–7
   uniforms 92, 96, 182

Z Cars 204

www.ingramcontent.com/pod-product-compliance
Lightning Source LLC
Chambersburg PA
CBHW071813300426
44116CB00009B/1298